A Distant Thunder

The Storm of Peace, Love, and Harmony

REVEREND KENNETH AND
ELIZABETH HERZOG

ISBN 979-8-88851-179-4 (Paperback)
ISBN 979-8-88851-180-0 (Digital)

Copyright © 2023 Reverend Kenneth and Elizabeth Herzog
All rights reserved
First Edition

All biblical citations were taken from the New International Version of the Holy Bible (NIV)

All rights reserved. No part of this publication may be reproduced, distributed, or transmitted in any form or by any means, including photocopying, recording, or other electronic or mechanical methods without the prior written permission of the publisher. For permission requests, solicit the publisher via the address below.

Covenant Books
11661 Hwy 707
Murrells Inlet, SC 29576
www.covenantbooks.com

Contents

Introduction vii
The Season of Advent 1
  A Distant Thunder 1
  Preparing for the Storm 8
  The Rope of Three Cords 14
    The Cord of Repentance 16
    The Cord of Conversion 17
    The Cord of Baptism 17
  A Journey of Faith, Hope, and Love 19
The Christmas Season 25
  The Movie of Creation 25
  The Birthday Party 30
  Forever Silenced 37
  The Tent 42
  Unexpected Angels 48
    The First Lesson: Prayer Involves the Ministry
      of Angels 50
    The Second Lesson: God Protects His Children 52
    The Third Lesson: God Brings Us Home to Him 53
The Season of Epiphany 56
  The Living Light 56
  Emerging from the Water 61
  New Life for a Broken World 66
  Satan Goes to Church 72
  The Mountaintop 76
The Season of Lent 82
  The Cross of Ashes 82
  The Desert Retreat 90
    The First Temptation 92

- The Second Temptation 94
- The Third Temptation 95
- Turning Points 97
- Jesus Weeps for You 103
- The Grace Period 109
- The Holiest Week 114
  - The Holy Paradox 114
  - The Night Time Stood Still 122
  - The Scapegoat 129
- The Season of Easter 138
  - This Is the Day! 138
  - Running 145
  - Second-Guessing God 149
  - The Stranger 155
  - Directions 163
  - Fallen Soldiers 169
  - Jesus Prays for You 177
  - Coming Full Circle 183
  - The Cosmic Christ: A Theory by Fr. Ken 191
- The Season of Pentecost 193
  - Wildfires 193
  - Roots and Wings 200
  - Who Is My Neighbor? 207
  - The Maggie Principle 216
  - An Act of Forgiveness 224
  - The Tapestry of the Living Bread 233
  - Jesus on the Moon 240
  - A Lowly Widow 242
  - The Royal Wedding 248
  - Arrows and Targets 254
  - The Golf Ball Analogy 260
- The Season of Thanksgiving 271
  - The Greatest Gift 271

Dedication

We dedicate this book to our son, daughter-in-law, and grandchildren who fill our hearts with pure love and joy. May their lives abound with God's blessings, the greatest of which is love!

We know that in everything God works for good with those who love Him and who are called according to His purpose. (Romans 8:28)

Love, Nana and Paken

Introduction

The pastor during my teenage and young adult years was one of the most compelling and inspirational preachers I had ever known. He made a church service come alive with his passion for the Lord. His sermons could bring a congregation to tears, not with fire and brimstone but with honesty and warmth. And even as a young adult, I looked forward to listening to him preach, which was rather remarkable given my somewhat lackadaisical attitude about attending church.

He connected the Gospel to our daily lives in such a way that I left the service feeling like I could face whatever life threw my way. His sermons not only captivated my heart but also helped me grow closer to God. At that time in my life, I believed that no other sermon could even compare to his. That was, however, until the first time I heard my husband preach when we were in seminary at the University of the South in Sewanee, Tennessee.

The seminarians and their families gathered together every Wednesday night for a Eucharist, followed by a family-style dinner in the main dining hall. We worshiped in the "Pit," a large room with stadium-like seating located on the lower level of the building where classes were held. These Wednesday nights provided the opportunity to gather together as a church community, share the body and blood of our Lord and Savior, and reconnect with one another.

Even though most seminarians and their families attended the service, attendance was not required unless the seminarian was scheduled to read the Scripture, set the table, or preach. The professors celebrated the Eucharist, but they also evaluated the seminarian's sermon, which added even more responsibility to that person's required participation.

Reverend Kenneth and Elizabeth Herzog

I'll never forget how diligently Ken prepared for the first sermon he preached during a Wednesday night service. For weeks, he wrote and rewrote, read and reread, and practiced over and over again. Although I offered to listen to his sermon, he said he wanted me to hear it for the first time like everyone else. And as disappointed as I was at first, I was so blessed that he refused.

I can remember that sermon like it was yesterday. He walked to the pulpit, notes in hand, and then suddenly decided to step away and preach in front of the altar. My stomach tensed, my muscles froze, my heart raced. Then he started.

My husband's compelling words became the riveting brushstrokes that gripped our minds and captivated our hearts. It was as if my husband disappeared and, in his place, stood the eighth-century prophet Isaiah. We saw Isaiah's long silver beard, his worn sunbaked face, and his large leathered hands.

As we and Isaiah listened to the thunder bellowing in the distance, the dark clouds and the turbulent wind that engulfed the once peaceful serenity of the pale blue sky forced Isaiah to his knees and made us gasp for breath. The trembling earth sent shivers deep into Isaiah's soul, and we felt our bodies quiver with the anticipation of God's imminent return.

By now, the powerful wind pierced Isaiah's swollen face, and as he rubbed away the gritty sand stinging his wearied eyes, we wiped away the surging tears flooding our aching hearts. When Isaiah stood upright against the mighty storm, stretched his strong welcoming arms, and screamed, "O Lord God, that you would tear open the heavens and come down!" (Isaiah 64:1–4), we sat silent, paralyzed against the power of my husband's mesmerizing and cathartic words.

My husband brought the Gospel to life that Wednesday night. It was as if he knew our innermost thoughts, our greatest fears, our deepest regrets. He touched our hearts and our souls. And he took our breath away. By the time he finished, no one moved, not even Isaiah. The stillness that consumed the room that night stopped time.

At that moment, I knew God had given my husband the gift of bringing His word to life. Maybe his five years in the Roman Catholic seminary helped. Maybe his ten years of teaching Scripture to high school students added another layer. Maybe this; maybe that. But deep down, I knew, and he knew too. His professors certainly knew because at graduation, they awarded Ken the *William Porcher DuBose Excellence in Preaching Award*, the highest award given to a graduating seminarian.

You see, that first sermon on that first Wednesday night thirty years ago was just the start: the start of touching so many lives, so many hearts, so many souls. It was the start of our journey as a pastor's family that has since developed into an even greater appreciation for God's numerous blessings in our lives. And it was the start of our book.

We hope and pray that our reflections guide you as you struggle to find a balance between your secular and spiritual life. We understand that this struggle can leave us feeling confused, disappointed, and troubled. And when this happens, we often find ourselves questioning our place in the world, sometimes even turning away from God, searching for answers in the wrong places. Hopefully, our reflections will help you understand that with God's guidance, the answer is often found within the struggle itself.

Although intended for a Christian audience, the reflections offer relevant interpretations of scripture to all people. Unique in style, they provide imaginative narratives and practical lessons that will linger in your heart and mind, while serving as a catalyst for love, hope, and peace in your life.

Personally, I pray each reflection helps you feel like I did when my husband preached his very first sermon. I hope you wipe away a tear, laugh out loud, or gasp for breath as you feel God's love deep in your soul. I hope you revisit the reflections that speak to you the most and that you spend quiet time with God.

May God's grace and love and joy fill your life with His greatest blessings. And maybe, just maybe, time will stand still for you too, if only for a brief moment!

With love and prayers,
Elizabeth A. Herzog

PS: Sweet dreams!

The Season of Advent

*A*s we wait to celebrate the birth of our Messiah, rich traditions fill the warmth and anticipation of this glorious season. In our churches, in our homes, and in our hearts, our personal traditions help us prepare for the great celebration of Christmas: peeling away the Advent calendar, lighting the Advent wreath, decorating the tree, displaying the crèche, singing carols, sending Christmas cards, attending Advent programs, sharing festivities with family and friends, and other traditions that enrich our lives during this holy season.

A Distant Thunder

Almighty God, give us grace to cast away the works of darkness, and put on the armor of light, now in the time of this mortal life in which your Son Jesus Christ came to visit us in great humility; that in the last day, when He shall come again in His glorious majesty to judge both the living and the dead, we may rise to the life immortal; through Him who lives and reigns with you and the Holy Spirit, one God now and forever. (Collect: First Sunday of Advent, BCP, 211)

O that you would tear open the heavens and come down, so that the mountains would quake at your presence as when fire kindles brushwood and the fire causes water to boil—to make your name known to your adversaries so that the nations might tremble at your presence! When you did awesome

> *deeds that we did not expect, you came down, the mountains quaked at your presence. From ages past no one has heard, no ear has perceived, no eye has seen any God besides you, who works for those who wait for him. (Isaiah 64:1–4)*

A distant thunder rumbles on the horizon. For Isaiah, this day cannot come soon enough. He turns and sees dark ominous clouds slowly engulf the peaceful serenity of the pale-blue sky. The billowing clouds swell with moisture and gradually overshadow the sun's golden rays, transforming the sky into a threatening greenish-yellow cast. The sudden breeze announcing the powerful storm stuns him, chills his bronzed rustic face, and tousles his long silver beard. Cupping his ears with his dry, wrinkled hands, he listens intently, praying that each roar will bring God closer to him.

Crouching on his knees, he places his hands on the sunbaked desert sand and feels the earth tremble. He puts his ear to the ground, listening as he waits. As each vibration penetrates his worn body, his skin tingles, sending shivers deep into his very soul. Slowly, he tilts his head upward, looks out on the horizon, and feels the force of the storm's turbulent wind as it whips gritty sand into his weathered face.

Wiping his sand-drenched eyes, he waits for further signs that will usher in the advent of God's new age. His heart pounds with excitement, his eyes widen with anticipation, and his smile broadens with exhilaration. His soul lights on fire and consumes his very being, giving him the spiritual strength to stand upright against the strenuous storm and stretch out his welcoming arms, embracing God's imminent arrival. He takes a deep breath and screams at the top of his lungs: *"O Lord God, that you would tear open the heavens and come down!"*

+++

A distant thunder rumbles on the horizon. Dark ominous clouds slowly engulf the peaceful serenity of the pale-blue sky. From His heavenly throne, the Son of God sees the impending storm and knows that

His Father is sending Him to Earth a second time, bringing to fruition the pinnacle of salvation history. The Son knows that for thousands of earthly years, His Father has faithfully pieced together His vision for our souls' return, fulfilling the redemption of all creation, paid for on the cross. The Father joyfully anticipates reuniting all His children in the kingdom, and the Son not only shares his Father's joy but is also delighted for Him. Before the Son descends, He recalls the prophecy He gave to His disciples while on earth:

> *But in those days, after the suffering, the sun will be darkened, and the moon will not give its light, and the stars will be falling from heaven, and the powers in the heavens will be shaken. Then they will see the Son of Man coming in clouds with great power and glory. Then he will send out the angels, and gather his elect from the four winds, from the ends of the earth to the ends of heaven. (Mark 13:24–27)*

Today, the four winds of heaven and the four winds of earth collide, generating the Father's almighty storm of peace, love, and harmony. Today, the Son becomes one with the storm, bringing His everlasting light that shatters the darkened world. Today, the Son embraces His people, calming their yearning and restless souls. Today, the Son reveals His Father's immeasurable power and glory, as the Father reveals the final piece of His vision. Today, His Son's joyful shouts reverberate throughout creation: *"This is the day the Lord has made; let us rejoice and be glad in it" (Psalm 118:24).*

The mesmerized angels celebrate as they witness the most incredible moment known to humankind, initiating the advent of God's new age. The angels bolt to the four corners of the earth, transcending God's children from their earthly home to their heavenly one. And in the distance, Isaiah's powerful voice echoes throughout the universe: *"O Lord God, that You would tear open the heavens and come down!"*

+++

We come to church on the first Sunday of Advent expecting to hear a little of the Christmas story. After having been away from it for a year, we yearn to hear the story about Mary and Joseph, the little donkey, the angel, the shepherds in the field, and the three Wise Men. We think about Jesus being born in a stable among animals. We think about Mary wrapping Him in simple swaddling clothes and placing Him in a manger filled with hay. That's all we know. It's all we want. It's all we expect. These stories fill our hearts with peace, love, and joy.

But we never hear this story on the first Sunday of Advent. Instead of the tender story of the manger, we hear the frightening story of the Second Coming. On this Sunday, we learn that God is loving, protecting, and forgiving, but we also learn that He is uninhibited, unconditional, and unbridled.

God will not reveal this side of Him until the advent of the Second Coming, when He unveils His vision for our salvation and creates the distant thunder that will usher in a radical change. As we listen to this story, tension builds within us, even though Isaiah and Jesus smile.

+++

On the first Sunday of Advent, we light the candle of expectation on the Advent wreath and feel tension as we look back at the manger but look forward to the end of time. While the manger comforts us, the apocalypse frightens us. But the apocalypse refers to the final destruction of evil and the total triumph of good. So why the fear?

What is frightening about the advent of the Second Coming? How can something coming from God be anything but joyful? Anything but holy? Anything but life changing?

Jesus tells us not to be afraid: *"Now when you see these things take place, look up and raise your heads because your redemption is drawing near" (Luke 21:28).* Raising your head and looking up are not postures of fear. Jesus does not tell us to cower and hide in the corner because of our shame. Jesus does not tell us to run from His Second

Coming but to embrace it, take a deep breath, and scream at the top of our lungs: "*O Lord God, that you would tear open the heavens and come down!*"

+++

You better watch out
You better not cry
You better not pout
I'm telling you why
Santa Claus is coming to town!
(Haven Gillespie and J. Fred Coots, October 1933)

The secular world often pulls adults away from the true meaning of Advent. We get caught up in external activities: decorating our trees and homes, sending Christmas cards, planning and attending parties, wrapping packages with ribbons and bows, hanging children's stockings, planning Christmas dinner, along with a myriad of other secular activities we all know so well. These activities often divert our attention away from the spiritual, leaving us exhausted and sometimes feeling empty. When we wake up on Christmas morning, relieved that the Christmas rush is over and thankful that we can finally focus on Jesus, we recognize that our priorities have been misguided.

For children, however, a large part of the excitement and mystery of Christmas centers around Santa. In their eyes, Santa is real. Santa comes on Christmas Eve with his twelve reindeer and brings them gifts. While parents assume the role of the mythical Santa, most of them do not understand their profound connection with the spirit of the real Santa.

Santa is not only the jolly old man in the red suit who listens as children tell him their wish lists, but he is also the symbol of something much deeper. Jolly old Santa evolved from jolly old Saint Nicholas, a fourth-century bishop, known as the patron saint of children who left gifts for them outside their homes late at night. Because of his genuine love for children and his strong devotion to the faith, he encouraged them to pray, attend church, obey their parents, and behave themselves: "He knows when you are sleeping. He knows when you're awake. He knows if you've been bad or good, so be good for goodness' sake" (Gillespie and Coots).

During this season, the secular and the spiritual arrive simultaneously, seemingly in competition with each other. The faith focuses on Jesus; whereas, the secular focuses on shopping. However, it's futile to separate the two, so we must find a way to connect them. Our secular activities should be ways to celebrate Jesus' birth. Our gifts to each other should be ways to celebrate God's gifts to us. We should not buy gifts out of a sense of obligation but with the joy of jolly old Saint Nick. Shopping for gifts should not make us weary but should bring us spiritual refreshment.

Advent calls us to prepare our hearts for the coming of Christ, not only the first time but also the second. Christians try desperately to keep the reason for the season and keep Christ in Christmas. Traditions like putting up the crèche, making the Advent wreath, following the scriptural Advent calendar, attending church services, and participating in Bible studies provide spiritual focus.

But how do we prepare for the Second Coming? The distant thunder on the horizon of Christ's Second Coming is just as much of a mystery to us as His First Coming was to Isaiah: *"O Lord God, that you would tear open the heavens and come down!"*

We ask ourselves: When will Christ come again? How will He return? What signs will we see before His arrival? How will He redeem the entire world? Will we be ready?

+++

The Yardman

> *But know this: if the owner of the house had known at what hour the thief was coming, he would not have let his house be broken into. You also must be ready, for the Son of Man is coming at an unexpected hour. (Luke 12:39, 40)*

Elizabeth and I grew up in Southeast Florida where many people are snowbirds, like the retired couple who lived across the street from us when we were first married. They spent their winters in Florida and their summers in New Jersey.

They owned a large piece of property with a big circular driveway, a perfectly manicured lawn, a variety of colorful flowers, and an assortment of tropical fruit trees. The man spent hours working in his yard and took great pride in its beauty. He would occasionally bring over a bag of fruit, filled with the bounty of his hard work: mangoes, lemons, limes, oranges, and avocados.

When they left for New Jersey at the beginning of each summer, they hired a yardman to maintain their property. Year after year, summer after summer, the yardman did nothing until about a week before the man and his wife returned. He would then work for a few days, from early morning until early evening, getting the yard ready.

One summer, the man and his wife returned early. Guess what they found? Grass and hedges growing wild, an abundance of nasty weeds, dried flowers decaying in the sun, and rotten fruit lying everywhere. Everyone in the neighborhood knew what was going to happen. And it did. The yardman was cast out into the darkness where there was weeping and gnashing of teeth: *"You must also be ready, for the Son of Man is coming at an unexpected hour"* (Luke 12:40).

If the Son of Man were to come tomorrow, how long and how hard would you need to work today to get your life ready?

Granted, each of us has a little yardman inside: times when we took what we could and neglected our responsibilities, times when we were never wrong until we got caught.

We always felt sorry for our neighbor when he returned. But we felt especially bad for him when he finally realized that he had been taken advantage of all those years. It must have made him sad and angry at the same time.

We should have warned that yardman. We should warn all the yardmen. We should tell them it is wrong to manipulate such a kind and loving and benevolent Master, God our Father. He gives each of us the fruits of His Spirit. When He returns, we hope He will not find His fruits rotting on the ground. We should tell all the yardmen to stay awake and keep watch.

We are trying to tell you though. Please, be ready. We know the date of His First Coming, but we don't know the date of His Second. We must keep our lives in order; we must prepare ourselves every day for His next arrival.

The yardman became complacent. The yardman did not stay awake. The yardman did not keep his watch. He thought he had more time to take care of the matter at hand.

Have you ever thought you had more time but later realized you didn't? Are you like the yardman? Have you become complacent in your life? Have you allowed the weeds to choke the fruit in your life? Is your commitment to God part-time? How much of the yardman do you have in your life?

To the yardman, it was just a yard. It was just a part-time job. It wasn't like it…was…the…end…of…the…world!

There is a distant thunder on the horizon.
Be silent and cup your ears.
Can you hear it?
It is coming!
Come, Lord Jesus. Come!

+++

This week…
As you decorate your home to celebrate His First Coming,
buy an ornament that anticipates His Second.

Preparing for the Storm

Merciful God, who sent your messengers the prophets to preach repentance and prepare the way for our salvation; Give us grace to heed their warnings and forsake our sins, that we may greet with joy

> *the coming of Jesus Christ our Redeemer; who lives and reigns with you and the Holy Spirit, one God, now and forever. Amen. (Collect: Second Sunday of Advent, BCP, 211)*

On the second Sunday of Advent, the candle of preparation continues the tension in the Christian's heart between the First and the Second Coming and urges us to prepare for the storm on the horizon. The scriptures on this Sunday introduce two dominant yet diverse voices of Advent, Isaiah and John the Baptist.

First, we hear from Isaiah, a well-educated prophet who lived around 750 BC in an upper-class family in the city of Jerusalem during a tumultuous time when the Assyrians threatened the Israelite nation. During this turmoil, the source of Isaiah's eternal optimism was the Prince of Peace, who would eventually bring harmony to a tenuous world:

> *But a shoot shall sprout from the stump of Jesse, and from his roots a bud shall blossom. The spirit of the Lord shall rest upon him. Then the wolf shall be a guest of the lamb, and the leopard shall lie down with the kid. The calf and the young lion shall browse together, with a little child to guide them. The cow and the bear shall be neighbors, together their young shall rest; the lion shall eat hay like the ox. The baby shall play by the cobra's den, and the child shall lay his hand on the adder's lair. There shall be no harm or ruin on all my holy mountain; for the earth shall be filled with the knowledge of the Lord, as the water covers the sea. (Isaiah 11:1, 6–9)*

By blending captivating imagery, alluring poetry, and compelling metaphors, Isaiah's exquisite writing whispers with imagination, eloquence, and beauty. His message flourishes with grace and sophistication, giving us a lofty vision of the Messiah's transformation of the world: *"There shall be no harm or ruin on all my holy mountain, says the Lord, for the earth shall be filled with the knowledge of the Lord as the water covers the sea" (Isaiah 11:9).* Animals will coexist with their natural enemies, babies will play with cobras, and children will pet the viper's newborn.

Standing in stark contrast with Isaiah, John the Baptist's lifestyle, persona, and writings vastly differ from his Old Testament counterpart. Following the Nazarite vow since birth, John never shaved or cut his hair *(Luke 1:16)*. And unlike Isaiah's elegance, John's hard demeanor, accentuated by his dark, penetrating eyes and his fiery, bellowing voice, cuts our hearts and grips our souls. Even the scribes and the Pharisees couldn't break away from the intensity of this grizzly man who left them in dismay and gave them much to think about as they returned home, *"You brood of vipers! Who told you to flee from the wrath to come? Show some evidence that you mean to reform" (Matthew 3:7, 8)*!

Even though John appreciated the beauty of Isaiah's captivating message, he knew that Isaiah's idealism would never move the people to repent. So out of frustration, he turned to the fearless prophet Elijah for inspiration. Elijah's power and determination solidified John's fiery voice, roaring with realism, confidence, and judgment, which offered an alternative approach to Isaiah's lofty vision.

John proclaimed a baptism of repentance for the forgiveness of sins, as it is written in the book of Isaiah,

> *The voice of one crying in the wilderness: Prepare the way of the Lord, make straight his paths. Every valley shall be filled, and every mountain and hill shall be made low, and the crooked ways be made straight, and the rough ways made smooth; and all flesh shall see the salvation of God. (Luke 3:3–6)*

As difficult as this is for us to hear, John's tough love, filled with wrath and judgment is, nonetheless, love. Wanting us to prepare our hearts through repentance, John understands the connection between self-deceit, admission of guilt, repentance, and forgiveness.

He understands that once the sinner overcomes the mountainous obstacle of self-deceit, this sequence flows naturally. By working backward, we learn that forgiveness comes only through repentance, repentance comes only after the admission of guilt, and the admission of guilt comes only after recognizing self-deceit.

When we light the candle of preparation, John asks us, "Who will fill the valley of despair? Who will lower the mountains of obstacles? Who will straighten the paths of sin? Who will smooth the challenges of life?"

We automatically assume the Lord will do all of this work. But John believes otherwise. He tells us to *"prepare the way of the Lord,"* not as an invitation to observe but as a command to participate. When we spend too much time waiting for God to perform some mighty act in our lives, we must remember that it is God who waits for us. The Lord God waits patiently for us to discover our higher purpose. God revealed His plan, and now He waits for us to prepare for the advent of His first and second arrival.

+++

When our son was a toddler, he had a fleet of small construction toys. By the time he was four, he could distinguish among a backhoe, frontend loader, earthmover, bulldozer, box blade, bobcat, excavator, and other types of heavy equipment, all of which became commonplace in his vocabulary.

These toys cluttered our cars and our home but also filled our hearts with joy as we watched him spend hour after hour maneuvering them, imitating the hum of their engines, and working on construction projects. At first, Elizabeth and I thought that his fascination with construction vehicles would eventually waiver, but it never did. In fact, as he got older, his fascination turned into a passion.

When Elizabeth and I picked him up from kindergarten one day, a large flatbed truck, used to haul drywall and concrete blocks, pulled alongside us at a red light. As the truck pulled up, he threw his hands up in the air and shouted, "Look! I can see his drivetrain turning!" At that moment, Elizabeth and I knew we had created a "gearhead."

A few years later, we visited Elizabeth's sister and her husband in Atlanta.

At that time, they owned a large construction company, and our brother-in-law gave us a tour of one of their job sites. Our son was in his glory when our brother-in-law took him from one piece of heavy equipment to the next, allowing him to shift gears, pull levers, and turn wheels. Leveling out, straightening up, filling in, and smoothing over the road, our son was not an observer but an operator, not a spectator but a participant, not a bystander but a "driver."

As Elizabeth and I watched his passion for engines and machinery mature, we realized that we must be active participants in our own lives. We must fill in the valley of despair with God's love. We must lower the mountain of obstacles with God's blessings. We must straighten the path of sin with God's forgiveness. We must smooth the challenges of life with God's guidance. And we must heed John's command, *"Prepare the way of the Lord,"* not as an invitation to observe but as a command to participate.

+++

Isaiah, the eloquent writer, provides the vision; John, the pragmatic preacher, provides the path. Isaiah soothes us with God's tenderness and mercy; John awakens us with God's judgment and righteousness. Isaiah gives us hope and encouragement, while John demands honesty and reform. Isaiah helps us see the light in our darkness, but John tells us how we entered the darkness in the first place. Isaiah covers our spirituality with the sweet nectar of honey. John reveals our deceit by peeling away the layers of our sin.

However, we need both of these men during the season of Advent. We need both because God has given us both. It is by His divine design that we hear from both of these great prophets who influence us during this holy season, each in their unique way. Without the hope of Isaiah, there is too much despair. Without the judgment of John, there is too much fluff. Their voices not only capture our hearts but also give us much to think about as we return home.

+++

There can be no Advent without spiritual preparation. Every charitable act, every humble repentance, every kind word, every selfless sacrifice, and every heartfelt prayer prepares us for the Messiah's arrival. Reforming our lives should not bring fear but joy during this holy season. Even so, our hearts tug between Isaiah and John.

But we must remember that we are being called to a higher order, a more personal relationship with our Lord and Savior, Jesus Christ. Preparing for His holy birth and glorious return must transform our lives! His birth is humanity's rebirth; His return is creation's rebirth.

During this holy season, we must eradicate all negative energy and fill our lives with positive thoughts, words, and actions. We must not be critical but complementary, not tear down but buildup, not show anger but give love: *"You must love the Lord your God with all of your heart, mind, and soul, and you must love your neighbor as yourself"* (Deuteronomy 11:1). The King is coming. We must prepare the way. Is your heart ready?

John tells us: Prepare the way of the Lord. Repent of your sinfulness. Change your ways. Mend broken relationships. Forgive those who have offended you. Pray for your enemies. Love one another. Isaiah tells us to open our arms to God's mercy and fill our lives with hope, peace, and harmony.

+++

This week…
If you have offended someone, reach out to
that person and ask for forgiveness.
If you find your life filled with more negative thoughts than positive
ones, start each day with a prayer, asking God to "open your arms
to God's mercy and fill your life with hope, peace, and harmony."

Then copy Deuteronomy 11:1 and tape it to your bathroom mirror or on the door of your refrigerator or on your computer screen. Read it throughout the day. You may even want to share its message with a loved one, a friend, a neighbor, or a colleague…or all four. And before you say, "Merry Christmas," live a holy Advent!

The Rope of Three Cords

As it is written in the prophet Isaiah, "I send my messenger before you to prepare your way: a herald's voice in the desert crying, 'Make ready the way of the Lord, clear him a straight path.'" (Mark 1:1–3)

Thus it was that John the Baptizer appeared in the desert proclaiming a baptism of repentance which led to the forgiveness of sins. All the Judean countryside and the people of Jerusalem went out to him in great numbers. They were being baptized by him in the Jordan River as they confessed their sins. John was clothed in camel's hair and wore a leather belt around his waist.

His food was grasshoppers and wild honey. The theme of his preaching was *"One more powerful than I is to come after me. I am not fit to stoop and untie his sandal straps. I have baptized you with water, but he will baptize you with the Holy Spirit" (Mark 1:2–8)*.

John the Baptist, the last of the Old Testament prophets and the first one of the New Testament, keeps a foot in both worlds, making him the perfect precursor to Jesus and a resounding voice during the Advent season. For this reason, we focus on John without his Old Testament counterpart, the Prophet Isaiah.

During his formative years, the Essenes, a Jewish sect that followed a strict lifestyle of poverty, celibacy, and the reform of Jewish culture while also shunning the people of Jerusalem, greatly influenced John's ministry and message. Thus, when his father, Zechariah, died early in his childhood, John refused his father's temple allowance, which resulted in his and his mother's eventual poverty.

When John was twenty-eight years old, his mother passed away suddenly. Due to the Nazarite vow regarding contact with the dead, John was not notified about his mother's death until all burial arrangements had been made. After her burial, John entered a two-year period of mourning, giving what little he had to the Essenes. He then retreated into the wilderness to fast and pray and read the Scriptures.

During this period of isolation, John became especially fascinated with Isaiah and Elijah—Isaiah for his vision of the Messiah's transformation of the world and Elijah for his fiery temperament. But he was especially enthralled with Elijah. So much so that he dressed like him, preached like him, and developed his blunt speech and abrupt style. John saw himself as Elijah's counterpart: Elijah as one of the first prophets and himself as the very last. Thus, he proclaimed a new age with the advent of the Messiah's arrival.

For us, John, a combination of Grizzly Adams and the Desert Fox, emerges with a strong presence of the Holy Spirit. People were attracted to him, listened to what he had to say, and came to him for baptism. Unlike the Prophet Isaiah, however, John didn't go to the people in Jerusalem. Rather, he made them come to him in the inhospitable wilderness and, eventually, into the desert, leaving behind their homes, their friends, and their families.

John's appearance is not a graceful one. Rather, he bullies his way onto the scene, demanding and capturing the attention of those who hear him as the voice crying out in the wilderness, *"Prepare the way of the Lord...make straight His paths."*

+++

John teaches us that the good news begins in the desert, in the midst of trouble, tribulation, and torment: That's what makes it good news. What seems as a precarious and trying situation is actually a vehicle for triumph and victory.

Our Advent journey leads us into the desert to be with John. How often when we leave everything behind do we find the presence of God? Perhaps in your desperation and searching for answers, you too have been through a spiritual desert. In that desert, God becomes our refuge, our rock, our stronghold. Mind you, God is not responsible for the desert; however, He can use our time in a spiritual desert to His advantage. Thus, in an irony of faith, our prayer life intensifies, we search more desperately for God's presence, and we read the Word more passionately. And during these times, God asks, "Why is this so bad?"

+++

John uses a rope of three cords to support his tent, carry his water, and drag his firewood. This type of rope is the strongest, but it is also a strong spiritual rope that John uses to proclaim our salvation. Thus, John's rope becomes the rope of our repentance, conversion, and baptism. This is also the rope of Advent that we must cling to during the Advent season.

The Cord of Repentance

Repentance is the posture by which we receive the gift of God's Son at Christmas. While sin prohibits us from receiving God's love, repentance allows us to receive and embrace God's gift. We must prepare our hearts so when we nestle the Holy Infant close to us, He will hear our hearts beat in purity and truth, and we will hear His heartbeat with compassion and forgiveness. When this happens, our joy is God's love, but God's joy is a repentant heart. Repent and receive Him with great care and feel God's love.

However, we cannot receive the Son of God with a tainted heart:

> *If we say we have no sin we deceive ourselves and the truth is not in us. But if we confess our sins, God who is merciful and just will forgive us our sins, and cleanse us from all unrighteousness. (1 John 1:8, 9)*

The Cord of Conversion

Conversion leads to an amendment of life and a desire to break the cycle of sin. Jesus tells the woman caught in adultery, *"Go and sin no more" (John 8:11)*. Jesus forgives her, but her adulterous behavior has to stop.

But putting an end to all sin is humanly impossible, which can be overwhelming to think that we can put an end to all sin, so we should focus on one sin at a time. Those suffering with addiction live their lives one day at a time, one hour at a time. Keeping our guard, we must be vigilant and not complacent. Sin brings death. Conversion brings rebirth. If admission of guilt is the most difficult part of repentance, then amendment of life is the most difficult part of conversion.

True repentance brings conversion, and true conversion brings the power of the Holy Spirit. Only the Holy Spirit can turn your heart. You cannot repent and remain the same. You cannot apologize and continue the offense. That in itself is a sin. Amendment of life is intrinsic to the forgiveness of Jesus Christ. The Holy Spirit directs our new path. You must change your evil ways. As evil will be eradicated at the apocalypse, so too must you rid yourself of the evil in the present world:

> *You were taught to put away your former way of life. Take off your old self which is corrupt and deluded by its lust, and be renewed in the spirit of your minds, and to clothe yourselves with the new self, created according to the likeness of God in true righteousness and holiness. (Ephesians 4:21–24)*

The Cord of Baptism

> *I baptize you with water for repentance, but one who is more powerful than I is coming after me. I am not worthy to carry his sandals. He will baptize you with the Holy Spirit and fire. (Matthew 3:11)*

The fire John speaks about is not the fire of condemnation into which the chaff will be thrown. Rather, this baptismal fire is the fire of the Holy Spirit, the fire of Pentecost when the apostles' hearts were burning with passion over the resurrection of Christ. The water of baptism does not squelch this fire but spiritually ignites it. We struggle to live up to our baptismal vows. Living a Christlike life, requires daily repentance and a daily conversion. Therefore, baptism is present tense.

The third cord of baptism is woven tightly around the cords of repentance and conversion. John the Baptist recognized the connection between repentance and conversion and baptism, which occur through the power of the Holy Spirit. Baptism is a public statement that repentance and conversion have taken place and is also a crucial milestone in a person's relationship with Jesus Christ, marked by the anointing of the Holy Spirit. As a sign of a new covenant, baptism fulfills circumcision, which was the sign of the old covenant.

However, with infant baptism, the cords of John's rope are woven backward. John preaches the sequence of repentance, conversion, and baptism. Infant baptism disturbs this sequence by putting baptism first. By doing this, the church plays catch-up and tries to lead those who have already been baptized to repentance and then conversion.

Baptism leads us down a new road with Christ, and once baptized, we will never remain the same. You can't take off your baptism while you engage in a sinful act and expect to find your baptism when you return. Once you take your baptism into your sin, your baptism enters the chaos, which makes the Holy Spirit scream, "Get me out of here! Quick!" As Paul writes, with baptism, we enter God's family as His adopted children:

> *For you did not receive a spirit that makes you a slave again to fear, but you received a spirit of adoption. And by him we cry, "Abba, Father!" The Spirit himself testifies with our spirit that we are God's children. (Romans 8:15, 16)*

A Distant Thunder

While most Christians have heard of John the Baptist, he remains elusive yet fundamental during Advent. Yet his contributions to salvation history surpasses most others. John leads us to baptism and inclusion as adopted members of God's family. Without John, the theology of baptism would have been left undeveloped, and the themes of repentance, conversion, and baptism would remain unfulfilled. Thank God for John! Thank God for the desert nomad who initiates the good news of God's salvation. Thank God for this humble, fiery man who teaches us about ropes.

+++

This week…
Cut a piece of rope a foot long and keep it with you, in your home or in your car, to remind you of John's Advent message.

A Journey of Faith, Hope, and Love

The angel went to Mary and said, "Greetings, you who are highly favored! The Lord is with you." Mary was greatly troubled by his words and wondered what kind of greeting this might be. But the angel said to her, "Do not be afraid. You have found favor with God. You will conceive and give birth to a son, and you are to call him Jesus. He will be great and will be called the Son of the Most High. "How can this be," Mary asked the angel, "Since I am a virgin?"

The angel answered, "The Holy Spirit will come upon you and the power of the Most High will overshadow you. So the holy one to be born will be called the Son of God. "I am the Lord's servant," Mary answered. "Be it done to me according to your word." Then the angel left her. (Luke 1:28–32, 34–35)

In the darkness of night, a heavenly presence appears, not with wings but as a bright beam of golden radiant light, first on the outside, then passing through Mary's window. Astonished and filled with fear, Mary huddles against the wall in the corner of her bed. She grasps her worn blanket, pulls it up to her chin, and prays that the light brings no harm. The light breaks the silence with a gentle, reassuring voice, proclaiming to Mary and all generations that she is the chosen one. The light and the entire universe wait in hopeful silence for Mary's response:

> After the angel gave Mary the announcement but before her response, there ensued a cosmic silence. In that silence, all of the suns and all of the planets and all of the stars in the entire universe ceased to move and became perfectly still. When Mary replied, "Let it be with me according to your word," the universe once again resumed motion. The universe was never so dependent. (Brennan)

Mary speaks, and the universe rejoices! The more Mary trusts God, the more He reveals to her. Mary shows us the way of servanthood, humility, and acceptance:

- By emptying herself, Mary was filled.
- By giving her life, Mary lives eternally.
- By becoming God's servant, Mary becomes God's mother.

Even though her fear and bewilderment fade and are replaced with comfort and joy, her thoughts turn to Joseph: *I need his support. God needs his support. At first, everything depended on me. Now everything depends on Joseph. Please, God, help me!*

+++

Out on the fringes of the Christmas story, Joseph sits alone late at night in his modest workshop, pondering the angel's visit to Mary. The enormity of the angel's message overwhelms him. He questions how his meager means will provide for God's only Son. He worries how a simple carpenter can make any significant contribution to the world. He wonders if he will be a suitable role model for the Savior of humanity. Joseph bows his head, cups his dry, calloused hands over his troubled deep-set eyes and prays silently:

Lord God, what You are asking leaves me with many questions. I desperately need Your help, Your guidance, and Your support. As I raise Your Son, help me protect Him, guide Him, and teach Him. I ask that You protect me and Mary as we travel this journey together. Give us the strength, the wisdom, and the courage to remain Your obedient and faithful servants.

As his aching heart wrestles with his unsettled mind, Joseph stays silent. Pondering Mary's startling news, he now worries how this will change things between them. He worries about his role and what she expects of him. He feels betrayed and confused about their future. He wonders whom he can trust. He thinks about leaving her! Exhausted, Joseph curls his worn body underneath the window and falls into a deep sleep:

> *Because Joseph, her husband, was faithful to the law, and yet did not want to expose her to public disgrace, he had in mind to divorce her quietly. But after he had considered this, an angel of the Lord appeared to him in a dream and said, "Joseph, son of David, do not be afraid to take Mary as your wife, because what is conceived in her is from the Holy Spirit. She will give birth to a son, and you are to give him the name Jesus, because he will save his people from their sins." When Joseph woke up, he did what the angel of the Lord had commanded him and took Mary as his wife. (Matthew 1:18–20, 24–25)*

Raising his head, Joseph rubs his tired, weary eyes, stands and peers out his window at the brilliant starlit sky, sensing God's calming presence. As Joseph's mind and heart become one, he now knows that God is a faithful God who will not forsake him. At that very moment, Joseph's worries melt as he knows that God will walk with him and Mary on the most wondrous journey known to man.

Joseph's thoughts now become deeper and more spiritual. Now he understands; this is God's plan, not hers. Now he realizes that Mary needs him, that God needs him. Now he accepts what lies ahead is in God's hands, not theirs.

In a society that often misconstrues its definition of manhood, in a society where manhood is often boisterous, authoritative, and controlling, Joseph shows us that true manhood is none of these. Rather, Joseph shows us that manhood seeks not dominance but interdependence, not arrogance but obedience, and not assertiveness but humility.

+++

Like Joseph, our lack of confidence to face the challenges of the unknown often brings fear, which prevents us from accepting change. Even so, our lives seldom flow without change, making us feel anxious, insecure, and isolated. But we must trust God when facing the fear of change. We must remember that God does not reveal His plan all at once. Following Him sometimes brings holy insecurity. But our fear and lack of confidence must be transformed into trusting God and having humble obedience to Him. Mary and Joseph teach us that only with faith and trust can we face the challenges that lie ahead.

No doctrine is more important than the virgin birth to our understanding of Jesus as the Son of God. Through the power of the Holy Spirit, God becomes Jesus' Father, and Mary becomes His mother. Thus, denying the virgin birth denies the very core of Christianity, disregarding not only Jesus' divinity and humanity but also Mary's place in God's plan for His Son.

Mary holds a very dear yet reserved place in Christian hearts. She is the first among saints but not part of the Trinity. Through her, the Redeemer of the world became flesh. Mary knew that her Son had traits of the Holy Spirit, and the Holy Spirit knew that His Son had Mary's. She rejoiced at His birth. She wailed at His death. And she shares in His kingdom. The love between mother and Son has never been stronger. Did we mention that God's Son has his mother's eyes?

+++

After the Christmas story, we often underestimate Mary and Joseph's role, but their hard work had just begun. Mary and Joseph had the overwhelming responsibility and difficult task of raising, disciplining, and providing for God's Son. Protecting a precious gem in a small town with limited resources and occupied by the fierce and hostile Roman army required strong faith, deep trust, and constant prayer, along with a healthy marriage. Though different in many ways, their child would be the same in many others. And through it all, this holy couple sheds light on the fundamentals of married life and parenthood for all generations.

I Surrender All

All to Jesus I surrender, All to Him I freely give
I will ever love and trust Him, In His presence daily live
I surrender all
I surrender all
All to Thee my Blessed Savior I surrender all.
(Lyrics by Judson W. VanDeVenter)

+++

This week...
As you face change, no matter how big or small, turn to God and pray this prayer:

Reverend Kenneth and Elizabeth Herzog

> Lord God, the change I am facing leaves me troubled and fearful. I desperately need Your help, Your guidance, and Your support. Give me the strength, the wisdom, and the courage to face this challenge by replacing my fear with Your comfort and joy, knowing that You will walk with me as I face the challenge that lies ahead of me.

The Christmas Season

The Christmas season begins on Christmas Day and continues until the Epiphany on January 6 when we celebrate the arrival of the Wise Men. However, people often think they were celebrating the Christmas season as they decorated their homes, gave gifts, planned parties, and participated in a myriad of other celebratory traditions. That was Advent. But this is Christmas!

The Movie of Creation

God looked at everything He had made and saw that it was good. (Genesis 1:31)

Have you ever gone to a movie that captures your attention with the opening scene and keeps you enthralled from beginning to end? A love story where the plot seems real, the setting inviting, and the acting genuine; a love story that engages your emotions and leaps from fiction to reality. Have you ever been to a movie like that?

A little while into the movie, you think of a close friend who might love it as well. And as the plot unfolds, you grow more and more excited to call your friend.

Arriving home, you call and explain how the movie reminded you of your friendship. Your friend starts to share your enthusiasm, so you invite your friend to see the movie together. You make the arrangements. You offer to drive. You even pay the price of admission. Imagine that! You even pay the price of admission.

During the movie, you have one eye on the screen and one eye on your friend. As you watch together, your friend is enjoying the movie as much you had hoped and had anticipated. And during certain parts, you say to yourself, *Wait till this part comes. My friend is going to love it!* You wait and wait until the scene comes, and your friend laughs with you, filling you with joy. Your friend really loves it! And your friend is right there with you. And that moment is even more joyful than the first time when you saw it by yourself. With your friend by your side, the happy scenes seem happier and the sad scenes sadder. Your eyes hold twice the tears and your heart twice the joy.

After the movie, your friend turns to you and says, "Thanks. Thanks for thinking of me and thanks for sharing with me." You feel on top of the world. And your friendship reaches a new level.

+++

Like inviting a friend to a movie, God is excited about sharing everything He made with you. You bring God tremendous joy when you marvel at His creation. Therefore, you should never lose sight that God has included you in His design.

We should praise God for His creative work and should recognize it as a marvelous piece of artistry, much the same way that we admire beautiful paintings and the artists who painted them: Rembrandt, Picasso, and the like. How much more should we admire a painting that is alive! How many times have we seen a sunset shower the sky with vibrant colors or a flock of trumpeting geese flying in formation or the sun glistening on the ocean's waves that gently break against the shore? And how often do we stop, even for a moment, to praise God? When we do, we give God great joy. When we respond to His love story, He rejoices, which makes the bond of our relationship with Him grow ever closer.

It's amazing how God enables us to help write the script of His movie of creation. Even though God continues to bless us with different gifts and opportunities in life, He also gives us free will, allowing us to craft our own plot and determine its outcome. In this way, God's movie is unique to each person. God sits next to each of us and wonders where we will take His movie. As our storylines unfold, He shares the joy of our good times and the sadness of our difficult ones. His eyes hold twice the tears; His smile holds twice the joy.

However, God does something rare among moviemakers. God enters His own movie, steps onto the set, and begins interacting with the cast. God becomes human, one of us. Coming incognito, most people do not even recognize Him because His Presence is so simple, so humble, so unassuming. With the limitations of a newborn baby, the Eternal has chosen to reveal Himself. Outside a small town, inside a small manger, the Infinite is born. In a cruel, harsh world, Love becomes vulnerable. And the silent night becomes a holy night. And the Infant-God, the King of kings, the Savior of the world cries for milk:

> And the stars in the sky were the first Christmas lights
> And the wind sang the first Christmas hymn
> And the sheep and the cattle attended the first Christmas service
> Emmanuel: God is with us! God is here!
> God is human, and nothing else will ever be the same.
> God's love makes the movie real.

+++

In his book *Christus Veritas*, William Temple, the archbishop of Canterbury during the 1920s, imagines two very holy conversations the Father has with His Son. The first comes while God—Father, Son, and Holy Spirit—created the world.

The Father tells His Son, "Son, I want You to go to earth as a human and tell the people how much I love them."

The Son replies, "I will be honored to do that for You. Just tell me when to go."

The second conversation occurs after sin enters humanity.

The Father says, "Son, while You are on earth, You will have to pay for the sins of humanity. If You do not pay for their sins, then humans will have no way to enter our kingdom. It will cost You Your life, but I promise to raise You up on the third day. I promise."

The Son responds, "I understand, Father. I trust things will unfold according to Your plan. My death will further reveal Your love for all people. I will go because of My love for You and Our love for them."

+++

When God becomes human, He shows us that love is designed to be given away. Self-love becomes perverted and selfish. Unlike gravity that pulls everything down, the natural flow of love is outward and away from ourselves. God created us so He could give us His love, much the same way a parent loves a child. Yet parents' love for their children is only a reflection of God's love for us. We are not random acts; rather, we were purposely created by God:

> *For you formed my inward parts;*
> *you knitted me together in my mother's womb.*
> *I praise you, for I am fearfully and wonderfully made.*
> *Wonderful are your works;*
> *my soul knows it very well.*
> *My frame was not hidden from you,*
> *when I was being made in secret,*
> *intricately woven in the depths of the earth.*
> *Your eyes saw my unformed substance;*
> *in your book were written, every one of them,*
> *the days that were formed for me,*
> *when as yet there was none of them. (Psalm 139:13–16)*

Perhaps you have heard the story of a prince who lived in a royal castle and fell in love with a servant girl who lived in the village. At first, the prince hid his feelings for the girl, fearing that she would love him only for his wealth. But one day, the prince decided to disguise himself and live in the village among the servants. After they met, they eventually fell in love, and he revealed his true identity. He was convinced that her love for him was true and genuine, and they lived happily ever after.

This is what happened to us. The Son of God becomes human and lives among us with the hope of forming a true and genuine relationship filled with love.

If the Son came to us in royalty or as Himself, we would not be able to relate to Him, and a genuine relationship would not be possible. But coming to us in humility, the Son reveals His true nature and offers us an eternal life with Him in the kingdom. Could we have come to know Him in any other way? Could His love for us be revealed in any other form? Could our love for Him be any more real?

You don't have to be an angel to be touched by heaven.
You don't have to be a child to get lost in the mystery.
You don't have to be a wise man to see the light.
You don't have to be a shepherd to hear the glory being proclaimed.
("Breath of Heaven" performed by Amy Grant)

You must allow your love to flow outward, away from yourself. In order to live in God's love, you must give your love away. Like God, the magic of Christmas is the incredible joy we receive by giving our love away. Through gift giving, yes, but such gifts are only external and material signs of the love we have for one another.

From this day forward, we celebrate the greatest gift of all, the gift of love, given to us through His Son. God invites us into His movie and then gives us life to make love tangible. Love makes the movie real.

+++

This week...
Look for scenes in God's creation. Stop and give thanks to God for the beauty of His creation and share this moment with someone you love.
Merry Christmas...and to all a good night!

Reverend Kenneth and Elizabeth Herzog

The Birthday Party

While they were still in Bethlehem, the time came for her to deliver her child. And she gave birth to her firstborn son and wrapped him in bands of cloth and laid him in a manger, because there was no place for them in the inn. (Luke 2:6, 7)

Merry Christmas!

Tonight, as we sit in church, listening to captivating scripture, singing joyful hymns, and offering silent prayers, the angels, archangels, and all the company of heaven prepare for an incredible celebration. Tonight, the heavens rejoice, the angels sing, and the saints dance! Tonight, there's a majestic celebration in the heavens. Tonight, the Father gives a birthday party unlike any other. Tonight, Jesus, our Lord and Savior, is born!

Tables, covered with embroidered white linen tablecloths and set with gold-rimmed bone china, crystal stemware, and silver flatware, await the guests. The twinkling lights from the heavens flood the open-air room with a rainbow of dancing colors that accentuate the tables' towering crystal centerpieces, filled with an array of God's bountiful fragrant flowers. Music from a chamber orchestra floats gently throughout the heavens, providing peace, serenity, and tranquility for everyone who attends.

As the aroma of freshly baked unleavened bread fills the great hall, a dish of rich olive oil and bitter herbs along with hearts of palm and finely sliced heirloom tomatoes complete the first course. Waiters offer guests an assortment of fine wine, including smoky Palestinian cabernet and buttery Galilean Chardonnay. Champagne swirling gracefully to the top of each long-stemmed crystal champagne flute sparkles like dazzling diamonds, waiting for the Father's toast.

The entree of roasted lamb begins the next course: the lamb of the Passover Meal, the lamb of the Last Supper, the Lamb of God. Delicate roasted potatoes and sweet baby carrots sit gracefully around the roasted lamb. Small bowls of figs, dates, olives, and nuts accompany the main course. Waiters bring freshly steamed fish, served with a variety of legumes: broad beans, chickpeas, and lentils, and followed by an assortment of cheeses, nuts, and fruit.

After everyone is served, the Angel Gabriel invites God the Father to the podium to offer a toast to His Son.

Silence fills the room as everyone watches the Father gaze lovingly at His Son.

"My beloved Son, in You I am well pleased. Your humility and obedience inspire Me. You have accomplished everything I have ever asked of You, and You have fulfilled every request willingly, lovingly, and completely. The demands I placed upon You were almost insurmountable: to leave Your place here in the kingdom to become human. The disgrace You suffered while on earth and the horrific death You endured were too much to ask of any son. They were difficult to watch, and there were moments when the Spirit and I wanted to reach down and pull You back up with Us, but We realized that what You endured was necessary for the salvation of My people. Oh, how I wish You were here with Us on Easter morning! The heavens erupted as the stone was rolled back, and the saints sang songs of jubilation and praise!

Son, I love You dearly. You brought My message of love to them and revealed to My people My unconditional love, the power of mercy, and the glory of heaven. We owe You an eternity of thanksgiving. And so it is with great joy, everlasting gratitude, and deep appreciation that I offer this toast to mark the day of Your human birth so humanity may be reborn. Salute!"

After the Father's toast, Gabriel introduces a few distinguished guests to offer congratulatory remarks and remembrances. Mary, Jesus' mother, speaks first. With a soft smile and tender eyes, Mary gazes proudly on her Son as she recalls a moment from His childhood.

"I remember when You were twelve years old, and we went to Jerusalem to celebrate the Passover. Returning home in the caravan, Joseph and I were separated. When we finally found each other, You weren't with either one of us. Realizing You were lost, we became frantic!

At that moment, we thought we were the worst parents in the world. We had lost the Son of God for three days! We kept asking each other, 'Where on God's earth could He be? Will God ever forgive us?' Our hearts now break for every parent who has a lost child. You scared us, Son. But in finding You, You showed us the way."

As the guests applaud, John the Baptist makes his way to the stage. With genuine excitement and awkward clumsiness, John pays tribute to Jesus, his cousin.

"Down there I was always so serious, so ruff and gruff, so intense. But up here, it's glorious, fun, and joyful! While on earth, I gave my life to You, Jesus. I worked hard preparing the people for the advent of Your arrival: I proclaimed, screamed, and shouted, 'Prepare the way of the Lord!' I became hoarse from being the voice of one crying in the wilderness.

I remember when I baptized You. Wow! You blew me right out of the Jordan River water! How could anyone witness that event and not accept You as the Messiah? But You have to admit, Jesus. You were not what the people expected, not what they wanted, not what they believed. Down there, I felt called to proclaim Your message. Up here, I am honored to speak on Your behalf."

As John finishes his toast, the disciple Paul enthusiastically and energetically jumps up on the stage. Barely containing his excitement, he takes a deep breath before offering his words of praise.

"Jesus, I kept waiting for You to return, but it never happened. You are like the pot that never boils or the package that never arrives. I woke up every morning thinking, 'Surely this will be the day.' All those people whom I baptized and told that the end was near must have thought I was crazy! Well, maybe not. I see most of them here with us tonight. Jesus, don't keep it a secret for one more minute. Please tell me when the Second Coming will take place! Please tell us! Make a general announcement… But You aren't going to do that, are You? Hum!"

The heavens fall silent as they wait for Jesus' response. All eyes are on Jesus, hoping and praying that He will reveal His Father's final piece of salvation history. After what seems an eternity, Jesus rises, shrugs His shoulders, and proclaims, "Only the Father knows." And the inhabitants of God's kingdom know they must continue to wait.

Breaking the tension, Gabriel hurries to the stage and thanks Mary, John, and Paul for their kind words. "I could tell you a few stories of my own," he says, "but it's time to sing happy birthday and cut the cake."

Suddenly, from the back of the room, a glorious, saintly woman stands and stares at Gabriel as she makes her way to the stage. She is so glorious that Gabriel bellows for the crowd to wait. Turning his attention to the woman, their eyes lock as she makes her way to the front of the stage.

With determination and a commanding voice, she tells Gabriel, "I want to say a few words." But he responds, "I'm sorry, but the honored guests have already spoken. It's time to cut the cake."

Sensing her desire to speak and the urgency of her words, Jesus stands and tells Gabriel, "Please, let her speak." She turns to Jesus and nods her head in appreciation.

"Down there," she begins, "I was from Canaan. My people were despised by the Jews. But, Jesus, when I saw You, I realized that You were the only hope to cure my dying daughter. Oh, but You put up quite an argument and refused at first and even insulted me. For a moment, I considered the possibility that even the Messiah had an arrogant side. But I later realized that Your harsh words taught Your disciples a valuable lesson about prejudice and bias.

When You healed my daughter, I was overjoyed, but now in Your kingdom, I remain eternally grateful. Your compassion for all people shows that You are the Savior of the world. Your healing power will forever be remembered. And I will praise Your name and give You thanks forever. Now I would like all of the inhabitants of heaven to meet my daughter."

The woman's daughter rises from her seat in the back of the room, and the crowd explodes with applause and shouts of joy. The angels and saints give a standing ovation to Jesus. As the daughter rushes to the podium and embraces her mother, the thunderous roar continues for several minutes.

Standing at the podium, Gabriel quiets the crowd and proclaims, "The moment we have been waiting for is here!"

The two thousand candles on the angel food birthday cake are lit. It takes the breath of the Holy Spirit to blow out all of them. To honor Jesus' work on earth, each piece of cake receives a scoop of Rocky Road ice cream. And as the people wait for their slice, the waiters serve Heavenly Roasted Coffee.

By now, the chamber orchestra is replaced by the Sheep and a Goat, a lively rock band whose members are the shepherds the angel visited on the first Christmas, and their lead singer is the criminal who hung next to Jesus at His crucifixion. After leading everyone in singing the traditional Happy Birthday song, the dancing begins as the band plays the Beatles "Birthday Song":

> You say it's your birthday
> Well, my blessings to you;
> Today is your birthday
> We're gonna have a good time;
> I'm glad it's your birthday
> Happy birthday to you!

+++

After the children's service on Christmas Eve but while Ken was still at church for the later services, our son and I would come home and bake a birthday cake for Jesus. He always chose Pillsbury Funfetti, his favorite cake of all time! The vanilla frosting was topped with red, green, and white sprinkles and decorated with an assortment of small toys, usually mini John Deere tractors, bulldozers, and lawn mowers. He would carefully insert the multicolored candles, filling in the remaining gaps between his treasured toys. I can still remember his excitement and joy as if our time-honored tradition was only yesterday.

After our Christmas dinner, we would light the candles and sing "Happy Birthday" to Jesus. This special family moment added to the joyous celebration of our Christmas Day. Our son is now married and with children of his own, and he and his lovely wife continue this special family tradition, which Ken and I do as well.

The Christmas dinner you will eat in your home is an earthly extension of the heavenly one taking place in the kingdom. The presents you exchange with each other are preordained from the time the Magi first brought their gifts to the Christ Child.

Be sure to give the best gift to Jesus. Give Him one positive action you can do that will strengthen your relationship with Him: attend church more regularly, volunteer at a local food bank, read the Bible every day, set aside daily time for contemplative prayer. You get the idea.

While you give material gifts to everyone else, don't forget the most important gift of all!

The body and blood of Jesus Christ you receive at Holy Communion on Christmas day connects you to the heavenly banquet. Holy Communion looks forward to the time when you will be able to celebrate the birth of Christ with all angels and archangels and all the company of heaven. What an exciting day that will be! Such excitement and anticipation! This is the true hope of Christmas. This day should give you joy every day, knowing that the hope of Christmas provides comfort, even when times are not good.

+++

I make routine visits to Gerald, a man dying of liver cancer. The man has been a faithful and very active parishioner for ten years, and I have come to love him like a brother. His chemotherapy sessions have taken a toll on his health, weakening his motivation and reducing his powerful voice to a whisper. But his frail body hasn't depleted his love and joy for Christmas. Gerald leaves his artificial Christmas tree up all year, which he plugs in its lights and sings a Christmas hymn every morning.

When I bring him Holy Communion, he insists that I read part of the Christmas story from either Matthew or Luke. We have a mini Christmas service, no matter the time of the year. During this time, Gerald refuses to talk about his cancer; he only speaks of the joy, the hope, and the love of Christmas, which brings me as much joy as it does him. Gerald has taught me that my heart should always be filled with Christmas joy.

On my last visit with Gerald, I knew the end was very near. He picked up that I gazed at him a little longer.

"What are you looking at me for?" he asked.

"I just want to know if you want me to administer Last Rites?"

"Last Rites? To me? Don't be silly. When are you coming back? I'll have my sister make a batch of Christmas cookies."

Less than a week later, his sister called and asked if I could meet her at Gerald's house to administer Last Rites. Finding him barely conscious, I prayed over him and anointed him for the last time. I remember thinking, *I'm losing a dear friend, but heaven is gaining a joyful soul.*

+++

Overwhelmed by the beauty and majesty of the kingdom and with eyes wider than life, Gerald is enraptured by the joy of the birthday celebration. Juggling his plate of cake and ice cream while balancing his cup of coffee, Gerald moves toward the edge of the room. Still in awe by the incredulous scene, he turns his attention to the center of the room. In the midst of many well-wishers, his and Jesus' eyes lock as Jesus makes His way to him.

"Welcome to the party," Jesus begins.

With a trembling voice, Gerald responds, "The entire place is unbelievable. I never dreamed…no one can ever imagine what this is like."

"I know," says Jesus. "That is a large part of the problem. Gerald, you have been waiting to celebrate Christmas in heaven for your entire earthly life: leaving your tree up all year, reading the story of my birth over and over and over, singing Christmas hymns even in the middle of the summer. It gives me great joy that you are finally here with us."

Overcome with emotion, Gerald responds, "Happy Birthday, Jesus!"

"Merry Christmas, Gerald!"

+++

This week...
Make a birthday cake for Jesus, buy balloons and streamers
and candles and party hats and anything else to honor
our Lord and Savior's birthday! After dinner, light
the candles on His cake, gather your family
and friends around the table,
and sing with love and joy and at the top of your lungs,
"Happy birthday to Jesus!"

Forever Silenced

When Herod saw that he had been tricked by the wise men, he was infuriated, and he sent his soldiers and killed all the children in and around Bethlehem who were two years old or under, according to the time that he had learned from the wise men. Then was fulfilled what had been spoken through the prophet Jeremiah, "A voice was heard in Ramah, wailing and loud lamentation, Rachel weeping for her children; she refused to be consoled, because they are no more." (Matthew 2:16–18)

Reverend Kenneth and Elizabeth Herzog

> God's devotion
> Blameless baby
> Doomed future
> Innocent infant
> Destroyed lives

Roars of distant thunder from horses of bloodthirsty and vicious soldiers
Swords and nails pierce Israel's newborn as mothers mourn, cry, and wail
Blood flows from faultless cribs to cruel Calvary, victims of evil's victory
Precious innocent blood drips and sanctifies the old rugged wooden cross

> Herod's revenge
> Thumping hoofs
> Fractured doors
> Desperate shouts
> Forever silenced
> Holy Pieta aches
> Babies' gasps fall
> New lives ended
> Dim lights faded
> Tiny eyes closed

Abraham Lincoln wrote, "A man's true character can be found by giving him a little power." Written two thousand years after Herod the Great, Lincoln's words provide an apt description of this ruthless king. But often power comes with immense insecurity, including the dread of usurpation, which consumed Herod's recurring fear. Herod's angst overwhelmed him so much that he ordered the deaths of three of his sons, believing they were plotting his death and subsequent seizure of the throne.

Herod's fear reached new heights when he realized that the Wise Men had tricked him by taking an alternate route home after visiting the Christ Child. His insecurity, his fear, and his temper formed the perfect storm of his evil acts, not only against his sons but also against the newborn King. In essence, Herod became Satan's newest pawn.

The result? Infanticide of all Israelite babies two years and younger, not just in Bethlehem, but the surrounding areas as well. This evil, bloodthirsty king sought revenge and, in doing so, placated his own insecurity. Assured that the future King could not have survived his act of terror, Herod slept peacefully.

Even though this atrocity took place after the Wise Men visited the Christ Child on the Epiphany, we remember this atrocity, the Feast of the Holy Innocents, on December 28. This trauma, which abruptly thrusts us back into darkness and evil so soon after celebrating the birth of light and love, reminds us that the good news will always have enemies who attack quickly and viciously.

But who wants to confront this infanticide so soon after Christmas? After all, the joy of Christmas still lingers in our homes and in our hearts. Decorations sparkle. Friends and family linger. And the excitement of New Year's Eve builds. Thus, we often overlook the martyrdom of these infants. And yet just as Jews do not forget the Holocaust, so too must we never forget the deaths of these innocent children. But we do!

+++

Every year, an unmarried, childless woman in our parish asked me to remember the Feast of the Holy Innocents with an evening service. This tragedy that took place so long ago filled her with compassion. But I never honored her request because I didn't want to lead my parishioners back into darkness. Besides, I was exhausted and looked forward to spending time with my family after the busy Christmas services. So I told her that attendance would be sparse and that the Christmas season should crescendo and linger, not be cut short. Who wants to remember the massacre of babies while their own children delight in the gifts they just received from Santa?

So instead, I wrote an article in our monthly newsletter reminding people of this horrific event. But I now realize I was wrong. She was right. I was blind. A deeper contemplation of this tragic event reveals a deeper truth of God's mercy.

+++

Reverend Kenneth and Elizabeth Herzog

In this broken and sinful world, glory and tragedy often intertwine, not in God's design but in the corruption of a fallen humanity. In the midst of life, we find death. In the midst of death, we find life. And just as the third day after Christmas brings death, the third day in the tomb brings life. Life and death will intertwine until Jesus' Second Coming restores all life.

The Son of God takes on flesh to give new life to those who lose it. The Christ Child, with humility but also with glory, celebrates the season of His birth by remembering the holy innocents and protecting their lives forever. God is timeless. And so the grace of His Son's cross over thirty years later is already available to God, enabling the holy innocents to inherit the kingdom. God reveals that His Son's birth does not create a perfect world on earth but a redeemed world in the kingdom. Thus, tragedy becomes glory; dying becomes rebirth.

The human mind can't possibly comprehend the magnitude of the Son's human birth. His birth engulfs the totality of humanity: our joys and holiness, our sorrows and suffering, even Herod's evil. No matter how Herod tried, the darkness of his evil couldn't extinguish the light of God's goodness. Nothing escapes the magnitude of His birth: neither its light nor its redemption.

By remembering the Feast of the Holy Innocents, we are not pulled back into the darkness of evil; rather, we are brought into the light of redemption, just as a stained-glass window gives beauty to tragedy, hope to despair, and life to death.

+++

As a priest, I have counseled numerous families who have lost a child. I identify with their grief because when I was seven years old, my brother who was five died. He was the second youngest of the five children in our family and my only brother. When he died, I lost my best friend, my constant companion, my cohort in mischief. I lost part of my heart.

Gene went to the hospital for a routine tonsillectomy, a simple procedure that doctors regularly performed. And the surgery went well and was successful. My mom spent that night in the hospital with him, while my dad returned home to care for me and my three sisters.

Late that night, a nurse came in and gave Gene a shot of penicillin that was prescribed for the little boy in the next bed. Gene had an immediate allergic reaction and died in my mom's arms.

Our family was turned upside down that night. My sisters and I huddled together, crying long, desperate tears, sometimes with sobs, sometimes with screams, sometimes with silence. I can recall my dad trying to remain strong after Gene's death but also seeing the devastation and grief in his tired eyes. And it was the only time that I can ever remember seeing my dad cry.

My mom has recalled that night only once in my adult life, and when she did, it was still extremely emotional for her. I'll never forget how distant she looked and how suddenly her tears came, as if she were holding Gene all over again. That moment was just as heartbreaking as the night he died.

Now that I'm older and with a family of my own, I can only imagine the anguish of the scene: a mother holding her dead son… the Pieta. While my mom held Gene for only a short time, the grief of Mary holding her crucified Son must have seemed like an eternity.

The death of a child is the strongest emotional grief any mother can experience. The natural bond of love is torn away. I witnessed this grief first with my mom and then again on two different occasions: when I presided at the burial of a three-year old boy and when I was suddenly called to the hospital to baptize a stillborn baby girl.

The death of a child at any age is emotionally devastating and spiritually challenging for both parents. If you have experienced the death of a child, then you can better understand this black hole of life.

I think of Gene often and sometimes I even speak to him. I tell him how much I still wish that we could have grown up together, sharing childhood secrets, experiencing teenage disappointments, and rejoicing in adult accomplishments. Sometimes, when my life takes an unexpected turn, and I'm faced with insurmountable problems, I tell him how fortunate he is that he entered the kingdom so early and never had to face the drudgery of mortal life. During these times, I actually become a bit jealous of him.

Reverend Kenneth and Elizabeth Herzog

When I enter the kingdom, I will look for him first. But then again, he will probably be right up front to greet me. I thank God for this hope! God gives this hope to everyone: to those who have lost a child, a sibling, a spouse, or any loved one. It is the very heart of God's compassion and comfort for us in this life.

+++

This week…
Give thanks to God for the many blessings in your life.
If you have lost a loved one, do something to honor that person. Plant a small tree, buy and hang a windchime
outside your front door, volunteer
at a local food bank or at a nursing home or
at a food kitchen… Do something
to remember your loved one.
And above all, know that God's compassion and
love will comfort you.
All you have to do is reach out to Him. He will answer!

The Tent

In the beginning was the Word, and the Word was with God, and the Word was God. He was in the beginning with God. All things came into being through Him, and without Him not one thing came into being. What has come into being through Him was life, and the life was the light of all people. The light shines in the darkness, and the darkness did not overcome it. And the Word became flesh and dwells among us, and we have seen His glory, the glory as of a father's only son full of grace and truth. (John's Prologue 1:1–5, 14)

Covered in the void of total darkness and unaware of its Creator, the formless, lifeless Earth waits. Hovering over the water, the Spirit waits for the Father's thunderous voice: *"And God said 'Let there be light.' And there was light" (Genesis 1:1–3)*, thus forming a perfect world of all living things.

As one of the most important pieces of scripture and part of an early Christian hymn, we hear John's Prologue every year on the Sunday following Christmas Day. Poetic and powerful, its inspirational message warms our hearts with hope and joy, so much so that we can almost hear the heavenly angels glorifying God with their cathedral voices:

In the beginning was the Word.
And the Word was with God.
And the Word was God.

The Word is God's Son. With God from the beginning, the Son comes to Earth at Christmas in the human person of Jesus and brings the Light of Love. Jesus tells us what the Father wants us to hear: God is the Light of Love, and the Light of Love is God.

But humanity's sin, beginning with the first Adam, infiltrates the Light of Love with darkness, bringing chaos and evil. However, as John explains, the darkness does not conquer the Light.

The most profound verse of John's Prologue is *verse 14*: "*The Word became flesh and dwells among us.*" The Greek word for "dwells" refers to a tabernacle or a tent. The Son of God leaves His heavenly Mansion, comes to earth, and lives among us in a tent, giving us a new perspective of God's desire to have a closer, down-to-earth relationship with us. John's Prologue reveals that the joy of Christmas brings an encounter with the Word, the Light, and the Truth.

+++

Reverend Kenneth and Elizabeth Herzog

The joy of Christmas brings with it an encounter with the Word

Jesus invites you into His tent that has no walls, no emotional barriers. Your invitation includes no one else but you. He assures you that your conversation will be personal, private, and confidential. He stands at the open flap and invites you in.

But you run away as fast as you can, too frightened to look back. After nights of wrestling with yourself, you finally go. As you approach His tent, you are overwhelmed with doubt, insecurity, and fear.

You walk toward the entrance, not able to look at Him but sensing He has not taken His eyes off of you. Taking a deep breath, you step through the open flap. But there is nothing inside: no walls, no barriers, not even a bedroll. Not even Him.

Confused, you move to a corner, turn, and there He is! He calls for you, but you can't move. Your mind races with doubt as your heart screams with fear. You want to run, run back to your life, run anywhere! But your frozen body can't move. He beckons you again. This time, He sits on the dirt floor and motions you closer. Taking another deep breath, you muster all your strength and sit next to Him. Just you and God's Son sitting together on a dirt floor.

Overwhelmed, nervous, and hesitant, you say nothing. But He wants you to speak openly, freely, and truthfully as He promises to listen lovingly, patiently, and unconditionally. Your heart races. Your body shakes. Your head pounds. After what seems like an eternity, you finally speak. You find yourself telling Him everything. You pour out your soul to Him: your deceit, your greed, your anger, your regrets, your secrets, your doubts, your fears! Your words are raw and hard and brutal. But He listens, lovingly, patiently, and unconditionally. And the more He listens, the more you speak. And the more you speak, the more He listens.

He tells you how much He loves you, over and over, again and again. He is your one true love Who wants so desperately for you to love Him! He calls for you. He longs for you. He waits for you.

You finally allow Him into your heart! You are His, and His Word consumes you, filling you with His love. Just…for…*you!* Your conversation now becomes so personal and intimate that you feel you are the only one He cares about, the only one He knows, the only one He loves. He takes away your fears and anxieties. He removes your sins, buried with anger, enveloped with regret, drowning in sorrow. He reassures you that you are worthy, worthy of Him! He wants you to believe. He wants you to open your arms and allow Him into your life! He wants you to rest, knowing that He is with you, now and forever. He is your Lord and Savior. And He will never forsake you!

How could you ever stay outside? Remaining outside Jesus' tent is life without the Word, life without His love. Staying outside exposes you to the elements of a life without Jesus. Void of His Word and love, you will face the evil one alone. You will be weakened, and you will be easy prey. You will be forced to face life's greatest tribulations alone. Without Jesus, Satan will take over, slowly but determined to overpower you, confuse you, deceive you. Without Jesus, Satan will win! And Satan will smile.

Go inside; He waits for you! Just *go*!

The joy of Christmas brings with it an encounter with the Light

Jesus comes and lives among us in a tent. When darkness falls, you may have small lights: a flashlight or a lantern or even a spotlight. But these lights are not enough to protect you from the elements of darkness, elements that can trip you and trap you and cause you to fall, darkness where animals lurk on the fringes.

But His tent is filled with bright light. Jesus *is* the Light. Light radiates from Him. In His tent, you do not need a flashlight. As you stand outside in the darkness, you can see His silhouette against the wall of His tent. Jesus invites you into the light of His tent. He knows where you are in the darkness. He wants to protect you from the evils lurking there. He waits patiently for you.

The only other option is to remain in the darkness, outside of the Light. The farther you are from the Light, the more difficult it is to see. Even during the daylight, if you are not in His tent, you are in darkness. The Light lives among us in a tent.

Go inside; He waits for you! Just *go*!

Reverend Kenneth and Elizabeth Herzog

The joy of Christmas brings with it an encounter with the Truth

In Jesus' tent, you are one with the Truth. You look Truth in the eye. The Truth is not filled with fear but enlightenment. Jesus engages your true self. The Truth will set you free and release you from the bondage of self-deception and lies that mask the true you.

Inside His tent there are no walls or barriers to the Truth. Jesus is the Truth, and He wants to reveal Himself to you. The search for Jesus is the search for the Truth. When you find one, you find the other. You say things to the Truth that you normally wouldn't say. When someone asks you to tell the Truth, that person is asking you to say what Jesus would say. In His tent, there is no room for excuses, explanations, finger-pointing, and name-calling. There is no room in His tent for the past. Once inside, there is no place to hide from the Truth. Jesus *is* the Truth. Once inside, no secrets are hidden.

The only other option is to remain outside and not face the Truth. Lies and self-deceptions are traps of the evil one lurking in the shadows. The Truth will place you on the road to the eternal. Life outside His tent is life without the Truth. It is a life of sham, forgery, and fraud. It is the life of Satan.

The Truth becomes flesh and lives among us in a tent. Jesus invites you in. Go inside; He waits for you! Just *go*!

+++

Summer Camp

Every summer from the time our son was in fifth grade to the time he graduated from high school and went to college, he and I would go on a two-week camping trip while my wife, Elizabeth, visited her family. We left the day after school finished for summer break. Just the two of us…one-on-one…every summer. Northern Georgia… Tennessee…up through the Carolinas. I doubt there is a camping ground or a state park in those areas that the two of us have not camped.

You can get to know someone pretty well in a tent: little idiosyncrasies of your personality, your joys and fears, your thoughts on a variety of issues, personal plans, and dreams you have held for years. We took a small tent so there were no interior walls or barriers. I am convinced that my relationship with my son today has its roots in that tent. A tent can right a lot of wrongs. A tent can heal a lot of wounds. A tent can bring a brighter light than the day before.

I long for those camping trips with our son. I wish I could relive just one. I miss cooking dinner together and laughing as we mixed together leftovers to make our own camping recipes, giving them funny names: Bolognese Burgers, Dos Huevos con Pollo de Dios, Atomic Pork Chops, and my all-time favorite, Aunt and Uncle Pasta.

I would always get stuck doing the dishes, but it was a small price to pay. I miss the campfire conversations the most. The preface "Don't tell Mom, but…" always led to a funny story that revealed a part of my son I never knew. There was so much trust between us. The campfire conversations were the heart of the camping trip. They always led to a deeper talk once we were inside the tent.

Our son is married now with children of his own. He and his wife bought an RV. They take the family camping…North Georgia…Tennessee…up through the Carolinas. They camp in some of the same campgrounds and state parks the two of us stayed in. It gives me great joy. It tells me that he enjoyed our trips as much as I did, if that's possible.

That is the kind of relationship Jesus longs to have with you: personal, just the two of you, one-on-one…one without walls or barriers. Many people don't treasure such a relationship. They don't want certain parts of their heart exposed. They keep deep secrets hidden in the darkness. But Jesus knows. So why your secrets, your fears, and your doubts? Why? He knows everything, so why try to hide from Him? Why remain silent in the dark? The Truth becomes flesh and lives among us in a tent. Jesus invites you in.

Go inside; He waits for you! Just *go*!

+++

This week…

Be a child again and make a tent. Make a tent, some place where you can be alone without the distractions of the world. Hang a sign: "Do Not Disturb."

Turn off all of the lights and invite Jesus into your tent. Open your arms as you tell Him how much you love Him. Ask for His understanding, His forgiveness, His compassion. Remain silent and listen for His word. Receive His love, knowing that He loves you more than you could ever imagine. He is the Word, the Light, and the Truth. You are His and He is yours!

Go inside; He waits for you! Just go!

Unexpected Angels

An angel of the Lord appeared to Joseph in a dream and said, "Get up, take the child and his mother, and flee to Egypt, and remain there until I tell you; for Herod is about to search for the child, to destroy him." Then Joseph got up, took the child and his mother by night, and went to Egypt, and remained there until the death of Herod. This was to fulfill what had been spoken by the Lord through the prophet, "Out of Egypt I have called my son." (Matthew 2:13–15)

Distressing cries form droplets of sweat on his tightened forehead. Darkness approaches, echoing a menacing thunder. Something is terribly wrong. Danger lurks. The hunter intends to inflict serious harm: death, no doubt. As the predator draws closer, its eyes penetrate his soul. Paralyzed, Joseph's frozen legs don't offer strength for escape.

"Move, Joseph! Move!"

Barely audible, exhaling from his gut, he weeps. "I can't!" Shivering, he buries himself in their quilt, praying it will disappear. Mary stirs.

Suddenly, before death strikes, a radiant light appears, a familiar presence. Familiar but unrecognizable. "What!" Joseph insists. "Help me!" he pleads. Drawn toward the light, rubbing his heavy eyes, Joseph recognizes the Angel Gabriel. Relieved, Joseph sighs, knowing his ordained safety will end the hunt.

"Joseph, you must take the baby and his mother and flee! The child is in serious danger! Flee, Joseph, flee! Wake up, Joseph! Wake up! Joseph go…NOW!"

Startled, Joseph sits straight up in bed. Sweat trickles down his brow as his wide eyes stare at the angel. Alarmed and frightened, Mary wakes and turns toward her husband. "Joseph, you're all wet. What's wrong? Oh, Joseph," she moans. "You've had a bad dream."

"Mary, we must go. Mary, we must go now!"

"Joseph, it was a dream. Go back to sleep."

"Mary, it was the angel."

"The angel!" Mary knows that Joseph would only obey the angel.

"Mary, we must go and go now. The baby is in danger. Now, Mary! Now! We must be on our way!"

Shaking, Mary gets up and stares at her husband from the side of the bed. "Where?" she pleads. "Go where? It's the middle of the night."

"We must go," he insists.

"Go where?" she yells.

"I don't know! To Egypt."

"What! To Egypt? Are we going to Egypt? Are you sure this is what the angel told you?"

"Yes, I'm certain."

"Are you sure, Joseph?"

"Yes, Mary. We must go to Egypt. Don't ask again. Just trust me. Trust the angel."

Once again, in perfect obedience to the angel and to the Father, Mary obeys. Leaving everything except their faith, Mary wraps the child in a warm blanket, and within minutes, they are on their way.

Because the dream warns Joseph about Jesus' safety, the child escapes Herod's infanticide. The angel tells Joseph that they must flee. In other words, *now*! Don't wait until the morning. Don't delay another minute. Trusting the dream and recognizing the angel, Mary and Joseph comply. The good news of Jesus' birth suddenly turns perilous. And the Holy Family run for their lives.

Our journey with Jesus hastens. There is no time to gather our things, no time to waste, no time to question. Sometimes God's timeline allows us to pray, ponder, reflect, and pray some more. Sometimes our window of opportunity is small, and God does not want to miss it. Other times, God calls for immediate action. In this chaotic and ominous turn of events, we learn about holiness, faithfulness, and God's providential care.

+++

The First Lesson
Prayer Involves the Ministry of Angels

The common image of an angel resembles human form, dressed in a white robe with large wings. Angels appear throughout Scripture: Jacob wrestled with one all night. The prophets Isaiah and Ezekiel received visits from angels. The Angel Gabriel appeared to Mary and Joseph several times. When angels appeared to the shepherds announcing Jesus' birth and again when they appeared to the women inside the empty tomb at His resurrection, they have always been described with human semblance and have always been a part of God's master plan.

But for many people, believing in angels requires a leap of faith, which most people either don't understand or won't accept. For many people, angels are too mysterious and invisible, often compared to ghosts. As a result, we seldom recognize their presence in our lives.

This is regrettable because angels speak to us the same way Gabriel spoke to Joseph. Angels are our messengers and protectors who appear in different forms and who surround us with God's presence. Angels are God's messengers to us, not our messengers to Him. God resides within them. We shouldn't pray to angels; rather, we should pray to God the Father, Son, and Holy Spirit. God's answer often comes through angelic intervention, which we do not fully understand. Their presence is often unrecognizable because angels interact with us in ways that we don't perceive. Sometimes we look back and ask, "Could that have been an angel watching over me?"

+++

> An angel stood and met my gaze, Through the low doorway of my tent; The tent is struck, the vision stays; I only know she came and went.
> (James Russell Lowell)

Ken and I slipped away for an overnight. Just the two of us, no agenda, no expectations, no worries. Just us, away for a day and a night.

We enjoyed a clear, sunny day—a slight breeze offset the brilliant sun, warm but welcoming. After enjoying a leisurely lunch outside, we strolled through the park, filled with flowers bursting with spring colors, feeling the pressures of the week slowly fade away. As we listened to a young man playing his guitar and the laughter of children, we felt not only the love we share but also the love God shares with us.

The sun-kissed sky soon gave way to twinkling stars, a glowing golden moon, and a cool breeze that swayed with the inviting music floating out of restaurants dotted on the other side of the park. A perfect day followed by a perfect night! Until the next morning!

I don't enjoy drinking coffee from a paper cup, so I went downstairs to the restaurant for two mugs of coffee. As I balanced the mugs of steaming coffee, I struggled to push the outside elevator button. Once inside, I pressed the button for our floor. The doors closed; the elevator moved. All was well, until a jerk brought the elevator to an abrupt halt! My body stiffened, my heart leaped, my fingers pressed buttons. By this time, with hot coffee streaming down my arm, I didn't care what floor as long as the doors opened.

Just as I pressed the "call" button, the elevator's back door opened. A man, dressed in a dark-gray shirt and pants, with an even darker-gray laundry bin, appeared. But then the door closed. By this time, I kept praying, "Please, God, please *help* me! Please! Please!" But nothing! Silence! Frantically, I pressed the "call" button again. No movement, no sound, nothing!

All of a sudden, the back door reopened. And the same man appeared but this time without the laundry bin. Shaking, feeling threatened, gasping for air, I sputtered, "I'm scared and don't know what to do!" Just then, a voice came on the speaker asking, "Where are you? What's the problem?" The man quietly assured the anonymous voice that everything was fine, and he would "take care of this!"

Feeling even more trapped, I prayed out loud, "God, please help me! Please, God! Please!" Suddenly, the front door opened, and as I turned to see where he was, he was gone. I didn't stop to question. I didn't stop to think. I didn't stop to breathe. I took the mugs of coffee and bolted, just as the doors were closing.

After Ken and I talked about the entire episode, we realized that the man dressed in dark gray was an angel, God's messenger and protector who surrounded me with His loving presence. God answered my prayers that morning. And even though fear blocked my understanding, I know now that He sent an angel to my rescue.

+++

The Second Lesson
God Protects His Children

It's not safe for the baby Jesus to be in Israel, so God leads the Holy Family to Egypt to protect His Son. Thirteen hundred years earlier, it was not safe for God's people to be in Egypt, so God told Moses to lead His people to Israel. What an extraordinary twist of holy irony!

The manner of God's protection remains a mystery that we don't understand. However, trusting God's wisdom and discernment gives us confidence that He will guide us in the right direction, even if it seems unfavorable to our will. If we live in God's will, He will protect us, making other options a moot point. It's a matter of faith.

But what happens when we don't pray? Does God forsake us? Does God ignore us? Absolutely not! But when we don't pray, we can't recognize His wisdom and discernment, which leaves us fearful, doubtful, and uncertain about which option to choose. Part of the mystery of God's love is that He continues to protect us even if we don't ask for His guidance. Like most parents, He loves us unconditionally. Like most parents who guide and protect their children, even when their children don't ask for or accept their guidance, God's protection and guidance remains.

Does this mean if we pray, tragedy will never happen? Does this mean people who encounter serious problems aren't leading a faithful life? Absolutely not! This was the Old Testament belief of the Jews, but Jesus has taken us to a new understanding. Even though these mysterious questions have no mortal answers, we must continue to pray and trust God's will. A life in Jesus provides us with confidence and an awareness that a life outside of Him does not.

+++

The Third Lesson
God Brings Us Home to Him

God's well-planned design to protect the Holy Family from the infanticide of the holy innocents leads them out of Egypt after Herod's death and returns them to Israel, which fulfills Hosea's prophecy, *"Out of Egypt I have called my son" (Matthew 2:15)*. After returning to Israel, they settled in Nazareth, Mary's hometown, where they lived before they left for Bethlehem to register for the census when Jesus was born. Thus, God brings the Holy Family full circle.

The entire plot of salvation history is simple: We had it. We lost it. We want it back. Our unity with God begins in the garden of Eden, a symbol of the kingdom. We lost our unity with God because of our sinfulness. Once we are reunited with God in the kingdom, our unity with Him will be restored. God stops at nothing to bring His children full circle.

Walking into our home after a long journey, how often do we say, "It's good to be home." This is what our spirit will say when we are home in the kingdom. And God will embrace our spirit and say, "Welcome home!" The earth is not our home; it's just temporary housing. The kingdom is our home. Like Mary and Joseph who knew their time in Egypt was temporary, we will one day return to God who will bring us full circle.

Beth and I know several couples in the military who are separated for six to eight months at a time. While their spouses are away, they know their separation is temporary, and they count the months, weeks, and the days for their joyous reunion. God also knows that our time away from Him is temporary, and He counts the years, the months, the weeks, and the days for our return. He too looks forward to our joyous reunion.

Because God continues to work within us, salvation history is ongoing.

Each day, God shapes us, forms us, and prepares us for the kingdom. This perspective opens our eyes to see His work in our lives. God will not rest until we are all seated at the heavenly banquet, and Jesus will say the blessing.

+++

Our daily problems, as difficult as they may be, are only temporary. But sometimes our problems overshadow the glorious day when we will return home. Our faith rises above earthly concerns and refocuses our attention beyond our earthly life to our heavenly one. This level of faith makes it easier for us to cope with the problems of life.

Our faith should begin with a prayer of discernment, which aligns our will to God's will. Faith is a bicycle built for two. We take the front seat, steering and pedaling our way through life, taking great comfort knowing that Jesus is on the back seat along for the ride. However, faith comes when we stop the bike, get off, and change places with Jesus, allowing Him to steer.

What faith! What trust!

This is the trust and faith that Joseph and Mary had as they participated in the history of salvation. It's now our turn.

+++

This week...
When you encounter a difficult decision, say a
prayer to discern God's will. If it means
changing directions from your current path, don't
be alarmed. Fully rely on God *and let His*
angels take charge over you. They are perched, waiting to hear from you.

The Season of Epiphany

*H*ave you ever watched a movie wearing a pair of 3D glasses? The images on the screen appear to jump out at you, making them seem larger than life. But 3D glasses are an optical illusion, created by enhancing our depth perception.

Have you ever thought about God's activity in your life? Unlike the optical illusion created by 3D glasses, God *is* larger than life. And if you look for Him, He will jump out at you, appearing in events that you often consider commonplace.

The season of Epiphany is a time to wear your spiritual glasses. By becoming more aware of God's presence in your life, each day can bring spiritual epiphanies. But you must allow God in your life. And when you do, you will see how holy and anointed the world really is.

The Living Light

In the time of King Herod, after Jesus was born in Bethlehem of Judah, wise men from the East came to Jerusalem, asking, "Where is the child who has been born king of the Jews? For we have observed his star at its rising, and have come to pay him homage." When the wise men saw that the star had stopped, they were overwhelmed with joy. On entering the house, they saw the child with Mary, his mother; and they knelt down and paid him homage. Then, opening their treasure chests, they offered him gifts of gold, frankincense, and myrrh. (Matthew 2:1, 2, 10, 11)

In all liturgical churches, the Feast of the Epiphany is celebrated on January 6, the twelfth day of Christmas, ending the Christmas season. The Feast of the Epiphany celebrates the arrival of the Wise Men to see the Christ Child. Unfortunately, by January 6, most people have taken down their tree and packed away their crèche. By the time the Wise Men arrive, it's as though Jesus has come and gone. No wonder they had to stop and ask, "Where is this newborn King?"

Traditions from the Eastern Church maintain that there are three Wise Men: Gaspar, Balthasar, and Melchior. But Matthew's gospel, the only biblical reference to their visit, does not identify a specific number of them and does not exclude the possibility that there could have been more than the three we recognize today. Matthew simply states that Wise Men from the East followed a star, searching for the Christ Child.

One of the main reasons only three Wise Men were identified is because there were only three gifts: gold, frankincense, and myrrh. Each gift foreshadowed a significant aspect of Jesus' life. Gold foreshadowed Jesus as king. Frankincense, used in temple sacrifices, foreshadowed the sacrifice of Jesus on the cross. And myrrh, an expensive ointment used to prepare dead bodies for burial, foreshadowed Jesus' death.

Matthew also mentions that the Wise Men entered a house, insinuating that the Holy Family is no longer in the manger, stable, or cave where Jesus was born. This could have been twelve days after His birth since the Feast of the Epiphany is the twelfth day after Christmas Day. But since Herod murdered all Jewish babies two years and younger, their visit might have been a couple of years after Jesus' birth. Nevertheless, the Wise Men were the first ones outside of Israel to see the Christ Child, indicating that Jesus is not only the Savior of the Jews but also the Savior of the world.

The Feast of the Epiphany points to Jesus' worldwide ministry, indicating that we all belong to the same "catholic" (universal) Christian church, which brings salvation to all. Thus, the Feast of the Epiphany invites everyone to the kingdom. Those denominations that act like they have a lock on the kingdom could use an epiphany.

+++

Reverend Kenneth and Elizabeth Herzog

Elizabeth and I had an epiphany after the 7:00 p.m. Christmas Eve service this past year. Knowing that we had a couple of hours before the 11:00 p.m. service, we took a walk around the plaza where our church is located. After being in church for the past few hours, the crisp night air, clear sky sprinkled with shining stars welcomed us as we walked. The plaza was filled with cheerful people enjoying the Christmas music that serenaded them as they strolled along the plaza, adding to the spirit that is uniquely Christmas.

As we made our way back to the church, we were greeted by a most beautiful sight. The lights in our church illuminated our stunning stained-glass windows. They are beautiful in the daytime as we see them with the light streaming in, but they are even more glorious at night with the light shining out. At night, the light shines outward, which makes our windows look like sparkling jewels.

The great feasts of Christmas and Epiphany proclaimed a single glorious message for us that night. As the Prophet Isaiah proclaimed, *"The people who live in darkness have seen a great light" (Isaiah 9:2)*. We wonder if Isaiah was not only given a vision of the Messiah but also a vision of our church.

As the people in the church gathered on Christmas Eve to celebrate the birth of our Savior, the people in the plaza only had to make their way through the darkness to follow the light where the Christ Child lay. While the Wise Men traveled miles to find the Christ Child, the people in the plaza only had to travel a few steps.

Isn't that the purpose of the church? Isn't that why the church exists: to be a shining light that leads others to Christ? We bask in the light on Sunday mornings to worship and honor our King, and like the Wise Men, we bring our gifts and offerings to lay down in front of Him. However, we must not stop there. We must be a light for those who are still in the darkness outside the church and outside of God's love. On Christmas Eve, there were many more people in the dark than there were inside the church in the light. So we must find those people who live in the dark and then lead them into the Light.

+++

Who led you to Christ? Who has been the star that you followed through the darkness to find Jesus? Who has been the majestic stained-glass window through whom you found the glory and majesty of the Christ Child? Who has been your star?

If you have found the Light, what is preventing you from stepping further into the Light? Maybe you have not accepted the invitation. Why have you not stepped into the Light?

Why have you not had your epiphany with Jesus?

You can be the star for someone else. You know someone living in darkness. Don't leave that person there. Someone brought you to the Light. Now it's your turn.

But many Christians are not good evangelists. We share recipes, names of favorite restaurants, hairdressers, nail technicians, doctors, etc. But we do not share our faith. When it comes to faith, many people remain private because they don't know what to say or because they are not sure what they believe. Some people feel that if they express what they believe, and someone questions them, their relationship with God is disturbed.

> *You are the light of the world. A city built on a hill cannot be hidden. Men do not light a lamp and then put it under a bushel basket. They put it on a stand where it gives light to all in the house. In the same way, your light must shine before all so that they may see goodness in your acts and give praise to your heavenly Father. (Matthew 5:14–16)*

If you struggle with bringing people to Christ, try one of these suggestions.

The next time you wait in line, hum one of your favorite worship hymns or songs, like "Amazing Grace" or "How Great Thou Art." If someone notices, smile and say, "This past Sunday in church, we sang this hymn, and I can't get it out of my head." Boom! You're in. Let the Holy Spirit take over.

When you step into an elevator, say something like, "We are going up, right?" When the person nods or answers yes, say "Good.

One day I hope to meet Jesus." Hopefully, that will spark a conversation. Boom! You're in. Let the Holy Spirit take over.

Put a small statue of an angel on your desk at work. Wear a necklace with a cross on it and display it outside your shirt. Use a coffee cup with the name "Jesus" printed on it or use a coffee cup from your church. Purchase a spiritual tie or scarf and wear it to work. Do bold things for Jesus who does bold things for you.

Be creative and confident! Say something or do something that promotes Jesus Christ. Jesus defended you to His Father. The least you can do is to proclaim Him to the world. Plant a seed. Give the Holy Spirit something to work with. Do it to honor God. Be a light to the world.

One great and glorious day, you will be in the kingdom. One great and glorious day, you will stand in the presence of the Living Light. You stand in the presence of Jesus Christ. Wouldn't it be amazing if someone in heaven moved close to you whispering,

> You were my Star. You led me to the Light.
> You were my John the Baptist.
> You pointed me to Jesus.
> You were my Isaiah. You gave me hope
> when I was filled with despair.
> You were my stained-glass window.
> You showed me the glory of God.
> You were my Star.
> And I now stand with Him
> because you stood with me.

+++

This week...
Do something bold for Jesus.
Not something incidental but bold.
Do something out of your comfort zone.
Have fun with it; notice the reactions of others.
Let the Holy Spirit take it from there.

Emerging from the Water

> *In those days Jesus came from Nazareth of Galilee and was baptized by John in the Jordan. And just as he was coming up out of the water, he saw the heavens open and the Spirit descending like a dove on him. And a voice came from the heavens, "You are my Son, the Beloved; with you I am well pleased. (Mark 1:9–11)*

At midmorning on a crisp spring day, a hundred people gather along the bank of the Jordan River. John the Baptist stands waist high, braving the chilled water, proclaiming his fiery, passionate message. His tunic, stained by the brackish sediment, stands as a symbol for the sins of all. With a compelling voice, John beckons the people to repent their sins and be cleansed through baptism.

Slowly, they enter the river, approaching John, one by one. With a dark, penetrating stare, he asks, "Do you repent?"

"Yes" comes the reply.

Probing into their darkest secrets, he commands, "Do you repent of all of your sins from the time of childhood?"

"Yes, I repent all my sins."

With a forceful hand on the top of the head, John plunges the repentant sinner underneath the water. The bubbles of sin leave the soul and reach the surface just before the newly baptized is cleansed and receives new life. With a jubilant smile, John's now compassionate eyes engage the newly washed soul. "God bless you," he proclaims emphatically.

As the scene repeats itself over and over, the newly baptized emerge from the chilly water and warm themselves by the fire of the Holy Spirit.

On this crisp spring day, the Holy Spirit compels Jesus to the bank of the Jordan River. At first, Jesus stands in the periphery, observing the people's baptisms. Eventually, He feels called to join them, but they do not know Him. Waiting His turn to enter the river, He bends down and removes His sandals. Entering the river,

He approaches John whom He has not seen in quite some time. John's humble eyes can barely engage the Messiah. Confused why Jesus has come, John leans in and softly whispers, *"I need to be baptized by you, and do you come to me" (Matthew 3:14)*?

Sensing that something incredulous is about to happen, Jesus responds, *"Let it be so now; for it is proper for us in this way to fulfill all righteousness" (Matthew 3:15)*.

Confused but with a trusting heart, John honors Jesus' request. Knowing that Jesus is without sin, he does not question Jesus about repentance. John places his forceful hand on the top of Jesus' head and plunges Him under the surface of the water. No bubbles of sin leave Jesus' soul, but as He emerges from the water, the Holy Spirit descends as a dove, and the Father's voice comes from heaven: *"You are my Son, the Beloved; with you I am well pleased" (Mark 1:11)*, and at that moment, one of the most amazing epiphanies takes its place in salvation history.

+++

We hear the account of Jesus' baptism every year on the first Sunday after the Epiphany. But why would Jesus, who has no need to repent, ask John to baptize Him? As Jesus explains to John, *"It is proper for us in this way to fulfill all righteousness" (Matthew 3:15)*. While John preached a baptism of repentance to prepare the hearts of the people for the coming of the Messiah (*Matthew 3:11*), Jesus preached a baptism of repentance to prepare the people for the coming of the kingdom (*Matthew 4:17*). Thus, Jesus' baptism becomes the personification that fulfills the baptism of all of Israel.

Unlike us, Jesus didn't need baptism to remove sin because He was sinless. Unlike us, Jesus didn't need baptism to be adopted into God's family because He was already God's Son. But like us, Jesus needed baptism so the power of the Holy Spirit would be awakened and energized and would also ignite the fire of His ministry.

Though the unfolding of this epiphany will continue after His baptism, He emerges from the Jordan River unified in body and spirit and retreats to the desert for further discernment. Only through frequent prayer and long conversations with His Father does His humanity become aware of His divinity.

It's no coincidence that Jesus' baptism occurs during the season of Epiphany. God reveals Himself in an awesome, amazing, and powerful way, not only to the people there but also to Jesus Himself. For the first time, all three Persons of the Trinity reveal themselves simultaneously to humanity.

Jesus' baptism reveals that He is not only the Messiah but also the Son of God. Our faith proclaims that Jesus is 100 percent God and, at the same time, 100 percent human. Because of His humanity, He did not have all of the answers available to Him. Prior to His baptism, His divinity and humanity swirled within His self-image, often clouding His awareness that He is the Son of God.

At the Incarnation, His divinity took on human form, allowing Him to express the Father's love to us. But at the same time, His humanity imprisoned His godliness, which yearned to burst forth from stringent mortal restraints. Rising from the Jordan River was the first time Jesus felt His divinity rising out of His flesh, much like an out-of-body experience. The few minutes of His baptism thrusts His soul into a deep and profound epiphany, altering His very being.

+++

Jesus' baptism has major implications for Christians: You are not a body that contains a spirit. Rather, you are a spirit wrapped in a body. The anointing of the Holy Spirit at baptism makes us one with Him. Our spirit becomes His Spirit. *"The Spirit himself joins with our spirit to affirm that we are children of God" (Romans 8:16).* As Jesus needed baptism to unify His humanity and divinity, we too need baptism in the same way. The way Jesus thinks of Himself and the path He takes dramatically changes after His baptism. In like manner, the way we think of ourselves and the path we take changes after the anointing of the Holy Spirit.

The human body that wraps the spirit within us is 80 percent water. At our baptism, the water in our body is anointed by the Holy Spirit. We become living fountains of anointed, holy water. Medical experts tell us that we need to hydrate the body by drinking plenty of fluids. In like manner, we need to hydrate the water of our baptism through those things which empower the Holy Spirit.

The spirit is fed through prayer, reading the Bible, and attending church. The spirit is fed and nourished through the body and blood of Jesus Christ in Holy Communion You would never think of going a long time without feeding the body, yet some people go long periods without feeding the spirit. They go long periods of time without praying or reading the Bible or weeks without attending church. They go weeks without receiving Holy Communion. Consequently, the spirit starves. Unfortunately, we become so consumed and embedded in the secular world that our mortal flesh imprisons our spirit. And like Jesus, our spirit yearns to burst forth from such stringent mortal restraints.

Years ago, Elizabeth and I owned a Border collie who used to look at us as if to say, "I am much smarter than you give me credit for." She wanted to learn new tricks. She wanted us to challenge her intelligence. She yearned for new and deeper levels of thinking. In a similar way, our spirit is not satisfied with surface mortality. Even with our material successes, the spirit tells us that we are capable of much more. Our baptism awakens the Holy Spirit within us, thrusts our soul into a deep and profound epiphany, and alters our very being. Slowly, gradually throughout our life, we constantly struggle with the awareness that we are children of God.

+++

The first person I ever baptized was Jack, a seventy-five-year-old man. He had a fun, outgoing personality and a warm, engaging smile. He had been attending our church for a couple of years before he finally expressed an interest in baptism. During our baptismal preparation, I asked him why he had not previously thought of baptism. He explained that he had felt the call for several years, but he wanted to be baptized in the Jordan River, even though his life's circumstances never allowed him to travel there.

We set his baptism for Pentecost Sunday and, as God would have it, a week before Jack's baptism, a good friend of mine brought me a vial of water from the Jordan River, which I used for Jack's baptism. It was another incredible example of the Holy Spirit at work, a glorious day and a glorious baptism! During the ceremony, Jack and I were both in tears.

+++

One of the unique and beautiful parts of the Episcopal Church is that our theology not only has a high doctrine of God but also a high doctrine of humanity. What does this mean? It means that while all denominations consider God all powerful, omnipotent, and eternal, Episcopalians also believe that humans are the pride of God's creation, not in an arrogant, self-righteous way but in a godly, loving, and holy way. Our image of God is one of a loving, merciful, forgiving Father. What warms the Episcopalian's heart is that God loves us so much that He sent His only Son to be with us.

God loves us beyond our wildest imagination, and He will do anything to have us be with Him. This is the heart of the Episcopal message. Everything else flows from there. During the season of Epiphany, the way you think of yourself must change. Stop thinking of yourself the way you usually do and start thinking of yourself the way God thinks of you: the beautiful person you are, the vision God has of you, the child God adopted into His family, and the earnest desire God has for you to be with Him in His kingdom. Let that affirmation be your epiphany during this holy season.

+++

This week...
Walk through the world the way Jesus walks through it. Think of the world the way Jesus thinks of it. Say things Jesus would say. Do things that He would do. Treat people as though you are willing to die for them.

Reverend Kenneth and Elizabeth Herzog

New Life for a Broken World

> *Then Jesus, filled with the power of the Holy Spirit, returned to Galilee, and a report about him spread throughout the surrounding country. He began to teach in their synagogues and was praised by everyone. When he came to Nazareth, where he had been brought up, he went to the synagogue on the Sabbath day, as was his custom. He stood up to read, and the scroll of the prophet Isaiah was given to him. He unrolled the scroll and found the place where it was written: "The Spirit of the Lord is upon me, because he has anointed me to bring good news to the poor. He has sent me to proclaim release to the captives and recovery of sight to the blind, to let the oppressed go free, to proclaim the year of the Lord's favor." And he rolled up the scroll, gave it back to the attendant, and sat down. The eyes of all in the synagogue were fixed on him. Then he began to say to them, "Today this scripture has been fulfilled in your hearing." (Luke 4:14–21)*

Filled with the Holy Spirit yet concerned about the day, Jesus and His family leave their home and begin the dusty two-mile walk to the synagogue. On this Sabbath, Jesus' family will take their turn to present the service's prophetic lesson. The family selects Jesus as their spokesperson, a role He knows will be difficult yet a role He anxiously embraces. Along the way, the family engages in lively conversation, but Jesus remains silent, pondering the next few hours.

"Is there something wrong, Son?" Mary asks, noticing His reflective mood.

"No, Mother. I'm just reviewing the lesson I will teach."

The lesson has robbed Him of sleep for the past few nights. The assigned lectionary calls for *Isaiah 61:1–3*, a passage where the great prophet proclaims the Messiah's reign, the good news He will bring, and the power of His coming. Jesus knows that the great prophet speaks of Him, and that only He fulfills this prophecy. He knows that the Holy Spirit orchestrated God's anointed prophecy: the day, the family's rotation to speak, the passage itself, and the chosen privilege to teach. Jesus knows the day has come for Him to reveal that He is God's Messiah, the anointed one, the chosen one, the expected one. With each step He takes, this moment of destiny rapidly approaches. And although His stomach squirms not knowing what He will face, He will not back down from His words. He will not disappoint His Father. But the people's reaction still concerns Him.

As the family and other residents of Nazareth arrive at the synagogue, they stop at the Mikveh, a place of personal prayer. According to Jewish custom, they purify their hearts before entering the large wooden doors of the synagogue. They gather for the Sabbath's morning service and sit on the dirt floor while the rabbi, the canter, the board of elders, and the town dignitaries sit on wooden benches that line the three adjacent walls. Everyone sings and chants ancient hymns, prays, listens to the Word of God, and hears insightful interpretations of the Scriptures. This morning, one of these interpretations will change their lives, and the synagogue at Nazareth will forever be remembered.

Once inside, Joseph points to a section of the dirt floor large enough for the family to sit together. And as the Messiah of the world takes His place, a sacred silence fills the house of God. Only the clap of sandals and the whoosh of tunics disturb the anointed air.

At the appointed time, the blowing of the shofar announces the beginning of the service. The cantor rises and steps up to the bimah, a raised platform with a pulpit located off to the side of the front wall. From there, he chants the appointed psalm for the day. After each half verse, the people offer a dutiful response that they know by heart.

The cantor leads a second psalm and then an ancient hymn. One of the board of elders comes forward to lead prayers thanking God for His blessings and asking further prosperity for all of Israel. More chanting comes from people as the rabbi approaches the binah carrying the Torah, the Book of Law. He reads the assigned text and then sits in the Moses chair, a chair reserved only for the rabbi who speaks with the authority of Moses when he interprets the Torah.

Jesus knows that He will speak after the rabbi's teaching, a scene that has been playing in His mind for a few days. Since early that morning, He has been in constant prayer, asking the Father to calm His anxious heart. And now He will reveal one of the greatest epiphanies in salvation history.

In an adjacent room, the thirty-nine scrolls of the Hebrew Scriptures are kept in the ark, a sacred wooden box that is carefully overseen by an attendant. The scrolls, hand copied by the scribes in Jerusalem, are the Word of God and the main focus of worship.

Jesus stands at the binah, and the attendant hands Him the scroll of the predestined prophecy written by Isaiah. He senses something startling is about to happen, which heightens His anxiety because He knows that the next few minutes will test His favorable reputation. But He also knows that Isaiah has waited 750 years for Him to breathe life into His prophecy. And His Father has waited since creation for Him to breathe new life into a broken world. Jesus knows Isaiah and His Father cannot wait any longer. Taking a quiet breath, He closes His eyes as the Holy Spirit breathes courage into His heart. And at that very moment, Jesus proclaims to all: *"The Spirit of the Lord is upon me, because he has anointed me to bring good news to the poor. He has sent me to proclaim release to the captives and recovery of sight to the blind, to let the oppressed go free, to proclaim the year of the Lord's favor" (Isaiah 61:1–3)*. Rolling up the sacred scroll, Jesus hands it back to the attendant who replaces it in the ark.

Even though prophetic readings and interpretations always take place at the binah, Jesus moves away and confidently walks toward the center of the room, stopping in front of the Moses seat. The people gasp! Dare He sit down? Jesus sits, shocking the people. The rabbi squirms. The people stare. He returns with a single stare. Anticipation consumes the air. After what seems like an eternity, Jesus speaks: *"Today, this scripture has been fulfilled in your hearing."*

+++

The Spirit of the Lord is upon me, because he has anointed me to bring good news to the poor.

God wastes no time announcing His Son's mission when He sends the good news of Jesus' birth to the lowly shepherds. God's highest priority brings the good news to the poor, the outcasts, and the marginalized: *"Happy are those who consider the poor; the Lord delivers them in the day of trouble" (Psalm 41:1)*. The least on earth are the first in heaven. When Jesus says that He came only for the lost sheep of Israel (*Matthew 15:24*), He does not mean only Israel, as if to limit His ministry to His native country; rather, He means all lost sheep. *The shepherd will leave the ninety-nine faithfuls to find the lost one (Matthew 18:12).*

While Jesus walks with us every step of our lives, He draws us even closer to Him during troubled times. When we feel isolated, He does not abandon us. Just as He showers us with compassion, Jesus expects us to extend His compassion to anyone suffering in any capacity. We must not ignore the destitute; rather, we must embrace those in need and bring His good news to the lost sheep of our world.

> *He has sent me to proclaim release to the captives.*

People in prison are criminals and sinners, removed from society and living in isolation as punishment. But these lost sheep also must hear the good news, which will hopefully help them reform and amend their lives. Through the prison ministry, many criminals come to Jesus while serving their sentence. But because of their police record, they carry the stigma of their arrest, marginalizing them the rest of their lives.

While crime offends civil law, sin offends the law and the will of God. Estranged from the life of Christ, the punishment of sin brings death (*Romans 6:23*). Sinners must hear the good news of repentance and forgiveness in order to receive God's grace afforded by the blood of Jesus Christ on the cross. Jesus comes as a deliverer and breaks the bondage of sin. But the sinner is held in bondage until the grace of repentance completely frees him from the death sentence. Instead of isolation and a lifetime stigma, repentance restores the sinner's unity with God, eliminating the prior offense.

He has sent me to proclaim recovery of sight to the blind.

While Jesus cured many blind people, the most intriguing is when He cures a man blind from birth *(John 9)*. Jews believed that serious disabilities resulted from personal sin. Thus, the disciples question if the man's blindness could be a result of his parents' sin. Jesus tells them that there is no connection between the man's blindness and his sin but that "*he was born blind so that God's works might be revealed in him*" *(3)*. Even so, the Pharisees doubt Him because they had never heard of anyone blind from birth recovering sight *(32)*. After questioning the man, his parents, and some bystanders, the Pharisees are forced to believe that Jesus cured this man. Like the Pharisees, spiritual blindness makes us unable to see the presence of God active in our lives. People who don't connect events in their lives to the hand of God at work refer to these events as coincidences and luck. What we must do is raise our spiritual antennas and tune into not "coincidences" but "God-instances" that produce incredible epiphanies that color the mundane world with the miraculous touch of a personal God who cares about you and who calls you to notice Him. Once we make these connections, life becomes exciting and sustained by one revelation to the next.

He has sent me to let the oppressed go free.

The Lord God told Moses, "*So indeed the cry of my people has reached me, and I have truly noted that the Egyptians are oppressing them. Come now! I will send you to Pharaoh to lead my people out of Egypt*" *(Exodus 3:9, 10)*. Thus begins the Exodus story after 420 years of slavery in Egypt, ending in the promised land and providing freedom to God's people.

Related to those held in captivity, the Lord uses the word *oppressed* because the Egyptians subjected the Israelites to harsh and cruel treatment. God's people were not only held in captivity as prisoners but also as slaves of the ruthless Egyptian taskmasters. Exodus, chapter 5, further reveals the cruelty and harshness of the taskmasters who made the Israelites' lives unbearable.

Similar to the Israelites, Black Americans, Native Americans, the Jews in Nazi Germany, the Kurds in Iran, and many other racial and ethnic groups have all cried out for their God-given rights. Their hope rests in God's compassion and that He will put an end to their suffering. The persecuted depend upon the healing power of Jesus Christ. And His mission, as difficult as it may seem, is to end the hatred, the injustices, the prejudices, and the stereotypes and to unite the world through the love of the Father. We will never have world peace until the power of love overcomes the love of power.

> *He has sent me to proclaim a year of the Lord's favor.*

This part of Jesus' mission statement has a twofold agricultural reference from the Old Testament (*Leviticus 25*). The Lord told Moses that every seventh year was a Sabbath Year, which provided the land a year of rest. The Lord assured Moses that whatever the land produced on its own would be enough food for each household, cattle, and flock (*1–7*). The Lord also told Moses that every fiftieth year would be a Year of Jubilee when the people would return home to their clan and celebrate the Lord's blessings (*8–13*). Rest, celebration, and trust in the Lord were essential virtues for these two feasts.

Standing in front of the people in the synagogue, Jesus proclaims He fulfills these two feasts: He is the source of rest and comfort, the center of celebration, and the reason to trust God. He tells the people that they must take time from their busy lives to reestablish their relationship with God. Jesus' covenant between God and His people establishes a new beginning, a fresh start, a new year: a year of the Lord's favor.

But what happened to our new beginning, our fresh start, our new year, our year of the Lord's favor? Prior to the early '70s, America's "blue laws" closed businesses on Sundays, mandating a day of rest, which slowed American lives and gave them time to attend church services, time to reconnect with the Lord, and time to spend with one another. But Americans cried for their rights: Open the doors on Sundays! Once this happened, Americans experienced a cultural shift that slowly moved them away from their day of rest, away from their day of celebrating the Lord, away from their trust in God, propelling them deeper into the fast-paced world of consumerism.

The result? Max Lucado says it best in his book, *Anxious for Nothing: Finding Calm in a Chaotic World*:

> The United States is now the most anxious nation in the world. The *Journal of the American Medical Association* cited a study that indicates an exponential increase in depression. People of each generation in the twentieth century "were three times more likely to experience depression" than people of the preceding generation. (6)

As we find ourselves becoming more and more anxious, depressed, and troubled, we must return to the synagogue in Nazareth and listen to Jesus. It's time for us to rest, to celebrate, and to trust! If we will open our hearts, move away from our busy lives, and trust God, He will calm our chaotic world. He will, you know!

+++

This week…
Spend quality time with the Lord! Talk a walk, marveling in His blessings…the array of colorful flowers, the crisp blue sky, the melodious birds flying overhead, the gentle breezes moving the white billowy clouds. Listen to Him. Celebrate with Him. Trust in Him. As you do, He will shower you with His calming presence. He will, you know!

Satan Goes to Church

> *They went to Capernaum, and when the Sabbath came, Jesus went to the synagogue and*

began to teach. The people were amazed at his teaching, because he taught them as one who had authority, not as the teachers of the law. Just then a man with an unclean spirit cried out, "What do you want with us, Jesus of Nazareth? Have you come to destroy us? I know who you are—the Holy One of God!" Jesus said sternly, "Be quiet! Come out of him!" The unclean spirit shook the man violently and came out of him with a shriek.

The people were all so amazed that they asked each other, "What is this? A new teaching—and with authority! He even gives orders to unclean spirits and they obey him." News about him spread quickly over the whole region of Galilee. (Mark 1:21–28)

Every time Jesus meets someone who possesses an evil spirit, He kicks the demon out. Jesus does this because demons don't have power over Him; therefore, they must obey His authority. But what happens to those demons who never meet Jesus? That's when Satan wins, and although Satan may win some battles, the final victory belongs to Jesus. Thus, Satan knows his time is limited, so he works hard to beat the odds of time.

This Gospel is unique because it is the only time that Jesus casts out a demon in a synagogue, which tells us that even Satan goes to church. But why would the devil go to church knowing that Jesus is there? Satan isn't after Jesus; he's after us, hoping that he can infiltrate our hearts and our minds while we worship in God's house. And he will do anything to disturb and disrupt the congregations' focus on Jesus.

For example, Satan loves it when we criticize the service: The music is bland, the reading is too long, the sermon is boring, there is a mistake in the bulletin, on and on and on. He also loves it when our minds wander during the service: *I have so much to do this afternoon, I have to improve my golf swing, I think I'll have an omelet at brunch, I'm concerned about the stock market, I'm worried about my math test tomorrow*, and on and on and on. He will disturb, disrupt, and distract. The more often we lose our focus on Jesus, the more battles Satan wins, even in the house of God.

So how does Satan enter God's house? In this Gospel, he attached himself to a good man, a faithful man, a believer who was in the synagogue worshiping God. But if Satan came to church dressed as himself, the usher would not even give him a bulletin. So he attaches himself to the hearts of those walking through the door and sometimes even before they arrive.

+++

Satan is a good theologian. He also knows that there is only one God and that he is not the one. Satan also believes in the Incarnation and knows that the Son of God became human. In this Gospel, he not only addresses Jesus as Jesus of Nazareth but also calls Him the Holy One of God.

Satan is not only a good theologian; he is also the master of division. He can split a marriage, a family, a church, a country. He can pin even the most faithful believers against themselves, not stopping until chaos erupts. Division and chaos are Satan's mission.

Satan has no power to create, so he sends demons on his mission to taint God's goodness.

Satan's demons play havoc with our lives, infiltrating almost every aspect of our spiritual, emotional, and physical well-being. And when this happens, Satan smiles. But we must remember that Jesus is the only one who has power over Satan. Therefore, we must pray using the name of Jesus to cast out Satan's demons.

+++

It's Sunday morning in church. The priest is at the pulpit preaching the sermon. Some of the people stir, some look away, others stare, but you slouch wanting to hide. This is too personal, too raw, too in-your-face. This is not why you came to church!

His words pierce your heart as you try desperately to clear your throat, wipe the corners of your eyes. But it's too much to bear.

Almost ready to leave, your spirit speaks ever so softly, but then you stand, and with a compelling voice, your demons cry out: "*What do you want with us, Jesus of Nazareth? Have you come to destroy us? I know who you are—the Holy One of God!*"

He knows your heart. He knows your soul. He knows your demons: "*Be quiet! Come out of him!*" But this is not why you came to church!

But your demons resist, making you tremble, trying desperately to catch your breath. Suddenly, the burden you've carried for years is now lifted, lightening your shoulders, freeing your soul as a trail of tears stream down your face. Now you can finally take a deep breath. They're gone; you're free!

And the people, amazed, are staring at the vacant air, the place where He was, but they could not see. So they ask the priest: "*What is this? A new teaching—and with authority! He even gives orders to unclean spirits and they obey him.*"

+++

Everyone comes to church with their demons. The church is not a country club for the faithful but a hospital for the sick. We don't come to church to be convicted, but we are. We don't come to church to be healed, but we are. The power of worship is not the nice, warm, fuzzy feeling of singing our favorite hymns and then leaving with our egos filling us with the false pride of being a good Christian.

However, the power of worship is when our frailty meets a powerful and eternal God. The power of worship is when our weaknesses meet the rock of our salvation, when our sicknesses are healed, when our demons are expelled, when our tainted hearts are made pure by the presence of the Holy One.

Our worship must center around Jesus. Sundays are not for us; Sundays are for God. The question is not, "How much did I get out of the service knowing God was there?" Rather, "How much did God get out of the service knowing I was there?" Check your ego at the door. Enter God's house with a humble heart, knowing that you are a sinner. Come to Jesus for forgiveness, grace, and mercy. Praise Him with a joyful voice so the angels in heaven know that you are there.

If you do not attend church because you feel unworthy, you deny yourself a powerful source of hope. Everyone in church is a sinner. Everyone has demons, even the priests. But we come together in our weakness for strength in His holiness. In community, our mortality encounters the spiritual, and the two are made one. We must worship the loving God who created us. We must praise the Son who died for us. We must thank the Spirit who sanctifies us. Praise Him. Worship Him. Love Him.

There's no place for Satan in church, but there is a place for you!

+++

This week...
Put on the armor of God and kick Satan out of your life!
And when you do, give thanks to God during the church service that you attend this week.

The Mountaintop

Jesus took with him Peter, James and his brother John and led them up a high mountain, by themselves. And he was transfigured before them, and his face shone like the sun, and his clothes became dazzling white. Suddenly there appeared to them Moses and Elijah, talking with him. Then Peter said to Jesus, "Lord, it is good for us to be here; if you wish, I will make three dwellings here, one for you, one for Moses, and one for Elijah." While he was still speaking, a bright cloud overshadowed them, and from the cloud a voice said, "This is my Son, the Beloved; with him I am well pleased; listen to him!" 'When the disciples heard this, they fell to the ground and were overcome by fear. But Jesus

> *came and touched them, saying, "Get up and do not be afraid." And when they looked up, they saw no one but Jesus himself alone. (Matthew 17:1–8)*

Something's different, radically different: radiant, glorious, transformational. Like the butterfly leaving its cocoon, you have no remorse about leaving your earthly body. Powerful, glorious, radiant light not only defines you but also surrounds you. His presence and tender words capture your soul: *"You are my beloved child in whom I am well pleased."* As the Holy Spirit anoints you, the angelic witnesses are not fearful but welcoming, greeting you with loud shouts and songs of praise to the Lord God. As you join them, Jesus' glorious light surrounds you, welcoming you home.

+++

During the season of Epiphany, the Holy Spirit reveals a relationship between Jesus' baptism which is the first Sunday after the Epiphany and His Transfiguration which is the last Sunday after the Epiphany, two glorious lights that form the bookends of this holy season. The bright cloud, the Father's voice, the Spirit's presence, and the bewildered witnesses, present at both, illuminate a new direction in salvation history. The Father, shrouded in the mysterious bright cloud of the unknowing, proclaims His love for His Son. The Spirit anoints Jesus as the Messiah, the Son of God. The miraculous intermingling of the divine and the mortal overwhelms the bewildered witnesses, leaving them speechless.

Although the light at Jesus' baptism remains in the cloud, the light at His Transfiguration comes out of the cloud and into Him, changing His appearance: *"And he was transfigured before them, and his face shone like the sun, and his clothes became dazzling white" (verse 2).* This powerful description, appearing again on Easter Sunday, gives Peter, James, and John a glimpse of Jesus' resurrection.

The Transfiguration is actually the flip side of Christmas. At Christmas, the Son of God becomes one of us. At the Transfiguration, Jesus, who was one of us, appears as God. Thus, God becomes like us so we can become like Him. While Christmas reveals God's humility, the Transfiguration reveals God's magnitude. Christmas and the Transfiguration help us understand how Jesus' divinity was held captive by His humanity. In the human Jesus, the Son of God yearns to emerge.

Moses, the symbol of Old Testament law, and Elijah, the symbol of the Old Testament prophets, appear with Jesus at the Transfiguration, revealing that Jesus is the fulfillment of both the law and the prophets. Like an hourglass, everything in the Old Testament flows *through* Jesus, and everything in the New Testament flows *from* Him. Thus, everything in the Old Testament points to Jesus, and everything in the New Testament points toward the kingdom. Just as Jesus is the fulfillment of the Old Testament, the kingdom is the fulfillment of all Scripture.

+++

Like Peter, who stands in the presence of the Risen Christ and does not want to leave the mountaintop, we too, experience similar spiritual highs: a moving weekend retreat, a powerful revival, a church service that ignites our hearts, an encounter with the Holy Spirit, or other moments when the Almighty speaks to us. At these times, we, like Peter, don't want to leave the mountain. And even though we are aware that these moments will fade, we delay the descent for as long as possible.

Many adults have experienced either a spiritual or an actual journey to the top of a mountain. I faced mine when Ken went to seminary, which took us to the University of the South in Sewanee, Tennessee, located on the Cumberland Plateau. Moving away from the beaches of Southeast Florida to the mountains of Tennessee presented its challenges, to say the least.

I remember crying when we arrived, but I remember crying even longer when we left. Sure there were life adjustments at first, not only geographic but also cultural. South Florida's fast-paced lifestyle differs dramatically from Sewanee's laid-back community. When friends and family first asked me how life was in Sewanee, I responded with a small smile saying, "Different." But when asked the same question near the end of our first year, my smile was replaced by joyous tears and a resounding, *"Our slice of heaven!"*

It's difficult describing Sewanee, or *on the mountain*, as the locals say. On one hand, it's a quaint college town, filled with everything a university has to offer. On the other hand, it's a holy place where you feel the presence of the Holy Spirit sitting beside you in All Saints Chapel or where you walk up the long narrow road which ends at the sixty-foot brilliant-white Sewanee Memorial Cross that towers over the valley or where you hike the Perimeter Trail and discover small creeks, endless wildflowers, and majestic cliffs and boulders or where you find yourself sitting under an enormous old oak tree, listening to its leaves tell the stories of generations who came before you; or where you speak to your soul and hear and feel and see the presence of our Lord and Savior.

But as difficult as it is to describe, Sewanee is even more difficult to leave. William Alexander Percy, Class of 1904, captures why so many of us return to this holy domain:

> *It's a long way away, even from Chattanooga, in the middle of woods, on top of a bastion of mountains crenelated with blue coves. It is so beautiful that people who have once been there always, one way or another, come back. For such as can detect apple green in an evening sky, it is Arcadia—not the one that never used to be, but the one that many people always live in; only this one can be shared.* (*Lanterns on the Levee*)

However, I must add that Sewanee is also a place of comfort, serenity, and tranquility. It's a place where you can open your heart and a place where *"the peace of God, which transcends all understanding, will guard your heart and your mind in Christ Jesus"* (*Philippians 4:7*). But when you must leave, one of His angels will carry you down the mountain, guarding you until you return.

+++

Reverend Kenneth and Elizabeth Herzog

After a long night of tossing and turning, the alarm sounds as the sun cracks the horizon. Making your way to the kitchen, you wonder why you had such a difficult time sleeping. While you wait for the coffee to brew, you sit at the kitchen table, turn on your laptop, and check your emails.

There's a knock at the door. What! At this hour? Who in the world would come at this ungodly hour? Peering through the glass, you see a Man who looks strikingly familiar from the many pictures you have seen of Him. But His movement assures you it's not a picture. Nah! It couldn't be! Jesus? He knocks again, waits, and then rings the doorbell.

Your heart pounds, your palms sweat, your muscles freeze. You don't know what to do. You take two steps toward the door and then quickly hide in the bedroom. The doorbell rings again. By His persistence, He knows you are home. You take a second look: Not a forcible entry, not a robbery; the Man respects your locked doors. Feeling an unexpected sense of calm, your fear turns into curiosity. As you move closer, the familiar stranger waits patiently for you to open the door.

Of all of the times Jesus has knocked on your heart, *and you have not let Him in, this time feels different.* Taking a deep breath, you open the door. Looking into His eyes, He calls your name, beckoning you to come with Him. And you follow.

He leads you to the high mountain. Coming from the Holy Spirit's brilliant light, a voice proclaims, *"This is my Son, the Beloved; with Him I am well pleased, listen to Him" (verse 2)*! You fall to the ground in repentance, and a newfound fear overwhelms you. But Jesus touches you. *"Get up and do not be afraid."* When you stand, He looks into your eyes and reveals that your dark sins are transfigured by the light of His love, grace, and mercy. In awe, you praise His name, crying out: *"Thank You, Jesus! Thank You, my Lord! Thank You, my Savior!"*

Your encounter with Jesus seems to last for hours. But you suddenly find yourself back at your kitchen table. The coffee maker beeps, and the aroma of freshly brewed coffee fills the kitchen just as the Holy Spirit filled your heart with God's unending love.

+++

Friends, this Gospel gives us a glimpse of heaven! We look forward to the day when we will stand in the presence of the Risen Lord. It will be beyond human comprehension. We can only imagine what it will be like. Or can we even imagine? As long as our lives point toward the kingdom, we can bask in the presence and the light of the Risen Christ.

And so as we say, "Farewell," to this great season of Epiphany and enter the darkness of Lent, let us pick up the cross of Jesus that makes us worthy. And let us not forget the two incredible lights that direct our way to the other side. There will always be hope. There will always be light outside the darkness. There will always be another epiphany.

+++

This week…

Sit in a quiet place and close your eyes, take a deep breath, open your heart, and invite Him in. Feel His enduring love, compassionate mercy, and endless grace and listen to His comforting words: "My peace I leave with you; my peace I give you. I do not give to you as the world gives. Do not let your hearts be troubled and do not be afraid" (John 14:27). Take up the cross of Jesus and descend the mountain, praising His holy name!

The Season of Lent

Sometimes, life is a treadmill, making it difficult to unplug, take a break, and slow down. Sometimes, societal demands play havoc with our personal, professional, and spiritual lives. Sometimes, these demands overwhelm us, not only emotionally but also physically. And as hard as we try to slow down, society puts us back on the proverbial treadmill.

However, the season of Lent reminds us to slow our lives by strengthening our relationship with God. Lent is more than giving up something; it is a time of giving, and the gifts are not tangible but spiritual. Granted, Lent is a long, arduous six-week journey of faith, reminding us that Jesus made this perilous journey in real life. It is a difficult walk but a necessary one. Are you ready?

The Cross of Ashes

> *Beware of practicing your piety before others in order to be seen by others; for then you have no reward from your Father in heaven. So, when you give alms, do not sound a trumpet before you, as the hypocrites do in the synagogues and in the streets, so that they may be praised by others. Truly I tell you, they have received their reward.*
>
> *But when you give alms, do not let your left hand know what your right hand is doing, so that your alms may be done in secret; and your father who sees in secret will reward you. And when you pray, do not be like the hypocrites; for they love to stand and pray in the synagogues and at the street corners, so that they may be seen by others.*

Truly I tell you, they have received their reward. But when you pray, go into your room and shut the door and pray to your Father who is in secret; and your Father who sees in secret will reward you. And when you fast, do not look dismal like the hypocrites, for they disfigure their faces so as to show others that they are fasting. Truly I tell you, they have received their reward. But when you fast, put oil on your head and wash your face so that your fasting may be seen not by others but by your Father who is in secret; and your Father who sees in secret will reward you. (Matthew 6:1–6, 16–18)

The priest smudges his thumb into the ashes of the palms from the previous Palm Sunday, connecting us to Jesus' triumphal entry into Jerusalem and emphasizing the joy of Lent. Tracing the ashes in a vertical motion, the priest begins the ancient proclamation:

Remember you are dust.

Then the Lord God formed a man from the dust of the earth, and breathed into his nostrils the breath of life; and the man became a living being. (Genesis 2:7)

The priest finishes the proclamation by making a horizontal motion that forms the cross:

And to dust you shall return.

Reverend Kenneth and Elizabeth Herzog

The vertical line of the cross points down toward us, representing the times in our lives when we focus on ourselves, not on Jesus. The horizontal line represents Jesus making His way into our lives. The left side of the horizontal line represents those times when we don't invite Him into our lives. Once we accept Jesus as our Lord and Savior, His line crosses and stays with ours, and we move with Him, and He with us. During these times, our hearts are for Him, not ourselves; our passions are for Him, not ourselves, and our love is for Him, not ourselves. Thus, we focus on God's glory, not ours! However, when we become more focused on ourselves, our relationship with Jesus blurs, moving us further away from God.

+++

The above passage is always the Gospel for Ash Wednesday, taken from Jesus' first sermon, *The Sermon on the Mount*. Jesus warns His people that their self-centered motives will not bring them closer to God. He commands them to do good deeds for the right reasons, not for notoriety. They must avoid becoming hypocrites, for when they do, their behavior mirrors those who *"sound their own trumpets"* and whose reward is temporal and not from God. Thus, if recognition is their motive, they will not bring goodness and righteousness into the world.

Jesus' *Sermon on the Mount* initiated His ministry of raising the people's moral center beyond the Torah's written law. For centuries, the Torah served as the authority for Jewish morality, and this was the first time that love was introduced as a foundation for morality. But the Jews saw Jesus' law of love as having no structure and no balance between what to do or not to do. They interpreted it as being no more than self-love and self-gratification. Because the Jews only accepted the Torah, they could not understand Jesus' law, which was *other-centered*.

+++

The *Oxford English Dictionary* defines hypocrisy as "the assumption of a false appearance of virtue or goodness, with dissimulation of real character or inclinations, especially in respect of religious life or beliefs; hence in the general sense: dissimulation, pretense, sham." We see hypocrisy as being dishonest, insincere, fraudulent, and even sanctimonious.

Why then do some Christians say one thing but do another? Why do some Christians hide their true motives behind the cross? Why do some Christians proclaim their love for Jesus but do not follow His law of love? Why do some Christians allow their ego-centered lives to overshadow their Christ-centered ones? In other words, why are some Christians living a life of hypocrisy?

And what is our reaction? Do we condemn our Christian brothers and sisters for their self-righteous behavior? Do we shun them as they enter God's house, knowing that their piety is a cover for their questionable behavior outside of church? Or do we grow weary of their moralizing because we know they don't live what they preach?

Yet where does this leave us? And who are we to say that we are any more pious, virtuous, honest, benevolent, honorable, decent, humble, or peaceful than our Christian brothers and sisters who sit in the pews with us? And who are we to judge our fellow sinners?

When asked what we learn from Jesus, Gandhi revealed that "Jesus was one of the greatest teachers that humanity has ever known. Jesus lived and died in vain if He did not teach us to regulate our whole of life by the eternal law of love." Thus, we should love one another, with all of our sins and transgressions.

+++

As a priest, I offer a variety of Bible studies. A few years ago, I led a men's Bible study, but not all of the men owned a Bible. Those who owned one had different versions. Because of this, the men said the scripture readings were difficult to follow. After a couple of weeks, Paul, a member of the group, purchased a Bible for each man so we all could read from the same translation.

When the Bibles arrived, Paul told me to distribute them but not to mention his name. After the first session with the new Bibles, a couple of the men thanked me. Without thinking, I said, "Don't thank me. Thank Paul. He's the one who purchased them."

Paul became upset with me. He explained that his reward was now in the eyes of the men and not with the Lord God. I felt terrible because I turned Paul's altruism into a self-serving act. I robbed him of the joy Jesus wanted for him, which is what Jesus wants for each of us when we do a good deed for the right reason.

Jesus wants our hearts, not how we appear to others. Our full attention must be on Him. He will have our hearts when only He sees our good deeds. Thus, we should seek His approval, not the temporal approval of others.

Hypocrisy emerges when we claim our actions are from God's will, but they only satisfy our selfish motives. Convincing others and even ourselves that our virtuous behavior is altruistic creates a gap between the truth and our arrogance and between God and deceit. And our self-righteous behavior can lead us more away from God than closer to Him. Thus, bridging the gap between God's truth and the ego's lie requires repentance.

Paul writes that *"all have sinned and fallen short of the glory of God" (Romans 3:23)*. When we sin, we offend our loving God who has given us life. However, we often look at this from our perspective when we should consider it from God's. While we justify our pretentious behavior, God weeps for us, waits for us, and longs for us to return home. *Ash Wednesday is God's hope.*

Ash Wednesday calls us to repent. The cross of ashes not only reminds us of our mortality but also those times when we satisfy our mortal needs at the expense of our relationship with God. Satisfying the first at the expense of the second is a sin, and sin requires repentance. On Ash Wednesday we are marked with ashes as a sign of our repentance: *"The wages of sin are death" (Romans 6:23)*, which combines our sin and our death. And unless we repent, we will be faced with both simultaneously.

Many people attend a morning Ash Wednesday service. By wearing ashes, the rest of the day *could* be a positive witness of faith if worn for the proper reason. If we wear the ashes to promote the faith and share our experience as a Christian, then this is righteous in Jesus' eyes. But if we wear the ashes to flaunt our piety, then we taint the faith. Thus, wearing the ashes should remind us of our human mortality and our true life with Christ. Anything less is self-serving and hypocritical. If Jesus spoke to us on Ash Wednesday, He would tell us:

> *Do not have your forehead marked with ashes just to show others that you are holy, for you have already received your reward. When you have your forehead marked with ashes, do so with the intention of dying to the world so that you can live in me. And when you sacrifice worldly pleasures, do not tell others of your sacrifice so that they will think more highly of you, for you have already received your reward. But when you sacrifice worldly pleasures, do so in secret. And your Father who sees in secret will reward you.*

Jesus calls us to the cross on Ash Wednesday, knowing that we are all sinners. He calls us to the cross because He accepts us—with our faults, our impiety, our sinfulness. He reminds us that we are "dust and to dust we shall return." He reminds us that we must follow His eternal law of love. We must allow His cross to lead us to a life devoted to our Lord, and we must invite Him into our lives.

So where does that leave us on Ash Wednesday, a day that marks the beginning of Lent? We often hear people say, "I can't possibly take time out from my busy work schedule and personal responsibilities to go to church on Ash Wednesday," or "It's not a 'Holy Day of Obligation,' so I don't feel hypocritical about not attending a service," or "There's no way I can make it to a morning service and get to work on time." These are just some of the myriad reasons we see so many empty pews on Ash Wednesday. How do we promote the faith and share our spiritual experiences with our Christian brothers and sisters if they can't or won't join us at church?

What's the solution? What's the answer? Well, if the people won't come to the church, then we should bring the church to the people. What started as the brainchild of the Reverend Jonathon "Jay" Edwards, a United Church of Christ minister, who organized the first Ashes to Go in 2007, has now evolved into an international way of bringing ashes to the streets, meeting God's people outside of church.

And that's exactly what happened on Ash Wednesday 2010 in the Chicago area:

> *Three Chicago-area Episcopal congregations independently took ashes and prayer to suburban train stations, and discovered commuters hungry for a moment of prayer, renewal, and grace. Those who had no time to attend services or had forgotten about the tradition were delighted to receive ashes with prayer as they began their day. Many responded with tears or smiles of gratitude that the church would come to them. By 2012 Ashes-to-Go went viral and national, with USA Today and CBS This Morning reporting the "good news."* ("Ashes to Go: Taking Church to the Streets")

When Ken and I first heard about Ashes to Go, I must admit that we were nonplussed, to say the least. Our strong liturgical roots were met with borderline confusion and disbelief. Honestly, we didn't know what to think. After discussing both sides, Ken finally saw Ashes to Go as "Ashes-without-Repentance," an easy way to make ourselves feel holy during one of the most important and spiritual times in our lives. Ken believes that Ashes to Go would have more meaning if the person was called to repent. And as much as I understood his point, I couldn't stop thinking about Jesus and what He would say.

Perhaps Jesus would agree with Ken. Perhaps He would see Ashes to Go as a "way out" of repenting and worshiping Him in His house. But maybe, *just maybe,* Jesus would say, "*If the people won't come to me, I'll go to them, on the streets, in subway stations, in coffee houses, or wherever they are."* In either case, Ashes to Go has become even more popular as we suffer the effects of the COVID-19 pandemic.

+++

As the priest smudges his thumb into the ashes of the palms from the previous Palm Sunday, connecting us to Jesus' triumphal entry into Jerusalem and emphasizing the joy of Lent, let us remember that Ash Wednesday calls us to repentance. And so we repent, lifting our voices to Him:

> *I regret the hours I have wasted*
> *And the pleasures I have tasted*
> *That you were never in*
> *And I confess that though your love is in me*
> *It doesn't always win me*
> *When competing with my sin.*
> *And I repent*
> *Making no excuses*
> *I repent, no one else to blame*
> *And I return, to fall in love with Jesus*
> *I bow down on my knees and I*
> *repent.*
> *I lament the idols I've accepted*
> *The commandments I've rejected*
> *To pursue my selfish end*
> *And I confess I need you to revive me*
> *Put selfishness behind me and*
> *take up my cross again.*
> *And I repent*
> *Making no excuses*
> *I repent, no one else to blame*
> *And I return, to fall in love with Jesus*
> *I bow down on my knees.*

Reverend Kenneth and Elizabeth Herzog

> *And I return, to fall in love with Jesus*
> *I bow down on my knees and I*
> *repent.*
> ("I Repent" by Steve Green, 1998)

+++

This week…
Take time out of your day to recite and/or listen to the words from "I Repent," written and recorded by Steve Green.

The Desert Retreat

Jesus, full of the Holy Spirit, left the Jordan River and was led by the Spirit into the wilderness, where for forty days he was tempted by the devil. He ate nothing during these days, and at the end of them he was hungry. The devil said to Him, "If you are the Son of God, tell this stone to become bread." Jesus answered, "It is written, 'Man shall not live on bread alone, but only by the word of God.'" The devil led him up to a high place and showed him in an instant all the kingdoms of the world. And he said to Him, "I will give you all their authority and splendor; it has been given to me and I can give it to anyone I want to. If you worship me, it will all be yours." Jesus answered, "It is written: 'Worship the Lord your God and worship him only.'" The devil led Him to Jerusalem and had him stand on the highest point of the temple. "If you are the Son of God, throw yourself down from here. For it is written: 'He will command his angels concerning you to guard you carefully; they will lift you up in their hands so that you will not strike your foot against a stone.'" Jesus answered, "It is said: 'Do not put the

Lord your God to the test.'" When the devil had finished all this tempting, he left him until an opportune time. (Luke 4:1–13)

Overwhelmed by His epiphany at His baptism, Jesus emerges from the Jordan River with the revelation that He is the Son of God, which condenses His life into this one shocking moment. The mysterious cloud of God's presence, the Spirit in the form of a dove, the gentle voice of His Father, and the astonished witnesses intensify within Him as He becomes aware that He is God's Chosen One.

Confused and dazed, Jesus steps out of the water and walks aimlessly. With each step, deep, fundamental, and profound questions spin and swirl in His heart and mind, taking Him further away from His previous life.

The Son's acceptance of His Father's mission prior to the Incarnation is now revealed in a new light as the human Jesus ponders His identity:

Who am I?
Why am I here?
What is My purpose?

Recognizing Jesus' vulnerability, the Spirit leads Him to the wilderness, a mountainous geographical area between the fertile land around the sea and the arid desert. Limited rain provides a scant food supply for the wild animals that graze on the weeds and shrubbery. Small caves offer shelter from the scorching heat, the biting windstorms, and the cold, hostile nights. After walking for hours in the searing sun, Jesus reaches the wilderness' threshold. The blistering heat penetrates His tunic, making Him feel as if He were on fire. His cracked lips, dry throat, and burning eyes cry for relief. Seeing a small pool of water hewed in a rock, Jesus stops to drink. Kneeling at the edge of the pool, He scoops the cool refreshing water into His swollen palms and splashes His parched face. Scooping more water, He drinks.

Bending even closer, He sees His reflection for the first time since His baptism. Startled, He turns away. But something calls Him back. Rubbing His eyes, He looks once again as His reflection gazes back. Jesus stares in disbelief as silent screams echo in His heart: *Who am I? Who is this Jesus? Yahweh, please help! Help, Yahweh, help!*

An unexpected slight breeze crosses the pool, causing gentle ripples on the water's surface. Peering even more intently, Jesus sees Himself as a small child and recalls a conversation with His mother, *Jesus, I must speak to You. Please listen. You were not born like everyone else.*

Responding with childlike innocence, He asks, *What do you mean? Are you not my mother? Where did I come from?* Waiting for her response, the tiny droplets from His beard disturb the ripples that form His mother's face as her answer fades into the water.

Perplexed and even more confused, He hears His Father's voice echo in His soul: *Jesus, You are My beloved Son. You must trust Me. Come with Me. Come, Jesus. Follow Me.* Led by the Spirit and His Father's voice, Jesus presses deeper into the wilderness. As the sun starts its golden descent over the horizon, He searches for shelter. Making His way through the narrow entrance of a small cave, Jesus takes refuge inside its mysterious chamber that offers a welcome respite from the intense heat.

His pleas for understanding dangle in the stale air. Exhausted, He folds His arms into a pillow and tries to sleep. The incredible images of His baptism and the long conversation with the Spirit quiet His pressing questions as He falls into a light slumber.

The First Temptation

The night's darkness enters His dream, *If you are the Son of God. If you are the Son of God...*

Startled, He awakens. His body aches from the rock bed of the cave, and as He slowly sits up, a deep voice pierces the silence.

"I know You are hungry and weary from Your arduous journey. Feed Your body as You would feed Your soul. Turn these rocks into bread, proving to me that You are the Son of God. Prove to Yourself that You are

the Anointed One, the Chosen One. If You do what I ask, we will break bread together."

"Jesus," warns the angel. "It is Satan. Beware. He attacks when You are vulnerable. He attacks at Your weakest moments."

"Yes," Jesus responds. "For some reason, I know him well."

Jesus would love something to eat, but the angel warns Him not to succumb to Satan's temptation. Satan's food is defiled, not fit for the body or the soul. Annoyed, Jesus tells Satan, *"Man does not live by bread alone."* Jesus would rather continue in hunger than prove to Satan something Satan already knows.

+++

Jesus stands at the opening of the cave and peers into the starlit sky. The night's crisp air brushes His face and cools His tunic as a sudden shiver travels throughout His body. Looking at the stars glistening across the dark sky, little does He know that He helped His Father and the Spirit create each one. From a distant star comes a voice.

"Jesus, You are My Son. Jesus, Your humanity does not remember the kingdom. The conversation We are having now is a conversation that You and I have had since the beginning of human history. My people need You. You are their Savior."

"But how? How can I save them? I do not understand."

"Of course, You don't. Things must come slowly. You can't know everything at once. Otherwise, My plan will overwhelm You, and it will take You even longer to understand. But know that the Spirit and I love You and will guide You as You make this journey. We miss You, and We long for the day when You return."

"When will that be? How will that happen? What do I do in the meantime? I feel caught between two worlds, and now I don't understand either one."

"Jesus, I am always here. Trust Me. You are My Son, and I will never abandon You."

The Second Temptation

Days in the wilderness turn into weeks. Scarce water makes His days long and challenging. Taking comfort in remembering how God's people fasted and prayed during difficult times, He continues His spiritual discipline. The cave remains His home, and campfires at night not only provide warmth but also keep the wild jackals away. Consumed by conversations with His Father and the Spirit, time slips away.

The Spirit strengthens and inspires Him, helping Him embrace His role as the Messiah.

Their conversations slowly reveal His nature, His self-identity, and the delicate balance between His humanity and divinity. As God's plan slowly unfolds, His understanding increases, making Him feel empowered to fulfill His place in salvation history. The Spirit reveals that He is the instrument of His Father's love, and all honor, power, and glory belong to the Father.

Lurking in the shadows, Satan's jealousy and envy reach new heights. His thwarted plan to kill the Messiah as a baby must now be revised for Jesus, the man. Stopping at nothing, Satan demands power. And while Jesus sleeps, Satan attacks.

"Jesus," says the menacing voice. *"Look! Wake up and look! From here You can see all the nations of the world. I will bestow the power to You if You bow down and worship me."*

Warning Jesus, the angel whispers, *"It is Satan. He comes again to destroy You, to attack You. Do not believe him. Truth is not his. He will not resign any of his power to You. You must not betray your Father's trust. Vanquish him! Tell him to leave and never return."*

Sitting straight up in a cold sweat, Jesus wipes His forehead. Bewildered, He adds dry branches to the dying embers that ignite not only the fire but also His soul. Recalling His dream and the angel's response, He cries, *"Father, I will never betray You. Who is Satan to drive a wedge between Us? I will only worship and serve the Lord. Go to hell, Satan. Leave me alone."*

During these two temptations, the scriptures come naturally to Him. He becomes aware of His passion for the scriptures and remembers how the great prophets captivated His heart when He was in school. He recalls a conversation with His teachers in the temple when He was twelve years old as His parents searched for Him in desperation. Difficult to recognize, the signs have always been there. And now, through the guidance of the Holy Spirit, they are coming to light.

The Third Temptation

Frail and weak, Jesus leans against the side of the cave near the opening. The tunic His mother made for Him hangs loosely over His sunken shoulders and drapes around His famished body. Rubbing His hands across His rib cage, He counts His bones. Yesterday, He fell on His walk to find water, and today, He fears the same will happen. He knows that He will have to end His fast soon, or else, the empty cave will become His final resting place where the wild animals will eat the body of Christ.

Even though the conversations with His Father and the Spirit have filled His soul with overflowing joy, His body craves food. He will spend one more night, build one more fire, and engage in one more conversation. Tomorrow, He will return.

Sensing that Jesus' time in the wilderness is short and knowing that the Messiah is vulnerable and delirious, Satan has one last chance to prey on Jesus' weakened heart. As Jesus struggles to stay awake, Satan comes to Him in a vision, and in his craftiness, he takes Him to the temple's pinnacle, the highest point of the holiest place. In a menacing deep voice, Satan challenges Jesus' identity, *"If You are the Son of God, throw Yourself down and see if the angels will catch You, for the Bible says that they will protect You, and You will not encounter any harm."*

Appearing behind Satan, the angel warns Jesus of Satan's ploy. Instinctively, Jesus understands. He whispers, *"I know who it is, and I know where it comes from."* Drawing strength from the Spirit, Jesus commands, *"Do not put the Lord God to the test."* Defeated but vowing to return, Satan leaves Him until a more opportune time.

+++

Just as Satan tempted Jesus, he also pulls us into turmoil until the line between right and wrong blurs. He lures us into his trap, enticing us just as he did Jesus. Tempting the mind to serve the body is Satan's prevailing ploy. After all, the mind and the body are corruptible and easy prey for the evil one: overspending, gluttony, lust, greed, envy, jealousy, and anything else that satisfies temporal cravings. Because the mind can easily become the enemy of the soul, Satan uses the mind to trick the soul. Paul teaches us that all sin originates in the flesh (*Galatians 5:19–21*). Even Jesus claims that *"the spirit is willing, but the flesh is weak" (Matthew 26:42)*. However, Paul also explains that the body is the temple of the Holy Spirit (*1 Corinthians 6:19*). The body, a vessel of holiness, contains the breath and presence of the Holy Spirit. The body is anointed at our baptism by the Spirit for the honor and glory of God, making it an expression of God's grace and mercy in a fallen world.

What tempts you to fall into Satan's trap? When have you fallen into his trap? Where have you fallen into his trap? How have you fallen into his trap? Why have you fallen into his trap?

The answer to these questions lies when we allow Satan to blur the line between truth and deceit, between right and wrong, and between good and evil. When we find ourselves struggling, we must draw on Jesus' internal strength, which will defeat Satan's external trap.

+++

This week...
Memorize this Bible verse from Proverbs 3:5–6:

> *I will trust in the* LORD *with all my heart and lean not on my own understanding but on His; in all my ways I submit to Him, and He will make my paths straight.*

When temptation comes knocking, drive him away with this verse!

Turning Points

There was a man who had two sons. The younger of them said to his father, "Father, give me the share of the property that will belong to me." So, he divided his property between them. (Luke 15:12)

From Shakespeare's *Hamlet* to Disney's *101 Dalmatians*, classic stories include five parts that work in a dramatic literary pattern: the conflict, the recognition, the turning point, the falling action and, finally, the resolution. The cycle of anger works in a similar way:

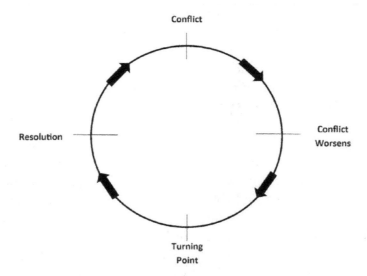

The parable of the prodigal son, one of the more recognizable Gospels during the Lenten season and taught by Jesus in *Luke 15*, is a classic story that follows this pattern.

The conflict begins when the youngest son asks his father for his share of the inheritance. This conflict is especially disturbing because in biblical times, sons were not eligible to receive the inheritance until the father died. For the youngest son, the father is not dying soon enough. The son does not want to wait any longer for his share of the money. For this reason, the father agrees because he does not want to go on living with his son wishing he were dying.

However, this parable falls short in explaining the father's deep anxiety. The son's selfish and greedy request requires the father to surrender half his assets, causing his father's fear: What will he do with the money? Will he take the money and leave? Will I ever see him again? While he ponders these questions, we fail to see the father's anguish. The conflict in the father's heart rivals the conflict he has with his son. Thus, the father's worst fear comes to fruition:

> *A few days later the younger son gathered all he had and traveled to a distant country, and there he squandered his property in dissolute living. When he had spent everything, a severe famine took place throughout that country, and he began to be in need. So, he went and hired himself out to one of the citizens of that country, who sent him to his fields to feed the pigs. (Luke 15:13–15)*

The youngest son earns high marks in low living. Not only is the father's greatest fear realized but ours is as well. According to Jewish tradition, working with animals, especially pigs, was a definite sign that you lost God's blessing. In his search for independence and freedom, the son finds himself imprisoned by his sad state of affairs. And since the father has not heard from his son, the father is filled with remorse over his decision. The conflict in the father's heart engulfs the conflict with his son, which intensifies the father's internal conflict.

At his lowest point, the son recognizes his sin:

> *He would gladly have filled himself with the pods that the pigs were eating; and no one gave him anything. But when he came to himself, he said, "How many of my father's hired hands have bread enough and to spare, but here I am dying of hunger. I will get up and go to my father and I will say*

> *to him, "Father, I have sinned against heaven and before you; I am no longer worthy to be called your son; treat me like one of your hired hands." So, he set off and went to his father. (Luke 15:16–20)*

The son's recognition brings the turning point, the most significant moment of the son's conflict: *"But when he came to himself."* What a great verse: *"When he came to himself."* This indicates that the son also finds himself in a twofold struggle, the external conflict with his father and the internal one with himself. Thus, he is no longer himself.

But before he can turn away from his sinful ways, he must end up outside himself, looking at himself as an observer. At this point, however, he has difficulty recognizing his sinful self and considers the sinner as a stranger, which alienates him to himself. *But when he came to himself:*

> The rebellious side *comes to* the compassionate side.
> The greedy side *comes to* the humble side.
> The false side *comes to* the truthful side.
> Once this happens, *he decides to go back to his father.*

The heart of the Lenten Season reaches its pinnacle in verse 17: *But when he came to himself, he decided to return to his father.* The son is hopeful that his father will take him back. And so the repentant son returns to his father with the hope that everything can be resolved, even if he has to work as a hired hand.

The repentance that Lent demands is not vague or ambiguous in this verse. We discover the absolute necessity of repentance if we are to be at one with our Father and ourselves. We find our true self in Jesus. The act of atonement, *"at-one-ment,"* must include the oneness of being with ourselves through God's grace and mercy. Repentance fills the empty void in our hearts, created by the alienation of sin. We are not ourselves when a wound we have inflicted on another does not include repentance.

If you had been a wayward child, then you depended on the forgiveness of your parents. If you had been the parent waiting for your child to return, then you depended on your child's repentance.

The son's humble repentance leads to the resolution:

> *But while he was still far off, his father saw him and was filled with compassion; he ran and put his arms around him and kissed him. The son said to him, "Father, I have sinned against heaven and before you; I am no longer worthy to be called your son." But the father said to his slaves, "Quickly, bring out a robe—the best one and put it on him; put a ring on his finger and sandals on his feet. And get the fatted calf and kill it, and let us eat and celebrate; for this son of mine was dead and is alive again; he was lost and is found! And they began to celebrate. (Luke 15:20–24)*

Upon his return, the agonizing grief of the younger son is overcome by the exuberant joy of his father. The conflicts, struggles, grief, and lonely pain for both vanish. Reunion and repentance and forgiveness and healing embrace the father and the son. This parable, also known as *the parable of the forgiving father*, teaches us that the son's repentance brings the conflict's resolution. Deserving the worst, the son receives the best: the best robe, the best fatted calf, the best seat at the banquet feast. The father's grace breathes life to the son:

> *For I was lost, but now I'm found.*
> *I was dead, but now I'm alive.*
> *Amazing Grace! How sweet the sound!*
> ("Amazing Grace")

+++

The father willingly and selflessly provides amazing grace. *Amazing grace!* What good and loving parent would not take back their child? What loving God would not take back His *own* creation? This parable is about the evils of greed and pride and lustful living. But more so, this parable is also about repentance and mercy and the absolute joy of reconciliation between the father and his son. However, it does not end with a peaceful resolution between the father's two sons:

> *The older brother became angry and refused to go in. So his father went out and pleaded with him. But he answered his father, "Look! All these years I've been slaving for you and never disobeyed your orders. Yet you never gave me even a young goat so I could celebrate with my friends. But when this son of yours who has squandered your property with prostitutes comes home, you kill the fattened calf for him!" (Luke 15:28–30)*

Like the two brothers, not all conflict ends with a peaceful resolution. In my personal life, a thirty-year friendship suddenly ended over a single uncharacteristic email that I sent, which Elizabeth read and warned me about the potential harm I could cause. Not listening to her advice, I sent the email. And the conflict worsened.

When the person told me our friendship was over, I finally recognized my offense.

Hoping for a resolution, I offered a sincere apology, pleading "I'm sorry. You know me better than this. Please forgive my insensitive words." But my pleas fell on deaf ears. My apology was not accepted. Consequently, there has not been a resolution, and the relationship has not been restored. And what's left? I'm left with one less friend, but he's left with a self-righteous, unforgiving heart!

+++

You will find plots and connections to this parable in your own life. Oh, there was a time when everything in life was moving in the right direction, when your marriage was healthy and strong, when your relationship with a son or daughter was simple, nurturing, and you cherished each other's company, when you shared family love with your parents and siblings, when your friend was a constant companion, when your job was promising and fulfilling, when the world was bright and filled with hopeful wonder.

But something happened. Didn't it? While some people can pinpoint a precise moment in time, for others, the conflict developed more gradually. Can you identify the time when the conflict cast darkness? Can you identify when your marriage took a wrong turn, when your child walked away, when your friend lost your trust, when your boss became overbearing, when the world lost its beauty? These are heartfelt, devastating times. They can move you to an awareness that all is not right with the world: times that can steal your joy, crush your strength, and smother your passion. When this happens, the conflict intensifies and leads to anger, resentment, and irresolution.

When you finally recognize your part in the conflict, then healing can begin. However, to bring healing, you must repent and ask for forgiveness, which can be the most difficult but also the most important part of healing. Why is this difficult? It's difficult because the evil one fills you with false pride, self-deceit, and self-righteousness, convincing you the other person is to blame, or you have been misunderstood. The devil tricks you into believing that you are the innocent one, the victim, making you the martyr and preventing you from repentance. Thus, the devil makes repentance even more difficult.

But a voice in your heart calls you to repent. Deep inside, you desire healing, peace, and joy. Once you admit your wrongdoing, repent, and ask for forgiveness, genuine healing can take place. This is the point when your true self emerges, and you realize the way you have been acting is not embedded in your character. Even if you are truly not to blame, you must embrace the humility of restoring the relationship. You must reach a point in the conflict when alienation is no longer acceptable, and you must do whatever it takes to bring healing. However, true healing is possible only when both people desire peace and restoration. True healing is possible only when we leave the past behind, step out of our self-righteous behavior, and burn all grudges.

You are the prodigal son.
You are the prodigal daughter.
You were so greedy, so rebellious, so self-centered.
And then you came to yourself!
It was the holiest moment of your life.
It was the first step in the long road back home.
And the Father begs you never to leave again.

+++

This week...
Review the five parts of a dramatic circle and apply
it to a person or a situation in your life.
Choose something where you have not reached the turning point.
In great humility, determine what you must do to
turn and then put the resolution in motion,
remembering that it is the first step in the long road back home.

Jesus Weeps for You

Now a man named Lazarus was sick. He was from Bethany, the village of Mary and her sister Martha. (This Mary, whose brother Lazarus now lay sick, was the same one who poured perfume on the Lord and wiped his feet with her hair.) So the sisters sent word to Jesus, "Lord, the one you love is sick." (John 11:1–3)

Grant, a vibrant twenty-five-year-old young man and a new member of our congregation, recently accepted Christ. I welcomed him into our church family, and the more I got to know him, the more I thought of him as my brother-in-Christ.

He and I spent weekly sessions talking about Jesus, the Bible, and his girlfriend. Thankful that God brought our lives together, I helped him find the hand of God in his life. And as I watched his life grow in Christ, our friendship flourished, bringing us closer to Jesus.

After one session ended, I couldn't wait for the next one. Our sessions were as valuable for me as he claimed they were for him. As he grew in the faith, so did I. It was exciting watching someone come to the Lord and remain hungry for more. The Holy Spirit hovered in my office when the two of us gathered in His name.

Then Grant suddenly and tragically died in a car accident. The news almost broke my spirit, leaving me with the worst grief I have ever known. Numb to life, I could not focus on anything else. Meeting his parents was especially difficult. In my office where Grant and I celebrated the joy of faith, his mom, dad, and I grieved as we faced the painful task of planning his burial service.

After his death, Grant's parents moved into the area and now attend our church. And even though I see them every Sunday, I can't look at them without thinking of Grant. Five years later, I still grieve. Grant is missing. And I miss him.

I know Grant is in the kingdom, but tragedies like these wound our souls and are not easily healed. His sudden and tragic death has been more difficult to process than even my younger brother's sudden death when I was a young boy and the prolonged deaths of my aging parents when I was an adult. I wish I could have just one more two-hour session with him. I wish he could ask me one more question. I wish I could receive one more text. I wish I could look out into the congregation and see his smiling face one more time.

A priest faces death with great regularity: administering Last Rites, providing grief counseling, planning and presiding at funerals, bringing light in the midst of darkness, proclaiming hope in times of despair. Because priests must maintain a balance between their personal feelings and their professional responsibilities, we are taught to remain objective at all times.

Remain objective in my profession. *Really?* At Grant's funeral service, I broke down during my sermon and became so emotional that I had to pause, take a deep breath, and collect my thoughts. I prayed, *Lord, please lift me up and surround me with your love, guidance, and strength.* And He did, which helped me continue the service.

But today, I'm jealous of God because He has Grant's spirit.

More than likely, you have suffered the heartbreak of a loved one's death. A person's death forms a natural community of love and grief. Sometimes it seems surreal that the person you shared so many memories with is now dead. How can this be? You try to rationalize something that seems irrational. But someone is missing.

Death is the opposite of life, yet death is a natural part of the life cycle. Attending a funeral service reminds us of our mortality and the inevitable reality of our own death. If something is inevitable, then it demands that we face the reality of it. We must face death, realizing that death gives time its value.

+++

Lazarus and his two sisters, Mary and Martha, were very close friends with Jesus. They enjoyed each other's company, looked forward to being together, broke bread together, shared fond memories, laughed at the table, and consoled one another in times of trouble. For Jesus, their house was His oasis, a respite from a long journey.

Knowing how much Jesus loved Lazarus, Mary and Martha sent a message to Him when their brother fell ill:

> *"Lord, the one whom you love is ill." But when Jesus heard it, he said, "This illness does not lead to death; rather, it is for God's glory, so that the Son of God may be glorified through it." Accordingly, though Jesus loved Martha and her sister and Lazarus, after having heard that Lazarus was ill, he stayed two days longer in the place where he was.* (John 11:3–6)

By the time Jesus arrives at their home in Bethany, Lazarus has been dead and in the tomb for four days. Overwhelmed with grief, Mary and Martha cry out when they see Him. Seeing Jesus brings back a flood of memories, which intensifies their suffering. For Jesus, seeing Mary and Martha intensifies His deepest sorrow. And He weeps.

Jesus weeps! Just imagine the agony, the anguish, and the heartbreak! His dearest friend, *His brother-in-Christ*, died. How He longs for one more dinner, one more laugh, one more smile, one more embrace. His tears are a witness to how much He loved His dearest friend.

Mary and Martha hope Jesus will take away their pain. They expect Jesus to say a prayer. Say some comforting words. Offer some advice. They believe Jesus could have cured Lazarus if He had arrived in time, but now it's too late. They don't expect a resurrection, certainly not a physical one. Otherwise, why would Martha complain about the stench when Jesus tells them to roll away the stone? They believe something will happen because Jesus has finally arrived, but their expectations fall short of the holy promise stirring in the tomb.

However, Jesus finds comfort knowing that He will soon bring joy back to life. He has already told His disciples that Lazarus' illness would not end in death but for the glory of God. So when Mary and Martha first greet Him, He explains that if they place their faith in Him, they will see their brother rise to life. However, the sisters agree that their brother will rise in the afterlife. This is an odd twist of holy irony because normally, Jesus is the one speaking on the spiritual level, and the people speak on the physical one. But on this occasion, Jesus knows differently.

Knowing that He will raise Lazarus from the dead, the weight and loss of Lazarus' death lifts from His shoulders. He knows that the Father's glory will soon prevail. He knows that He will be reunited with His dear friend, and they will break bread together once again. His heart fills with joy, knowing that Mary and Martha will see their brother alive once again.

But why does Jesus weep? Jesus weeps because death was not part of the original design of creation. This was not what God intended for us. Pain, suffering, disease, heartbreak and, ultimately, death do not come from the loving God who formed us in His image as His children.

Jesus weeps because sin has distorted God's vision of humanity. Jesus weeps because the people never knew God's original plan for humanity. Jesus weeps because all humans are now sinners; therefore, all humans suffer the effects of sin. Jesus weeps because Lazarus' death has broken Jesus' heart. Jesus weeps because He has been given another glimpse of His own death. Jesus weeps for you. Jesus weeps when you weep. Jesus shares your pain and suffering. Jesus weeps when you do not understand. Jesus weeps when you blame Him for your sorrow and when you become angry at Him and turn your back on Him. Jesus weeps for your grief over a loved one who has died. And these things press on His heart with every step He takes toward the cross.

But our greatest fear is that these sorrows will stay with us forever, and that death lasts forever. The good news of the Gospel tells us that this is not so. The caterpillar does not stay in the cocoon—it just passes through the cocoon, transformed into a glorious, delicate butterfly. And like the lowly caterpillar, we die but do not stay dead. Jesus tells us that death is just a passage into something incredibly *life changing*. Thus, our death brings us freedom, a transformation that leaves all sin, all pain, and all suffering behind. We die! We are free! We are given eternal life! *Then why be fearful?*

+++

Mary and Martha, along with Jesus' disciples and a throng of people, gather in front of the tomb. Knowing all eyes are on Him but also knowing His Father is with Him, Jesus looks up to the heavens.

> *"Father, I thank you for having heard me. I know that you always hear me, but I have said this for the sake of the crowd standing here, so that they may believe that you sent me." When he had said this, he cried with a loud voice, "Lazarus, come out!" The dead man came out, his hands and feet bound with strips of cloth. Jesus said to them, "Untie him and let him go." (John 11:41–44)*

Dazed and confused, Lazarus makes his way to the entrance of the tomb. Cautious and bewildered, he emerges from the peace of death back to the discord of life. His first cries are like those of a newborn, short, high-pitched sounds of new life pushing air in and out of the lungs.

For Mary and Martha: *What joy! What elation! What unbridled emotion!* They rush to him crying, *"Lazarus, our dear brother! Lazarus! Lazarus!"* As Martha caresses his hair and face, Mary nestles into the fold of his arm. Their earlier tears of sorrow and grief are now tears of exultation on the other side of death. Jesus' disciples along with the bystanders cry out with disbelief.

Jesus watches the resurrected reunion in great anticipation of His own, a short five miles away. As Mary and Martha thank Jesus with overwhelming gratitude and appreciation, Jesus looks up to the heavens, proclaiming "To God be the glory!"

But what about Lazarus? Lazarus must be torn between two worlds, the joy of heaven and the joy of his sisters. Given even a glimpse of this new life, we wonder if he was truly happy that Jesus brought him back into our world, a world of sin, of troubles, of despair. Lazarus will die again. And when he dies a second time, Jesus will breathe new life into him. Not again in this world but in the next.

+++

Jesus stuns the bystanders with the news that the life He offers is not just for the future, but it begins now. Jesus' promise for our future in the kingdom holds fast, but there is also a promise for the here and now, making our time on Earth important.

Christians believe in the afterlife; it is a tenet of the faith. However, many fail to see the full extent of how God is willing to work in this life. This passage is not about Lazarus. It's about Jesus. Jesus came not only to offer us eternal life but also to fill this life with His abundance. A resurrected life does not have to wait until the person dies. A resurrected life begins when we accept Jesus into our hearts. It begins now with this very moment!

The joy of the resurrected life begins long before we ever die. There is much glory, majesty, and beauty to be lived now. Every moment is precious and should be embraced. It's up to you to live and embrace each moment. *Love, learn, live, and smile, by God!*

+++

This week...
Walk through life like you have died and are here
for a second time. Answer these questions:
How would you change?
How would you pray?
How would you love?
How would you be different?
It's time to be the new *you!*

The Grace Period

Now a man owned a vineyard, and in his vineyard was a fig tree that was not producing fruit. So, the owner said to the gardener, "For three years I have come looking for fruit on this tree and still I find none. Cut it down. Why should it be wasting soil?" But the gardener replied, "Sir, leave it alone for one more year, until I dig around it and put manure on it and water it. If it bears fruit next year, well and good; but if not, you can cut it down."
("The Parable of the Fig Tree," Luke 13:6–9)

No matter how you pay bills, they all come with a due date accompanied by a late date and a late date fee. *But, of course, you know this! Right?*

The other day, Elizabeth and I were looking online at the bill for our automobile insurance. And there it was, front and center: the due date, the late date, and a late date fee.

So I decided to have some fun with the insurance company that soaks up a good chunk of our money each month. I called our insurance agent and inquired about the due date. Of course, I seldom speak to our agent. I'm usually passed on to a well-trained assistant, a go-between, so to speak.

After a brief cordial introduction with our agent's assistant, I asked, "When is our payment due?"

She replied, "On the due date, sir."

"But," I observed, "my payment can arrive after the due date, and it's still the same amount. Right?"

To which, she replied, "It is the same amount as long as it arrives before the late date."

Pressing her a little more, I asked, "Then it's not due on the due date. It's due by the late date. Right?"

"No," she politely insisted. "It's due on the due date, but we give you until the late date before you incur a penalty."

I asked, "Why the extra time?"

She explained, "Well, that's the *grace period* we extend to you."

Ahh...now we are getting somewhere. She was playing right into my hands, so I pressed a little more. "*A grace period, you say?*"

"Yes," she explained. "It's an extension that we give you to get your payment in without penalty."

A grace period! Imagine that!

> *The gardener replied, "Sir, leave it alone for one more year, until I dig around it and put manure on it and water it."*

"A grace period?" I inquired. "How very generous of you to give me a *grace period*. Do you extend this *grace period* to all of your customers?"

"Yes, of course, sir," she politely responded.

"That's a lot of *grace* you extend," I remarked.

"That's because most people have difficulty meeting the due date," she explained. "Most of the payments we receive arrive between the due date and the late date. If we didn't extend the deadline through the *grace period*, then almost everyone would be charged a penalty, and we don't want that to happen."

"How kind of you," I remarked.

"Sir, it's the service we offer," she explained.

In the *parable of the fig tree*, the gardener asks the owner of the vineyard to postpone his decision to cut down the tree that is not bearing fruit. In other words, the gardener asks for a *grace period*.

Hearing her exasperation, I assumed the assistant knew I was up to something. But I pressed on, "Is there a time when you run out of grace?"

Although I couldn't see her lips tighten and her eyes squint, by the tone of her voice, I knew that her previous polite response now took a sharp turn: *"Yes, as I've explained more than once, that would occur at the late date. After that, you are charged a penalty."*

I could tell that the assistant had had enough, especially since her silence bordered on complete frustration and total annoyance. Knowing she was ready to put an end to my absurd inquiry, I pressed one last time, *"What is grace then?"*

+++

Have you ever thought about grace? Have you ever asked what grace is? Could you explain grace to someone? If you struggle with the deeper meaning of grace, it might help to remember the acronym, *GRACE... God's Riches at Christ's Expense*. In other words, grace is God's generosity toward you, paid for you by Jesus Christ.

But Jesus doesn't just postpone the payment of your sinfulness, He pays your way to the kingdom by eliminating your sins. He pays through the grace that flowed from His blood on the cross. And while there was a limited amount of blood in Jesus' human body that flowed on Calvary, the grace it produced is limitless, an ever-flowing eternal fountain. It makes you worthy. It makes you righteous. It makes you holy. Grace is the essential element of your salvation, which gives you your place in the kingdom.

However, to receive grace, you must repent. And once you repent, you must respond by producing fruit: *"love, joy, peace, patience, kindness, generosity, faithfulness, gentleness, and self-control" (Galatians 5:22–23)*. Thus, it is by divine design that God places *the parable of the fig tree* during the season of Lent. And it is by divine design that God gives you *your grace period*.

But how long does our *grace period* extend? Only the Holy Spirit knows. Saint Monica prayed for over a decade that her son Augustine would repent for his sins. Her prayers were finally answered when her son not only repented but also became one of the most revered saints in the church. It took Augustine many, many years to repent. But once he did, God showered him with His grace.

How long will it take you to turn your heart? How long will it take you to answer Jesus when He calls your name? How long will it take you to stop resisting God's grace? How long will it take you to accept His forgiveness? How long will it take you to start producing fruit? God waits for you to answer His call. God waits for you to repent your sins. God waits for you to accept His forgiveness. And when you do, God will shower you with His grace.

God is the owner of the vineyard, Jesus is the gardener, and you are the fig tree. The gardener pleads with the owner for a grace period. The season of Lent is *your grace period*. The due date is Ash Wednesday. The late date is Good Friday. This is your time to answer Jesus, to repent your sins, to accept His forgiveness, and to bear the fruit of God's generosity.

> If you use this Lenten season to truly repent,
> If you bear fruit during this *grace period,*
> If you are refreshed by the water of your baptism,
> Then you will share in the joy of Easter Sunday.

+++

Instead of a click followed by a dial tone, I got a terse response, "Sir, I don't know what else to say to you. Would you like to speak to my supervisor?"

At this point, I came completely clean and explained the real reason for my call to which she responded, "I hope you have a nice day. Is there anything else I can do for you?"

"Actually, there is something I want you to think about. Wouldn't it be a wonderful thing if we never ran out of grace?"

"Well, that's not our policy," she remarked.

Smiling, I said, "I know there's nothing you can change about your policy, but I *do know* someone who never runs out of grace."

After a long pause, she asked, "Another insurance company?"

"No," I responded.

After an even longer pause and with some hesitation, she said, "I think this conversation is about something other than insurance."

"You are right," I said. "It has little to do with insurance. It has everything to do with grace." And I could hear her smile.

I thanked her for her time, her patience and, of course, her grace. As we hung up, I wondered if the insurance company offers a *grace period* to gardeners working in a vineyard. I'm sure they do, though not all need it.

+++

This week...
Purchase a flower, a plant, or a tree.
Let it be a constant reminder of the fig tree, the
owner, the gardener and, of course, the grace.
And make sure you pay your insurance bill on time!

The Holiest Week

The culmination of Holy Week leads us to Easter Sunday, the resurrection of our Lord and Savior. But we must endure the pain of Holy Week before we can celebrate the joy of Easter. Thus, Holy Week reminds us of God's gift, a gift given to us on Christmas Day, taken away on Good Friday, and given back on Easter Sunday. We walk with our Lord as He faces the people's admiration on Palm Sunday, eats His last meal on Maundy Thursday, spills His last drop of blood on Good Friday, and rises victoriously on Easter Sunday.

Holy Week should bring us on our knees, thanking Him for our salvation, thanking Him for the forgiveness of our sins, and thanking Him for facing the most difficult week in His life. Will you be on yours?

The Holy Paradox

As they approached Jerusalem and came to Bethpage on the Mount of Olives, Jesus sent two of his disciples, saying to them, "Go to the village ahead of you, and you will find a donkey there with her colt by her. Untie them and bring them to me. If anyone says anything to you, say that the Lord needs them, and he will send them right away."

The disciples went as Jesus had instructed. They brought the donkey and the colt and placed their cloaks on them for Jesus to sit. A very large crowd spread their cloaks on the road, while others cut palm branches from the trees and spread them on the road. The crowds went ahead of him and those that followed shouted, "Hosanna to the Son of David! Blessed is he who comes in the name of the Lord! Hosanna in the highest heaven!"

When Jesus entered Jerusalem, the whole city was stirred and asked, "Who is this?" The crowds answered, "This is Jesus, the prophet from Nazareth in Galilee." (Matthew 21:1–3, 6–11)

> He couldn't stay away.
> His faith demanded that He go.
> His love compelled Him to go.

The journey of a thousand miles begins with a single step. The journey of the Son of God to Earth begins with the Son's single nod of obedience to His Father. The journey of three years of His ministry begins with a single baptism. The final journey to celebrate the Passover meal in Jerusalem begins with a single leap of faith. And the journey that leads to our salvation begins with one faithful, obedient, and selfless act of love.

On our Lenten journey, Jesus leads us into the city of Jerusalem to celebrate the Passover meal later that week. Much will unfold before the day is done, including more than what meets the eye.

Palm Sunday is a paradox because of the intense struggle between Jesus' humanity and His divinity. It is a paradox because in the midst of exuberant shouts of joy from the crowd, Jesus is desperately alone. It is a paradox because on this day, Jewish authorities plot to kill the Messiah that God sent to Earth out of His love for us. It is a paradox because our Palm Sunday service begins joyfully but ends ever so tragically. And finally, it is a paradox because each joyful Christian heart is faced with the dilemma of Jesus' impending death.

+++

The struggle between Jesus' humanity and His divinity forms our first paradox. From the human side, Jesus entered Jerusalem to celebrate the Passover, as He has done faithfully for the past thirty-three years. For Jewish people, the Passover, a major Jewish feast day, celebrates their ancestors' release from 430 years of brutal slavery in Egypt, which was orchestrated by the providential hand of God and led by the prophet Moses. Jews observe this memorial institution and remember God's providential care even to this present day.

Even though the Passover meal can be celebrated at home, Jews from all over Israel make the pilgrimage to the Holy City of Jerusalem to participate in the festive services celebrated in the temple. On this day, Jesus and His disciples come to Jerusalem from nearby Bethany, the home of Lazarus and his sisters, and stay in a small upper room in a house that was probably owned by one of His disciple's parents.

This Passover is different from the jubilant celebration of years past. This year, His presence is bittersweet. On the one hand, the people are overjoyed to see Him because He has not been in Jerusalem since the Passover meal last year. On the other hand, He knows tensions are running high. Some of the Jewish leaders do not want Him in the city because He poses a threat to the Romans as the Jewish Messiah. He, more than anyone, understands the severity of the situation. Thus, His human side ponders, *"Should I go, knowing my life will be in jeopardy?"*

But the divine side of His struggle focuses on more than just the Passover meal as He must also face the events of Good Friday. And while His humanity continually battles His divinity over the certainty of Easter's resurrection, His thoughts focus on the cross. From the divine side, there is no question: He must go! A price must be paid, and He is the only One who can pay it. The hope of our salvation is dependent on His death because His death pays for our sins. Otherwise, everything is lost. He is very aware of the Almighty Plan, and He cannot and will not back out. Simply put, He wants to go.

Even so, Jesus enters Jerusalem with an unbearable tension in His heart. Look closely, and you can see it on His face. It is the tension of knowing what others do not know but not being able to reveal it. It is the tension of knowing what lies in the very near future while everyone else celebrates the present. Nevertheless, He goes. He can't stay away. His faith demands that He goes. His love compels him to go. But He never forgets why He is there.

+++

The Holy City is overflowing with cheerful people. The streets are noisy, filled with vibrant activity, alive with a festive mood. Vendors fill the brisk spring air with scents of unleavened bread baking in outdoor ovens; vegetables roasting in olive oil; and lamb, goat, and pigeon sizzling on an open flame. Wine flows freely from tall carafes. Friends and relatives, who have been separated since last year, smile and laugh as they embrace each other with the anticipation of celebrating another Passover together. Obviously, this is not a somber, reserved feast.

When Jesus enters the city, the excitement of the crowd reaches an unsurpassed level. The people welcome Him with open arms as they sing, dance, and spread palm branches on the road, and their shouts of adulation for Him fill the air with a thunderous joy. Riding on a simple donkey, Jesus passes by like a hero returning from a long journey. It is difficult to catch a glimpse of Him because of the raised hands waving palm branches high in the air. Fathers put their children on their shoulders, and mothers hold their toddlers in their arms to catch sight of Him. Looking at their children, they ask eagerly, "Can you see Him? Look, He is our Messiah. He is our Savior!" Raising their voices, the crowd proclaims, *"Jesus! Son of David! Hosanna to the King!"* Can *you* see Him?

In the midst of the people crying out His name, Jesus stands alone in the crowd as He is keenly aware of what is going on behind the scenes, including the conspiracy taking place in the dark corners of the Jewish council. The loving and genuine admiration shown for Him by the people in His presence will soon clash with the hatred and malicious plot planned against Him by the Jewish leaders in their secret chambers. As Jesus enters the Holy City, Satan also enters the hearts of those Jewish leaders. According to these authorities, Jesus' triumphal entry into Jerusalem confirms their conviction that His followers have gotten out of hand. And if you have ever felt terribly alone in a large crowd, then you have experienced a small slice of what Jesus faced on Palm Sunday.

The people, including His disciples, are unaware of this paradoxical tension. This tension has been mounting for over a year. His charismatic popularity with the people, His conflicts with Jewish authorities over rigid Jewish law, His miraculous cures and power over natural elements, and claims that He is the Son of God have caused great trepidation among the highest Jewish leaders. They nervously fear the Romans will crush them, destroy their temple, and banish them from their homeland unless present conditions settle down. And now reports of Jesus recently raising Lazarus from the dead have fueled the fires of adversity.

The paradox is that while the Jewish nation gathers to celebrate the Passover and their ancestors' freedom from slavery in Egypt, the leaders are gravely concerned about Roman slavery. The authorities feel as though they must be proactive and show the Romans that they can take care of their own business. In secret meetings, they draw the conclusion that Jesus' death is the only viable solution. The Sanhedrin, the high Jewish court, seals His fate. The joy of Palm Sunday ends with a plan to extinguish the Light of the World.

> *Then the chief priests and the Pharisees called a meeting of the Sanhedrin. "What are we accomplishing?" they asked. "Here is this man performing many signs. If we let him go on like this, everyone will believe in him, and then the Romans will come and crush both our temple and our nation." Then one of them, named Caiaphas, who was high priest that year, spoke up, "You know nothing at all! You do not realize that it is better that one man dies for the people than the whole nation perishes." (John 11:47–50)*

+++

This incredible and almighty paradox comes alive in each Christian heart during this Holy Week. You too are drawn into the dilemma of Jesus entering Jerusalem. On the compassionate side, you do not want Him to go to Jerusalem. Spare Him the pain. Spare Him the humiliation. Spare Him the death. Spare *us* the pain. Spare *us* the humiliation. Spare *us* the guilt of watching Him die. However, spiritually, you *do* want Him to go. You *do* want Him to be betrayed. You *do* want Him to be arrested. And especially, you *do* want Him crucified. *You are keenly aware* that unless He finishes the week, eternal life will be lost. In that way, we must side with Satan and confirm that the Sanhedrin is making the right decision, whether or not its members know the true reason from which they act.

Either Jesus goes, or He does not go, and you know the outcome of the decision. If He does not go, then the price of human sinfulness will be left unpaid, the kingdom is not an option for us, and humanity will spend eternity in hell. If He does not go, then He will be spared the cross, but His Father will be greatly disappointed. If He does not go, then He will return to the kingdom as the Son of God with His aborted mission and face in shame the heavenly host of angels. He will have to live with their disenchantment. Of course, they will forgive and understand because none of them would want the cross for themselves. If He does not go, then He returns to His Father in the kingdom, but we belong to Satan.

If He *does* go, then He will have to face the cross. He will have to face the unbearable pain of flogging, crucifixion, and dying the most gruesome death known to mankind. It will be the longest day filled with excruciating pain. But it will be over in one day. If He goes, then the price of human sinfulness will be paid.

If He goes, then we will live eternally. If He goes, then He emerges from the tomb as the Risen Lord, the Savior of the world, as the One before whom heads and knees will bow for all eternity, including those of every heavenly angel. If He goes, then He will return to the kingdom in triumph, and one day, you and I will join Him there. One day, we will all be together. The union of us with Him in the kingdom as one with the Father is Jesus' greatest desire and passion.

This decision will reach its climactic conclusion on Maundy Thursday in the garden of Gethsemane when Jesus addresses it one last time: *"Father, if it is possible, take this cup from me. Yet not as I will but your will be done"* (*Matthew 26:39*). Of course, He goes. He goes out of love. He couldn't stay away. His faith demands that He goes. His love compels that He goes.

+++

Present-day liturgical denominations attempt to capture the paradox and tension of Palm Sunday through liturgy. The Palm Sunday Liturgy begins joyously and celebratory, the way Jesus enters Jerusalem: the blessing of the palms, a festive procession around the church with people singing the glorious hymn, "*All Glory, Laud, and Honor,*" and shouts of "Hosanna in the highest!" The people wave palm branches in the air hoping to catch a glimpse of the first Palm Sunday. But soon the liturgy turns dark with ominous tragic reading of the scriptures that reference His suffering and death. We hear the reading of the Passion and then the Preface of Holy Week, *"For our sins he was lifted high upon the cross, that he might draw all people to himself"* (*BCP,* 379).

The mood swing of the liturgy reflects the mood swing of the first Palm Sunday. A day of triumph turns into a day of tragedy. We leave the Palm Sunday Liturgy with a heavy heart and in stark contrast to the joyful anticipation when we first entered. It is difficult to capture the day in the confinement of liturgical rubrics. It is difficult to capture the day in just an hour. As a result, most people do not know nor experience the Palm Sunday Jesus knows. Most people take their palms, go home after the service, and never imagine the paradox of the day, the decision nor the loneliness of Jesus Christ.

Jesus' dilemma to face the coming week is now your dilemma. As you desperately need Him to journey through the week for you, He passionately wants you to journey with Him. He wants you to walk by His side, to encourage Him, to show your appreciation, and to love Him. He wants you in church. He wants you to be with His disciples who witnessed His final days. He wants to see you. While Palm Sunday services always exceed regular Sunday attendance, *everyone* comes to church on Easter. Everyone loves a hero. But in order to rise with Jesus on Easter, you must first travel with Him this week and be with Him even to His death.

> *Do you not know that we who were baptized into Christ Jesus were baptized into His death?*
> *Through baptism into His death, we were buried with Him, so that, just as Christ was raised from the dead by the glory of the Father, we too might have new life. (Romans 6:3, 4)*

You cannot have a theology of glory without a theology of suffering. You cannot have triumph without conflict. The more tumultuous the conflict, the more glorious the triumph. You cannot celebrate Easter Sunday without first passing through the cross of Good Friday. If you do, you have "Cheap Grace," as the great German theologian Dietrich Bonhoeffer calls it.

Cheap Grace is grace that is nowhere to be found at the foot of the cross but shows up suddenly at the empty tomb. We want every day to be Easter. But some days are like Good Friday, filled with great sadness. I once asked one of my parishioners if he planned to attend Holy Week services. "Oh no!" he responded. "It's too dramatic. I'll see you on Easter." Suffering to glory, conflict to triumph, and death to life are too dramatic. Imagine that! Jesus loves you so much that He laid down His life for you so you may share in His new life. That is not too dramatic. That is filled with grace.

What are your plans for this Holy Week? Where will you be and what will you be doing when Jesus enters Jerusalem on Palm Sunday? Where will you be when Jesus eats the Passover meal on Maundy Thursday? Will you be with Him on Friday as He hangs from the cross to save your soul? What can be more important? Jesus asks, "Can you not spend one hour with me?" Where will you be and what will you be doing during that hour? When a loved one is at the point of death, you want to be by his/her side. Go to church this week and be by His side. As Jesus walks through this week for you, walk through this week for Him.

> You cannot stay away.
> Your faith demands that you go.
> Your love compels you to go.

+++

This week…
Spend time with Jesus. Be with Him as He enters Jerusalem, eats His last supper, and hangs on the cross. Be with Him because He does this for you. Go to church this week; make room in your heart for Him! *He did the same for* you!

The Night Time Stood Still

> *The blood shall be a sign for you on the houses where you live; seeing the blood, I will pass over you; thus, when I strike the land of Egypt, no destructive blow will come upon you. (Exodus 12:13)*

Setting the stage for His final destructive blow against the obstinate Egyptian pharaoh, the Lord God sends a series of devastating plagues upon all of Egypt until the great prophet Moses leads God's people from their brutal Egyptian slavery. After 430 years of the pharaoh's unbearable cruelty, God tells Moses:

> *I have witnessed the affliction of my people in Egypt and have heard their cry of complaint against their slave drivers, so I know well what they are suffering. Therefore, I have come down to rescue them from the hands of the Egyptians and lead them out of that land into a good and spacious land, a land flowing with milk and honey. (Exodus 3:7, 8)*

The year is 1300 BC. Using Israelite slaves to build enormous Egyptian cities, the pharaoh remains deaf to God's call through Moses to free His people. The pharaoh ponders why he should obey a God he doesn't believe or recognize. As a result, one by one, the Lord God sends nine devastating plagues upon Egypt: the water of the Nile turns to blood, frogs swarm the land and enter people's homes, lice crawl over the land and on people, flies infest the skies, a deadly pestilence kills Egyptian livestock, boils cover people's bodies, hail destroys crops and splits trees, locusts eat the fruit and vegetables, and darkness covers the land.

After each plague, the pharaoh informs Moses that his people are free to go, only to change his mind and command that they stay (*Exodus 7–11*). The tenth plague, the death of the firstborn in every Egyptian household, becomes God's decisive act, thus making them think that the pharaoh will release God's people on this night, so they must be ready.

To initiate the final plague, the Lord commands His people to procure a lamb (*Exodus 12:3–6*), slaughter it, dip some of its blood with a hyssop branch, and sprinkle the blood on the exterior doorposts and on the lintel as a sign of their faithfulness (*Exodus 12:6, 7*). They must roast the lamb over fire and eat it with unleavened bread and bitter herbs (*Exodus 12:8–11*). The unleavened bread will take less time to rise, and the bitterness of the herbs will remind them of the harshness of their people's slavery. If anyone is alone, that person will join a neighboring family. They must eat quickly, fully dressed with staff in hand and sandals on their feet, ready for the journey (*Exodus 12:12*). The tenth plague will finally free God's people on this night.

+++

Darkness covers the night sky while the full moon glistens with a ray of hope. The stars tell the story of their ancestors who lived and died under oppressive slavery in this alien land. Their distant memory adds to the urgency of the night.

The lamb is taken from the fire, placed on a platter, and set on a wooden counter inside the home. The fire warms the night air as the scent of baking bread draws the family together. The bitterness of the herbs is a foreign aroma, reminding them that this night will be different.

As the family gathers around a simple table, the light of a single candle reveals the first holy ordained Passover meal. Eyes glance at each other in expectant anticipation. Conversations remain hushed as only the children question this most unusual night. Knowing that the great Exodus may come at any moment, they sit on edge, eating quickly, waiting for the signal to leave.

The God they barely know but whom they have come to trust through the words of Moses will act mightily, powerfully, and decisively as He leads His people from the hands of the Egyptian pharaoh into His gentle, protective, providential hand. The Angel of Death leaves his heavenly post and begins his mission, setting into motion the night time stood still.

The Israelites sprinkle the doorposts and the lintel, not for the angel but for themselves. Thus, by God's design, they participate in their own salvation. The Angel of Death who passed over the Israelites' homes didn't need to see blood on the doorposts to determine whether or not the occupants were Israelite or Egyptian. The angel already knew who was inside. Angels just know. And besides, the Israelites are slaves. They lived on the other side of town. By sprinkling the blood, the Israelites demonstrate their trust in the Lord God and participate in the history of salvation.

The blood of the lamb saves them from death.
And God, in His almighty wisdom, gives us
a foreshadowing of His own Son.

The Passover meal, a holy meal celebrated and commemorated every year, is the heart of the Old Testament: *"This day shall be a memorial feast for you, which all your generations shall celebrate with pilgrimage to the Lord as a perpetual institution"* (Exodus 12:14).

+++

Being a faithful Jew, Jesus celebrated the Passover meal thirty-three times, once each year of His life. For Jesus and His disciples—1,300 years later—the celebration of His last Passover meal falls on a Thursday, the night before He dies. However, the holiness of this night is tainted with mistrust as Jesus knows that one of His beloved disciples will soon betray Him. The tension of Palm Sunday is intensified by betrayal. And Jesus knows it will be His Last Supper. He knows that at this very moment and with this very meal, His life will take a decisive turn that will lead Him to the gruesome cross of Good Friday. It is by divine design that Jesus' Last Supper was the Passover meal as this night set in motion the events that initiated Jesus' passing over from death to life.

After the meal, Jesus and His disciples retire to the garden of Gethsemane, a common gathering spot for them. It is late; His disciples sleep. But Jesus does not. He is the only one aware of the traumatic events which will unfold within minutes. He sits alone in solitude, conversing with His Father. Facing the cross with the deepest emotion, Jesus prays, *"Father, if it is possible, take this cup from me; yet not what I want, but what you want"* (Matthew 26:39).

Once again, His humanity and divinity clash, knowing what must be done yet praying for a different outcome. But there is no other option. There is too much at stake. There is too much invested. The blood of the Lamb must be shed. As the pounding sound from the ominous footsteps of the soldiers who come to arrest Him and the threatening thunder that roars in the distance draws closer, the course of history changes for Him and for us. Thus, for the last time in His humanity, Jesus surrenders to His Father's will.

And so it begins.

+++

The hopes and fears of all the years are met in Thee tonight. The word *maundy* denotes a mandate, a commandment. During His last Passover meal, Jesus proclaims two mandates, one that is obscure and the other well-known. The obscure mandate comes early in the meal: *"And during supper Jesus got up from the table, took off his outer robe, and tied a towel around himself. Then he poured water into a basin and began to wash the disciples' feet and began to wipe them with the towel that was tied around him"* (John 13:2b–5).

The other one follows the first: *"So if I, your Lord and teacher, have washed your feet, you also ought to wash one another's feet. For I have set an example, that you should also do what I have done for you"* (John 13:14).

> *The Master becomes the servant.*
> *The Glorified is humbled.*
> *The Savior bows in obedience.*
> *The Pure One washes feet.*

Many churches practice foot washing on Maundy Thursday. We wash one another's feet, not because our feet are dirty but because we follow His mandate. This humbling experience often brings tears that trickle down our cheeks and onto the other person's feet, connecting not only us to the other person but also both of us to Jesus.

Even so, there are those who resist and find the experience uncomfortable, like Simon.

> *Peter said to Him, "You will never wash my feet." Jesus said to him, "Unless I wash you, you have no share with me." Simon Peter said to him, "Lord, not my feet only but also my hands and head." Jesus said to him, "One who has bathed has no need to wash, except for the feet, but is entirely clean."* (John 13:8b–10b)

When you wash another person's feet, you touch that person in ways that you would not otherwise touch them. And because we find this uncomfortable, we often do the minimum while trying to maintain our dignity. Pour a little water. Touch a couple of toes. Quickly wrap the feet in a towel. Avoid as much contact as possible. But walk away claiming that we have imitated Christ. Really?

We must remember that washing someone's feet will not save us. It is, however, an opportunity to participate in our salvation, the history of salvation, and following Jesus. So go ahead. Roll up your sleeves, check your apprehension at the door, humble yourself for Jesus. Foot washing will not save you, but His humility will. By embracing Jesus' humility, He redeems us. Foot washing is where the sole of humility meets the road of salvation.

+++

The second mandate of this night connects to the meal itself. As Paul explains,

> *I also handed to you what I received from the Lord that on the night He was betrayed He took a loaf of bread, and when He had given thanks, He broke it and said, "This is my body which is given to you. Do this in remembrance of me." Likewise, He also took the cup and said, "This is my blood of the new covenant. Do this as often as you drink it, in remembrance of me." (1 Corinthians 11:23–25)*

Jesus doesn't just eat the Passover; He becomes the Passover, the slaughtered Lamb. Jesus is the Lamb of God. The next day on the cross, the blood of the Lamb will once again become the salvation of the people. God's wisdom wove together the tapestry of our salvation 1,300 years apart. God arranged the pieces that will lead to our eternal life. And we remember His Son in the bread and the wine.

The word *Eucharist* means thanksgiving. We gather in thanksgiving for the gift of God's Son. We praise and glorify His name for what He has done for each of us. Like the Passover meal of the Old Testament, the Eucharist is the memorial meal of the New Covenant. Celebrated as a perpetual institution, it is our Passover meal, and Jesus is the Lamb.

The Eucharist is the profound spiritual presence of Jesus Christ in the elements of the bread and the wine. We do not understand how this happens or when this happens. We just know it happens. We know by the time Communion is distributed to the people, the bread and wine become His body and blood. During Communion, it looks like bread. It tastes like bread. It must be Jesus. It looks like wine. It tastes like wine. It must be Jesus.

The Lamb of God enters our humanity. The Lord Christ comes and lives in us: heart, body, mind, and soul. Our Father knew this when He sent His Son to our humanity because when we receive Holy Communion, He lives in our humanity. The Son of God not only dwells among us but dwells within us. The climax of the entire Eucharist is when we consume the body and the blood of Jesus Christ. This piece of salvation history begins with the first Passover meal and builds until we receive Holy Communion. Receiving the body and blood of Jesus Christ in Holy Communion prepares us for the time of our own pass over from this world to the next. It is the most important way to prepare ourselves for the kingdom.

The first Passover meal points to the Last Supper. The Last Supper points to the Eucharist. The Eucharist points to the heavenly banquet. These events are connected. We are connected. Receiving the Eucharist opens the lifeline to God's spiritual family. Through the Lamb, we become blood relatives with the Israelites who ate the Passover meal and the Jews who eat the Seder. The apostles and early martyrs are present in the Communion of the saints. We become brothers and sisters with Christians in Poland, the Catholics in Ireland, and the persecuted in South Africa. The One who ate and drank with His disciples two thousand years ago now eats and drinks with His friends all over the world. You are connected to all of this through the Eucharist. Relish it. Appreciate it. Give thanks for it. But by God, participate in it!

Maundy Thursday provides the food of salvation history. As the body and blood of the Lamb hangs on the cross of Calvary, they touch your hands and lips at Communion. This night moves us forward to eternity. It is a holy night, a night when time stands still: the past, the present, and the future become one. Obey this second mandate and remember Him in the breaking of the bread.

+++

This week…
Go to church on Maundy Thursday, wash someone's feet, and receive the body and blood of our Lord and Savior. Humble yourself so you can praise and worship Him!

The Scapegoat

"Forgive Me, Father, for My hurtful words. Forgive Me for questioning Your faithfulness. Forgive Me for doubting You."

Silence engulfs the heavens, waiting for the Father's response. As the Father's compassion fills the silence with His grace and mercy, His tender words provide comfort to His bewildered Son:

"Suffer no more, My Son. Hearing Your prayer in the garden of Gethsemane, witnessing Your unbearable pain on the cross, and keeping a vigil over Your lifeless body in the cave, I ached for You. My heart bled for You. You are My Son, faithful, obedient, loving."

"My bones were out of joint. Like wax, my heart melted within my breast. My mouth dried up and my tongue stuck to my jaws. They could count all my bones. They gloated over me" (Psalm 22).

"Forgive them, Son, for they know not what they do."
"Yes, Father, let them have My body. My spirit is Yours. All is forgiven."

The heavens rejoice with joy!

Let us pray:

Almighty God, we pray you graciously to behold this your family, for whom our Lord Jesus Christ was willing to be betrayed, and given into the hands of sinners, and to suffer death upon the cross;

> *who now lives and reigns with you and the Holy Spirit, one God, for ever and ever. Amen.* (Collect for Good Friday, *Book of Common Prayer*, 221)

+++

The Old Testament Jews had seven High Holy Days. The highest one and certainly the most holy was, and still is, Yom Kippur. Literally translated, it means Day of Atonement, which dates back to 800 BC. Its first explanation appears in *the book of Leviticus*: to cleanse the people from their sins and to reestablish their relationship with God:

> *Aaron shall bring forward a live goat. Laying both hands on its head, he shall confess over it all the sinful faults and transgressions of the Israelites, and so put them on the goat's head. He shall then have it led into the desert by an attendant. Since the goat is to carry off their iniquities to an isolated region, it must be sent away into the desert.* (Leviticus 16:20–22)

The intention of this rite places the sins of the people onto the goat that is then led to an isolated place in the desert to die. When the goat dies, all of the sins of the people are forgiven. This is the origin of the term *scapegoat*.

This very act signifies the alienation of sin from the people. And with the removal of sin, the relationship between God and His people can now be reconciled.

But the desert holds another important spiritual significance for us. When we feel alienated or cut off from God, we live in a *spiritual desert*. Since Paul states that all sin has its origin in the flesh, he tells us that when we are in a spiritual desert, we must die to the sin that is in our flesh so we can be reunited with God in our spirit (*Romans 6:5–11*).

+++

"Son, You are their scapegoat."
*"I know, Father. My death provided the grace
for their reconciliation with You."*
"It was difficult watching You endure such a brutal death, My Son."
*"My heart ached for their cruelty. Yet I suffered for You, Father.
I suffered for them.
I suffered for Us."*

Good Friday is our Day of Atonement. Jesus becomes the scapegoat on whom the sins of the world are cast. When the scapegoat dies, our sins are forgiven, *"Lamb of God Who takes away the sins of the world, have mercy on us."*

Good Friday begins in the early morning with Jesus' trial before Pontius Pilate, the Roman governor of Jerusalem. Since the Romans will not allow the Jews to sentence one of their own to death without a Roman trail, Pontius Pilate has authority of life and death. But Pilate does his best to give Jesus a fair trial. He asks the Jewish leaders, *"What charges do you bring against this man?" (John 18:29)*. However, the Jewish leaders are not forthcoming with Pilate because they know that charges under their law will not result in a Roman condemnation. So Pilate calls Jesus out and questions Him. But Jesus, answering Pilate's legal questions with spiritual answers remains nebulous because our Savior knows that His death is absolutely necessary. Pilate gets nowhere with anyone, not even Jesus.

The governor finds himself cornered with an ethical conundrum. His conscience weighs on his heavy heart as he is at the crossroads of justice. Once again, he summons Jesus and fires several questions at Him: *"Are you the king of the Jews? What have you done?"* And finally, when Jesus explains that He has come to testify to the truth, Pilate asks, *"What is truth?"* Ironically, Pilate looks at the truth in the eye but does not recognize Him. How often we have been blind to the truth when it is right before us! Pilate's demise is not recognizing the truth, not seeing the truth, not knowing the truth, not engaging the truth, all of which opens Pilate's door to the chanting angry mob.

The bloodthirsty mob is incited by the Jewish leaders. The enraged crowd chants, *"Crucify Him! Crucify Him!"* Pilate's attempted compromise to release Barabbas is declined. The outraged pack wants nothing but the blood of Jesus. *"Crucify Him! Crucify Him!"* Thus, Pilate is faced with four dilemmas: moral, ethical, political, and personal. Should he sentence Jesus to die? The politics of the day—the escalating tensions between the Jews and the Romans—demand death in order to maintain peace. Pilate knows that Jesus has not committed a crime deserving death, but in Pilate's eyes, Jesus is just a lowly Jew. Is He worth a rebellion where many will be harmed, arrested, and perhaps even killed? The governor orders Jesus scourged at the post, hoping to give the crowd some of the blood they desperately desire. Not satisfied, the crowd chants louder and louder and louder, *"Crucify Him! Crucify Him! Crucify Him! Crucify Him!"* Their cries are deafening.

The crossroads of justice meets the crossroads of the morning. On the verge of rioting, the hysterical crowd pressures the governor to act against his wisdom. Pilate reasons that the death of one man to save many others seems reasonable. *"Crucify Him! Crucify Him! Crucify Him!"*

And through a dream, his wife warns him not to get involved in the death sentence. The tension and anxiety of this decision is overwhelming as it is the strongest that he has ever faced. The dilemma before Pilate is so great that he literally washes his hands of the issue, hoping to excuse himself. And so he succumbs to both social and political pressures, causing him to back down from what he believes and to sacrifice his position of authority, and by doing so, he gives the mob what it wants.

By picking up His cross, Jesus carries the weight of the world on His shoulders. He is not led into the desert but to Calvary, a garbage dump. He does not die in isolation but with public humiliation. The *distant thunder* is the curtain of the sanctuary being torn in two *(Luke 15:38)*. And through His suffering on the cross, the sinful world is reconciled with the Father.

+++

Pilate's dilemma continues this day for all Christians. Pilate's dilemma is now yours. Why does Jesus have to die? Do you want Jesus to die? You know He is innocent, but circumstances demand that He die in order for you to inherit the kingdom. If He does not die, then eternal life will be lost, and reconciliation with the Father is rendered impossible. The world needs a scapegoat, and only One will do. You stand in Pilate's sandals but for very different reasons.

So you share in Jesus' prayer in the garden of Gethsemane, "Father, if it is possible, let this cup pass from Him." But as you pray, you know that there is no other option but for Him to die. *He is the only One.* There is only one suitable plan, and that is God's plan. Jesus is the only One worthy enough to die for your unworthiness. Is it right to want Jesus to die so that you can go to heaven? Is that selfish? How do you feel? If you were in the crowd in front of Pilate's headquarters, you would clamor for His death. *They roared out of hate. But you cry out of love.*

+++

And now we understand the paradox of Good Friday. It is a paradox because the Gospel in which we place our hope and the world in which we live directly oppose each other. It is a paradox because the Son of God becomes the Suffering Servant. It is a paradox because the King dies for His people. It is a paradox because by His stripes we are healed. It is a paradox because death brings life. It is a paradox because what you don't want to happen on Good Friday is exactly what you want to happen.

So Good Friday becomes the most momentous paradox of all. God sells His Son to Satan, a necessary evil for a greater good. The death of one Man is traded for the life of the world—a heartbreaking deal for God the Father, the preservation of national security for Jewish authorities, a political decision for Pontius Pilate.

Wishing to remain innocent by washing his hands, Pilate seals Jesus' fate, and Jesus is given His cross to carry. God brings joy even to Satan's heart, if Satan even has a heart. All the demons in hell proclaim Satan as lord, and they watch in excitement from the pits of hell as our Precious Savior stumbles toward Calvary jeering and cheering each time He falls. The angels in heaven can only weep in extreme sorrow.

+++

While Jesus is carrying His cross, He meets Simon of Cyrene who is mentioned in only one verse in all four Gospels: *"As they went out, they came upon a man coming in from the country from Cyrene named Simon, and they compelled this man to carry Jesus' cross"* (*Luke 23:26*). He is present in only one verse, but Simon plays an unforgettable role in the history of salvation.

Cyrene is a homonym to serene, but when Simon approaches Jesus, the scene he witnesses is anything but *serene*. It is filled with bitter pain, chaos, screams of agony from the cross bearers; Roman soldiers whipping, lashing out, and beating down; and loud lamenting and hysterical weeping by the Savior's followers.

Simon meets Jesus through the cross. Being from Cyrene, he is most likely Jewish, and he is in Jerusalem to celebrate the Passover. He comes in from the countryside to find one of his fellow Jews on his way to be crucified. He doesn't understand what is going on. From the country, he rarely sees such a horrific scene. He stares intently at Jesus, and their eyes gaze upon each other; Simon's eyes with the judgment of a criminal, Jesus' eyes losing hope with each passing minute.

Up to this point, he does not know Jesus. How many people do we come in contact with who do not know Jesus? They find Him through the cross. They find Him through the forgiveness of their sins, paid for by Jesus on the cross. Simon finds Jesus by carrying His cross, and his mind and his heart are overwhelmed at the prospect of carrying a cross for a man he does not know. That is why Jesus tells us to pick up our cross and follow Him.

The cross you bear in your life cannot be heavier than the cross Jesus carried for us. Jesus struggles because His divinity does not diminish His humanity. Thus, Jesus' cross was not one ounce lighter because He is the Son of God. He is the Son of God, but God never lightened His cross. And because He is human, His burden exceeds His level of endurance, and He needs help.

Simon is randomly chosen to carry Jesus' cross just as life randomly chooses you to bear the cross you must carry. As Simon helps Jesus carry His cross, Jesus, because of His humanity, helps you carry your cross. Simon becomes the personification of others in your life who help you along the ever-demanding crossroads of life. Jesus can't make it alone, and we can't either. You must accept the help of others because even Jesus cannot make it to Calvary alone.

Simon must have an attitude of "Why me?" Don't you think Simon feels this way? Think of the timing. Simon just happened to be in the wrong place at the wrong time. In holy irony, Simon probably thinks it is unfair that he, an innocent man, must carry the cross of a guilty one. Who is innocent, and who is guilty? Simon represents all humanity. We sin, and yet we complain that we have to carry a cross.

You would do anything to help Jesus out, right? Wouldn't you be honored to help Jesus carry His cross? Wouldn't you feel blessed to give Jesus a break from His arduous journey so He could make it to Calvary to die there instead of on the way? Yet this is an ethical and spiritual dilemma. You want to help Jesus so He can make it to His death. The irony is that it takes two men to bear the cross; but one of these men is completely innocent. This quandary is at the heart of Christianity. The irony is twisted. *How Satan has tainted everything!* You are now faced with this eternal dilemma. In some way, you must respond to the paradox. You must now live in the irony. The paradox becomes personal. Go ahead and shout, *"Crucify Him! Crucify Him!"* Shout it as though your life depends on it. Shout it as though your salvation depends on it. Because it does!

You understand what His crucifixion means. And as much as you understand it, Jesus understands it even more. He wants it even more than you do. He wants you to be with Him in the kingdom more than you want to be with Him in the kingdom. You don't understand this as much as He does. You cannot begin to understand the magnitude of His death as much as He does. Nor should you. The Son of God is willing to die for your sins so that you can one day be in the kingdom with Him. He is willing to do this for you. God, the Father, commands; Jesus, the Son, obeys,

> *He stretched out His arms upon the cross, and offered himself, according to your will, a perfect sacrifice for the whole world.* (Eucharistic Prayer A, Book of Common Prayer, 362)

This sentence makes it clear that Jesus' death upon the cross is the perfect sacrifice for the sins of the whole world. It is the perfect sacrifice: *"He stretched out his arms upon the cross,"* and when He does, your heart breaks.

Your heart breaks because you know the Roman soldiers do not have to force Jesus into the crucifixion. Your heart breaks because you know Jesus will not struggle. There is no confrontation. He does not fight. He does not squirm. It is not necessary for two soldiers to hold Him down while a third drives the nails. Jesus simply surrenders.

He surrenders in perfect obedience to His Father for the salvation of the world. He gives all of Himself. The most brutal death is willingly and peacefully accepted. *He stretched out His arms upon the cross.* It is easy for the soldiers. It is the easiest crucifixion the soldiers ever administer. Jesus dies willingly. He dies willingly for your sins. Your heart breaks because you know that Jesus loves you with arms wide open.

On the cross, good and evil, love and hate, and life and death become one. And the Father watches His only Son die for the salvation of the world. For you, for me, for all. William Temple, the archbishop of Canterbury during the 1920s, wrote, "The manger and the cross are God at His best."

> *"Father, have mercy on them."*
> *"Suffer no more My Son.*
> *All is forgiven."*
> *And the heavens rejoice with joy!*

+++

The good death...
good because it saves your life.
Kill the scapegoat.
Kill the Lamb of God.
Lamb of God Who takes away the sins of the world...
Have mercy on us!

+++

This week...
Remember that our Lord and Savior died for us and our sins so we may have everlasting life. Knowing His sacrifice for us, how can you not go to church on Good Friday and worship Him!

The Season of Easter

𝒜s we celebrate Easter with an array of chocolate bunnies, colorful Easter eggs, yummy jelly beans, and as we gather with family and friends to break bread and to give thanks for this glorious day, we must also celebrate what Christ has given us: a new attitude, a new perspective, a new reason for living. The Humble King born on Christmas Day is now the Risen Christ who triumphs over every evil. Let our lives be a living testimony to our living God! This is a time of pure joy: "Alleluia! Alleluia! Alleluia!"

This Is the Day!

This is the day the Lord has made;
Let us be glad and rejoice in it. (Psalm 118:24)

Death is strong but life is stronger.
Stronger than the dark is light.
Stronger than the wrong is right.
Faith and hope triumphantly say,
Christ is risen on Easter Day
(Anglican preacher Phillip Brooks on Easter Day, 1732)

+++

For some people, Easter is a metaphor for spring, filled with resplendent tulips, the fragrant smell of freshly cut grass, and baby chicks that chirp the sound of new life. And even though signs of rebirth usher in this welcomed season, especially after a harsh winter, Easter is more than a metaphor; it is the celebration of our Lord's resurrection. *So let us be glad and rejoice in it!*

If we want to know the truth, we must go to the Word. Amen! And the truth is this: *Easter means resurrection.* Save the tulips for your garden. Save the scent of freshly cut grass for your family picnic. And let the baby chicks wander as they may. Do not allow the temporal world to diminish the celebration of the resurrection, *"Do not conform to this world, but be transformed by the renewing of your mind" (Romans 12:2).*

Gospel means good news. The good news of Easter morning is that the tomb is empty: *"The angels said to Mary, 'Why do you look for the living among the dead? The One you are looking for is not here. He is risen'" (Luke 24:5, 6).*

The good news is like the caterpillar that doesn't stay in the cocoon for long. *It's just a phase.* The caterpillar eventually transforms into a butterfly. "Excuse me. Just passing through. Can't stay long." Death, like the caterpillar's metamorphosis, begins a transition into transformation. If the butterfly could go back to the caterpillar and say, "Look! One day you will be like this," the caterpillar would quiver with eager anticipation.

On Easter Day, Jesus is the butterfly who comes back to us in His glory, opens His arms, and says, *"Look! One day you will be like this!" This* is what we celebrate today. Who would have ever thought that a butterfly could come from a caterpillar? Who would have ever thought that a heavenly spirit could come from a mortal body? *Easter is resurrection. Resurrection is transformation. Transformation is life eternal.*

Today, we begin a part of the church calendar called the Great Fifty Days. It is the most joyous time of the church year. The crescendo of the resurrection carries us to Pentecost Sunday, fifty days from now. During these Great Fifty Days, our personal lives should reflect this glorious, joyful time. For these Great Fifty Days, our hearts should be lighthearted. For these Great Fifty Days, our minds should be reassured. For these Great Fifty Days, God's radiance should flow forth from us into the world.

Imagine Jesus lying in the tomb, wrapped in the burial cloth. It is predawn on Easter Sunday morning. His cold, lifeless, bloodstained body has begun to decay. The Hope of the world lies in state for three days. The host of heavenly angels pay their respect. Abraham, Sarah, and their only son, Isaac, are front and center. Moses and Elijah, who appeared with Jesus at the Transfiguration, offer a heartwarming prayer at the graveside. Kings David and Solomon, who built the temple of Jerusalem, kneel in front of the lifeless body. The Angel Gabriel who announced to Mary that she would be the mother of God quietly passes by. A multitude of people wait in quiet anticipation before the small tomb that holds our precious Savior.

Suddenly, at dawn, He takes His first breath, ever so gently. The startled guards outside the tomb think they hear something. They look at each other in wonder. One of His eyes opens…and then the other. Still confined by the tightly wrapped blood-soaked burial cloth, His gentle smile widens as He proclaims, *"Alleluia! This is the day!"* The angels instinctively know what to do as they unwrap Him, carefully, thoughtfully, and graciously. He bursts forth in the glory of the resurrection! The blinding Light blurs the guards' sight. And the choir of angels rejoice with exultation: *"Alleluia! Christ is risen! The Lord is risen indeed! Alleluia!"*

And so we should join them. Lift your voices: *"Alleluia! Christ is risen! The Lord is risen indeed! Alleluia!"*

+++

We are so blessed to live on this side of Easter. We are so fortunate to experience the richness of the New Testament. Yet we ask ourselves, would it have been better to live when Jesus lived, to meet Him, and to witness the events of His life firsthand? But if we had, we would not fully realize the magnitude of His life. Or are we more blessed to live now, without meeting Him, without seeing His life unfold in front of us, but with a more enlightened realization of the astonishing events that were His life? Both have their advantages, no doubt. But we have no choice. And so we must treasure our time in salvation's history.

Easter changes everything! Easter begins God's new world. Easter conquers death. Easter brings eternal life. The source of all life, the power of the universe, shines because of Easter. The humble Father who watched His Son die three days earlier displays His glorious power on this most magnificent day. *Easter changes everything!*

In our life, death gives time its value. In our next life, death makes time eternal. Easter changes our priorities and our direction. We cannot celebrate Easter without leaving our current path. We cannot celebrate Easter without releasing our worldly burdens. As our Lord God alters the path of human history through the birth of His Son, the resurrection alters the path of our future. Easter changes the way we think, the way we act, and the way we pray. Easter changes our attitude, our approach to this life, and our expectation of life beyond the grave. Wow! *Where is that cocoon?*

> Amid the trumpets and other brass
> instruments at the Easter Service…
> Amid the beautiful music of the organ and voices singing hymns…
> Amid the triumphal prayers of God's people…
> The tomb remains empty.
> And at the entrance to the silent tomb lies our
> joyous celebration into eternal life.

+++

Every Sunday is a little Easter. Easter is not a day. It's an attitude. It's the way we live. It's a lifestyle. Every Sunday, we should go to church and enjoy the rest of the day with our families. It wasn't so long ago when families did this on Sundays.

We should not go to church on Sunday out of obligation or guilt. We do not gather for any self-serving motive. We go to church on Sunday to praise and worship Jesus Christ. Sundays are not for us. Sundays are for Jesus. The question is *not*, "What did we get out of the service knowing Jesus was here?" Rather, "What did Jesus get out of the service knowing we were here?" The question is *not*, "How much of Jesus do we have?" Rather, the question is, "How much of us does Jesus have?" We should not make our Sunday plans and then see if there is time to go to church. Rather, we should go to church and then see if there is time for our Sunday plans. This is what we do on Easter Sunday. This is what we should do every Sunday, every "Little Easter." It's not about us. It's all about Jesus.

+++

Jesus makes God personal, and Easter makes the resurrection personal. Jesus is the Savior of the world, but Jesus is your Savior as well. Jesus died for the sins of the world, but Jesus died for your sins as well. You are not left out. You are connected.

God loves us so much that He became one of us. At Christmas, the Son of God takes human form, and we celebrate his birth. On Easter, His rebirth points us to the kingdom. Jesus wants to take His relationship with us to the next level. Jesus wants to take us to the resurrected life. God becomes like us so we can become like Him. God meets us where we are, but He loves us too much to leave us there. The only question is, "Are we ready to follow?"

The church is not rooted in this life. The church is rooted in the next one. The church exists for the kingdom. Church leaders and their congregations must always keep this on the front burner. As the popular adage proclaims, "Keep the main thing the main thing." Going to church without making the kingdom our top priority loses our focus on the main thing. The church exists for no other reason than to help us get to the kingdom. It is the instrument of our salvation. There is no other reason to go to church than to praise and worship Jesus.

Easter is also a transformation, which demands change. We don't like it, so we avoid it. Change, especially the radical change of Easter, is met with resistance. Easter tells us that we have been traveling on the wrong road, and anytime we are on the wrong road we become unsettled. Easter proclaims that our priorities are upside down. Easter affirms that our temporal world is topsy-turvy. Easter demonstrates that our lives are scattered. Yet most of us have become very comfortable in this life, and we don't want to leave it behind.

We have worked too hard. We have invested too much. And we don't want to change directions. So what happens? We look for ways to transform our lives without radical change.

But without the transformation of Easter, the evil one diverts our attention away from the resurrection by cluttering our thoughts with temporal concerns. If the evil one cannot keep us out of church on Easter or on any other Sunday, then he will quickly settle us back into the Monday morning grind. Sadly then, Sunday's glory fades into Monday's pressure.

But this is counterproductive to the resurrected life. The resurrected life allows Sunday's glory to permeate worldly concerns throughout the rest of the week. Instead of being in church and thinking about the world, we can be in the world and think about Jesus. Now we are on the right road. This is the signpost where Jesus points, the road that leads to the kingdom.

When we look at Easter through the eyes of God, we see a Lover who is willing to do anything for the one He loves. And the one He loves is you. Have you ever loved someone more than the other person loved you? If so, then you know just a little about what it is like to be God. What else does God have to do to win over your heart? He is dying to have an intimate, personal relationship with you. Like a true lover, He longs to be with you. He wants to live with you forever in His house, the kingdom. Only the resurrection gives us this hope. Only the resurrection brings recreation. Only the resurrection brings the transformation in your relationship with Him for which He yearns, for which He has done everything to make it possible. Unless you embrace the resurrection and the radical change it brings in everyday living, then you will miss the greatest Love of your life.

If you have not already done so, open your heart to the One who truly loves you. Renew your commitment to Jesus Christ today. This will make Easter truly profound. Hand over your life to Jesus Christ right now so He can transform it:

> *Therefore, God exalted him to the highest place*
> *and gave him the name that is above every name,*
> *that at the name of Jesus every head shall bow. Every*

> *knee should bend in heaven and on earth and under the earth, and every tongue acknowledges that Jesus Christ is Lord to the glory of God the Father. (Philippians 2:9–11)*

+++

This is what Easter is all about. This is what every Sunday is all about. Can you proclaim Him as your Lord and Savior? *Can you do that?* Through God's hope, we know that there is more to come. Through God's promise, we know that God is always there for us. Something better is yet to come, and God is hard at work for you. He is calling you. Will you respond? Make the day of Jesus' resurrection your resurrection as well. This is the hope and the promise of Easter:

> *This is the day! This is the day that the Lord has made.*
> *Let us rejoice! Let us rejoice and be glad in it.*

+++

This week...
Don't just go to church on Easter Sunday and wait until Christmas to go again. Go to church on Easter Sunday with the commitment to make every Sunday a celebration of Easter Sunday.

Go to worship and praise our Lord and Savior whose resurrection promises us our salvation, whose resurrection promises us an eternal life with Him.

Celebrate our Lord's resurrection knowing that He will one day celebrate yours!

> *This is the day!*
> *This is the day that the Lord has made.*
> *Let us rejoice!*
> *Let us rejoice and be glad in it.*

Running

The angel said to the women, "Do not be afraid, for I know that you are looking for Jesus, who was crucified. He is not here; he has risen, just as he said. Come and see the place where he lay. Then go quickly and tell his disciples: 'He has risen from the dead and is going ahead of you into Galilee. There you will see him.' Now I have told you." So, the women hurried away from the tomb, afraid yet filled with joy, and ran to tell his disciples. (Matthew 28:5–8)

Like most of you, Elizabeth and I were browsing through the Easter cards this past week. There were some delightful cards, depicting the beauty of the season, filled with lilies, tulips, and little yellow chicks nestled in baskets. However, there were not many cards with Gospel scenes. There were not many cards with the bright light, the dead guards, or the angel in front of the empty tomb. There were a few, but not many.

One of the Gospel scenes we would love to see on an Easter card is the women running back to Jerusalem to tell the disciples that Jesus is risen. They are running. *Imagine that.* They are running in their long flowing robes. They are running to tell the disciples. They are running because their encounter with the angel alarmed them, a frightening experience in the presence of such heavenly power. It's out of the ordinary, and that scares us. Wouldn't we love to have a dollar for every time *"Do not be afraid"* appears in scripture! The priest would have a fancy alb with lace trim, a gold-plated chalice with jewels around the base, and stoles of every color that depict the seasons during the liturgical year. The discretionary fund would be large enough to cover every parishioner's request.

The women are filled with fear because their lives have just been changed, and they have not had enough time to process this change. It's too fast and overwhelming to comprehend all at once. However, their fear is surrounded with the joy of knowing that the

One they love is no longer dead. They are anxious to tell others, but what words could adequately describe how they feel?

So they run. They run away from the angel who frightened them and the news the angel revealed. They run to the disciples to tell them of the joyful news. The angel told them to go quickly. So they run.

Before I met Elizabeth, I always thought I would be a Roman Catholic priest. Attending Roman Catholic schools my whole life and taught by nuns who wore habits with long flowing robes was something I saw every day at school and church. When I was in sixth grade, I remember Sister Mary Claire who would play kickball with us at recess. She was not like the other nuns. She was *"nun"* of the above. This nun could run! *Run, nun, run! See nun run!*

When I hear this Easter story of the women running from the tomb, I think of Sister Mary Claire. I picture the women running to tell the disciples like Sister Mary Claire running to first base in her habit, in her long flowing robe. I would like to see that on the cover of an Easter card, the women running to tell others. Running. Running in their long flowing robes. *Run! Run! Run!*

+++

The funny thing is that some people's reaction to the Easter story is often that of running. But they run for different reasons, sometimes even running in different directions.

There are those who run away from the resurrection. Like the women running away from the angel, these people run away from the entire Easter story. The whole concept of a resurrection is too much for them to handle. It seems outrageous, radical. Therefore, they are not in church this Easter morning. Oh! They're running all right. They're running to a child's soccer match. They're running to catch a flight. They're running to buy a last-minute anniversary gift. It's not that their lives lack passion, but they are the skeptics, the doubters, maybe even the atheists. Yet they keep running. Running seems important to them. Sunday morning is a good time to go for a run. At Easter, flowers and little yellow chicks are good enough.

Flowers and little yellow chicks include them in the celebration of Easter, and so does their run on Easter morning.

And there are those who are running in place. They are on a spiritual treadmill. They do the right things. They say the right things. They attend church on Sundays. They have faith, but there is no commitment to grow. The flame of the Spirit is barely a flicker. Church is just something nice to do. They work and play and raise a family, but they get consumed by worldly concerns. The bunnies and the little chicks point to something, but they have no desire to find a deeper meaning, let alone a desire to tell anyone what they believe.

Then there are those who, like the women, run to tell others. Their faith is alive, and their excitement can't be contained. *They just have to tell someone.* These people have encountered the Risen Christ, and He reigns in their hearts. They have discovered that life's true meaning is not found in this world but in the next one. These are the Easter people. They run toward the kingdom in joyful expectation. They have a love for Jesus that can never be extinguished. An encounter with an angel may scare them, but they have left the bunnies and little yellow chicks in the secular world because their focus is spiritual, not secular.

Paul, in the New Testament, is an excellent example of an Easter person. He is always on the move, always on the run. Paul embarks on three extensive missionary journeys, preaching the good news. For one thing, Paul thought that the Second Coming was imminent, so there was little time to lose. More important than the shortage of time though, Paul embraced the radical change of the resurrection and the implications of eternal life. He could not sit still knowing that others had not yet heard. Like the women running to tell the disciples, Paul spent the later years of his life savoring each day's opportunity to tell someone new. The only thing missing with Paul was the long flowing robe.

+++

Which way are you running? Are you running away from the story? Are you running in place? Are you running to tell others?

Reverend Kenneth and Elizabeth Herzog

Chances are you were running a little late for church this morning. But at least you were running in the right direction. Like Sister Mary Claire, you have to run in the right direction to get to first base. Have you gotten to first base with Jesus? Is Jesus Christ your Lord and Savior? Do you go to church on Easter to celebrate the resurrection, or do you go because the family always goes to church on Easter? The Easter bunny cannot save you. He is soft and cuddly, but he has not contributed to your salvation.

Running begins with a single step. A step toward first base is a step in the right direction. Run to Him who promises you eternal life. In doing so, you will discover that the One who stumbled His way to Calvary on Good Friday runs to embrace you with new life on Easter Sunday.

Easter fills us with fear and joy at the same time. Like the women running to tell the disciples, the resurrection unveils our deepest fears and wraps them in the joy of the Risen Christ. However, under normal circumstances, our deep fears steal away our joy. Darkness and depression soon follow. But somehow on Easter Sunday, we purposely block out our worries and concerns, and we consciously put ourselves in a great mood, if even for a day. But Easter people do this every day. These people do not dismiss their concerns as though they do not exist. Rather, they confront their concerns with a positive light. Nothing can bring them down. Nothing can rob them of joy. How do they do this? Because they know how the story ends. They know how their story will end—in the presence of the Risen Christ who will take away all of their concerns and dry all of their tears. Easter people never lose sight of this vision.

For a Christian, Easter is not a metaphor for spring. The hymns we sing this season are not about the rebirth of tulips. The "Alleluias!" during our service are not because warm weather has returned. Easter cards that depict these scenes are generic. They appeal to everyone, believers and nonbelievers. Our secular society has taken the power of the resurrection and turned it into baskets filled with chocolate bunnies, small candied yellow chicks, colorful plastic eggs filled with an array of jelly beans, all resting on synthetic yellow and pink and green grass. This way, everyone can relate! And this is Easter?

While Jesus' ministry is all inclusive, He stood firm in the faith. He never compromised His faith for another's convenience. The true meaning of Easter is found specifically with Christians. Christ is risen! Christ has conquered sin! Alleluia! *"Death, where is thy sting?"* The followers of Jesus Christ understand the significance of the Easter sunrise.

On this Easter Day, we hope you receive some brightly colored eggs. We hope you receive tulips and yellow chicks and a chocolate bunny and an Easter card. But most of all, we hope this Easter Day reminds you in which direction to run. *Run! Run! Run to His loving arms!*

Alleluia! Christ has risen!
The Lord has risen indeed!

+++

This week...
After you enjoy the brightly colored eggs, the delicate tulips, the chocolate bunny, and your Easter Card, run...run to Jesus.
Run with all your heart, all your soul, and all your might.
Run to Jesus; keep your focus on Him.
He will provide the true meaning of Easter.
He will be your strength and your source of joy.
Run! Alleluia! Run!

Second-Guessing God

On the evening of the first day when Jesus appeared to the disciples, Thomas (who was called the twin) was not with them. So the other disciples told him, "We have seen the Lord." But he said to them, "Unless I see the mark of the nails in his hands, and put my finger in the mark of the nails, and my hand in his side, I will not believe." A week later his disciples were again in the house, and Thomas was with them. Although the doors were shut, Jesus came and stood among them and said, "Peace be with you." Then he said to Thomas, "Put your finger here and see my hands. Reach out your hand and put it in my side. Do not doubt but believe." Thomas answered him, "My Lord and my God!" Jesus said to him, "Have you believed because you have seen me? Blessed are those who have not seen and yet have come to believe." (John 20:24–29)

> Doubting Thomas, shame on you.
> Don't you know that it is true?
> He appeared...but where were you?
> Doubting Thomas, shame on you.

We hear this story of the Doubting Thomas every year on the First Sunday after Easter. It is very familiar to us. It is easy to point our fingers in judgment, shaking our heads in disappointment. *Doubting Thomas...shame on you.* Be careful, however. A judging finger often disguises your own doubts whether they are in matters of faith or in other areas of life. Be careful not to allow self-righteousness to excuse similar thoughts. Put yourself in Thomas' situation. How would you accept such radical news? It would be difficult. All of his closest friends whom he trusts are telling him that Jesus is risen, but his logical and rational side is telling him it cannot be true. He needs proof. In such dilemmas, your gut feeling often wins. How many times has God's love been so radical that it was too difficult to accept? Perhaps your judgment of Thomas should slowly turn into empathy.

Everyone has doubts at one time or another. Everyone questions at one time or another. And everyone struggles to understand. The other day, Elizabeth and I were leaving for work at the same time. She asked me, "Are the patio doors locked?" I said, "Yes, they are." But she went over to check. I said, "I told you they are locked." She said, "I just had to see for myself." People second-guess others and themselves all the time, especially in important matters. In matters of faith, we even second-guess God.

On Easter Sunday morning, when the women told Peter and the disciples that the rock had been rolled back, and the tomb was empty, Peter and John had to go see for themselves (*John 20:1–9*). Why don't we hear stories about Doubting Peter or Doubting John? Once again, God's radical love does not make rational sense.

Many people continue to question the resurrection even in the present day. There are Doubting Thomases all around us. Maybe at one point, you were one of them. Maybe you are one now. For a new Christian, the death of a loved one often leads to questions about the resurrection. These questions must not be dismissed too easily. They lie at the crossroads of faith. New Christians often get angry with God rather than question and struggle with the faith.

Anger is dangerous. It comes from the evil one. God is not responsible for death, but He can use it to deepen one's faith if we examine it deeper. We will never understand completely, but through the struggle, we can move to the next level of faith. An imperative prayer is the one asking God for help during difficult times.

If the resurrection is not true, then the foundation of Christianity crumbles, Jesus' ministry is in vain, and the entire New Testament is a fraud. If the resurrection is not true, then why are there so many people in church on Easter Sunday? Why do stores close? If the resurrection is not true, then why do people celebrate the Risen Lord? If the resurrection is not true, then what purpose does this mortal life hold?

Let us not be too quick to point our fingers in judgment of the present-day doubters like we do with Thomas. New insights into the faith bring a struggle to understand and accept. It takes time to process. Doubting and struggling are parts of the natural process that will eventually lead a believer to a deeper faith. Struggle is a good thing to grow as a Christian. It is better than a blind faith where nothing is questioned, and everything is just accepted. This kind of faith is spoon-fed theology and rarely leads to any depth.

God purposely has Thomas miss Jesus' first resurrection appearance to the disciples so Thomas shows us how to work through our doubts so we too can eventually proclaim Jesus as Lord and Savior. Thomas wants to believe but struggles to do so. He does not want a blind faith. Thomas has to struggle with the resurrection in order to make it his own and to make it authentic.

God makes Thomas miss that first resurrection appearance because He knew that you would be sitting in church on the first Sunday after Easter to hear this Gospel. God wants you to read this because He knows you are hurting. God uses your doubt to deepen your faith. He wants you to consider this story of Thomas in a new perspective, which will help you on your spiritual journey. He knows you are struggling, but He also knows you are reading.

The struggle you are presently undergoing is personal to you. No one else is going through it in quite the same way. It is as personal as your spiritual journey. It is as personal as your unique life. The reason you are struggling is because God is calling you, calling you personally to a higher level of understanding in some area of your life. You have probably been in this struggle for quite a while, and you probably have given up on it at some point. But God knows how important this struggle is in your relationship with Him, and He will not allow you to quit. He keeps making you confront what you are going through. He is about to reveal something incredible to you, and He does not want you to miss it. He wants you to pursue it and embrace it. Go to Him and ask Him for a share of His wisdom and understanding. It will come. In the meantime, rest assured that God is not trying to frustrate you but to show you a new way to love Him more.

Dr. James Dobson tells a story of a woman who was watching a butterfly as it struggled to work its way out of the cocoon. After a while, the lady began to feel sorry for the butterfly, and so she got a small paring knife and carefully cut the cocoon just enough for the butterfly to work its way free. She felt so good when the beautiful butterfly spread out its wings and began to flutter about. But about twenty seconds later, the butterfly took a nosedive, hit the ground, and died. What the lady did not know is that the struggle to get out of the cocoon makes the butterfly's wings strong enough to fly. God uses doubt in much the same way. God has us struggle through the faith *not* to cause our failure but to make us strong enough to spread our wings and fly to the next level.

+++

This is the beauty of the Episcopal Church. The Episcopal Church is called the thinking person's religion. We *want* you to question. We *want* you to struggle. We understand your struggle is part of your spiritual journey. Getting there is half the fun. The journey is part of the process of arriving at a meaningful faith. This is part of what Paul means when he tells the Philippians, *"Work out your salvation on your own with fear and trembling"* (*2:12*). The Philippians were hearing the good news for the very first time, and Paul invited them to struggle with it. In the book of Genesis, Jacob, the older son of Isaac, struggles with an angel all night and prevails. These episodes teach us that a struggle in the faith can lead to owning the faith, making the faith personal, significant.

Struggle implies growth. Confusion signals progress. It makes us examine our conscience and realign our priorities. You will come out of the confusion with more wisdom than when you went in. But Paul tells us to do this work with fear and trembling. In other words, just be sure that your struggle does not leave the norms and the basic teachings of the faith.

Make sure you do not sacrifice the doctrines of the faith while putting together the pieces of your life's puzzle. While struggling, make sure you align your life to the faith and not align the faith to your life. Sometimes we are more anxious to bring the struggle to an end than to take the time to form a spiritual conclusion. This is because we do not like to struggle. It is easier to hastily form a secular conclusion and move on with life. With this approach, it is easy to make a wrong turn and have your faith unravel. Rather, stay true to the Scriptures. Stay true to the teachings of the church. The Scriptures and the church must inform your understanding and not vice versa. Do not form your own conclusion and then look for a Bible passage to support it.

That is why it is important not only to go to church but to also attend a Bible study. If the leader is qualified, a Bible study will guide you to form valid conclusions that align with the true faith. You will also hear the witnesses of others in the group, and you can hold your struggle up to other's interpretation. In a Bible study, you will find companionship, support, and you will not have to struggle alone. Others will offer the clarity you may be missing. The struggle of faith is a struggle to love Jesus. And the more you know Jesus, the more you will love Him. Thus, don't fear struggle, but don't face fear alone. Call God!

Some people believe that doubt is from the devil. If doubt erodes trust, then it *is* from the devil. But if doubt leads you to question your faith in order to better understand your relationship with God, then He is at work. In that way, Thomas may very well have been the first Episcopalian!

If you are not questioning the faith in order to better understand it, then you may as well revert to a spoon-fed faith.

+++

Thomas finally encounters the Risen Lord through the nail marks of the cross. *"Put your finger here and see my hands,"* Jesus tells Thomas. *"Reach out your hand and put it in my side."* Thomas comes to know the *Risen Christ* through the *Crucified Christ*. It is then that he responds, *"My Lord and my God."* Look at any picture or statue of the Risen Christ, and you will see the nail marks of the cross and the mark of the spear. The cross gives the resurrection its power.

This was the message of Billy Graham for sixty years. Reverend Graham won over the hearts of his listeners through the sacrifice of the cross and then he led them to the resurrection and eternal life. His strategy was that of Thomas: The cross leads to the empty tomb. The empty tomb leads to thousands of people coming forward during Reverend Graham's altar call. Every Billy Graham crusade was a mini-Pentecost Sunday when three thousand people were baptized.

The same is true for you. You should come to know the glory of the Risen Christ through the sacrifice of the Crucified Christ. Through the blood of Christ, the Lamb, you are washed white as snow. The hope of eternal life comes only through the death of Calvary. We receive grace and mercy through the gift of Love by God's Son. This is why Thomas missed that first resurrection appearance. Thomas' doubt leads to your understanding. And the more you question, the more you understand God; the more you embrace

God, the more you accept Him in your life. Leave your struggles at the foot of the cross, where you will be given new life.

+++

This week...
Recall a struggle in the faith you encountered in the past that has never been resolved; a time when you doubted God or questioned Him or did not understand Him or even became angry with Him. Maybe it was losing a job or sustaining a serious injury or the death of a loved one. What sense did you make of it then, and how has your attitude toward it changed now? If you continue to struggle over this area of faith, then your struggle is not yet over. It is a sign that you are unable to reach a viable conclusion on your own. If so, seek the advice of someone you trust and who has deep faith. God is calling you to a deeper epiphany, and He is anxious to reveal it to you.

The Stranger

Now on that same day two of them were going to a village called Emmaus, about seven miles from Jerusalem, and talking with each other about all these things that had happened. While they were talking and discussing, Jesus himself came near and went with them, but their eyes were kept from recognizing him. And he said to them, "What were you discussing with each other while you walk along?" They stood still, looking sad. Then one of them, Cleopas, answered him, "Are you the only stranger in Jerusalem who does not know the things that have taken place there in these days?" He asked them, "What things?" They replied, "The things about Jesus of Nazareth, who was a prophet mighty in deed and word before God and all the people, and how our chief priests and leaders handed him over to be condemned to death and crucified him. But we had hoped that he was the one to redeem Israel. Yes, and besides all this, it is now the third day since these things took place. Moreover, some women of our group astounded us. They were at the tomb early this morning, and when they did not find his body there, they came back and told us that they had indeed seen a vision of angels who said that he was alive. Some of those who were with us went to the tomb and found it just as the women has said; but they did not see him." Then he said to them, "Oh, how foolish you are, and how slow of heart to believe all that the prophets have declared! Was it not necessary that the Messiah should suffer these things and then enter into his glory?" Then beginning with Moses and all the prophets, he interpreted to them the things about himself in all the scriptures.

As they came near the village to which they were going, he walked ahead as if he were going on. But they urged him strongly, saying, "Stay with us because it is almost evening and the day is now nearly over." So he went in to stay with them. When he was at the table with them, he took bread, blessed and broke it, and gave it to them. Then their eyes were opened, and they recognized him; and he vanished from their sight. They said to each other, "Were not our hearts burning within us while he was talking to us on the road, while he was opening the scriptures to us?" That same hour they got up and returned to Jerusalem; and they found the eleven and their companions gathered together. They were saying, "The Lord has risen indeed, and he has appeared to Simon!" Then they told what had happened on the road, and how he had been made known to them in the breaking of the bread. (Luke 24:13–35)

Church services on Easter Sunday are glorious. Easter lilies, with their large white trumpet-shaped blooms and crisp fragrance, adorn the altar. Every note and every word of the hymns we sing fill our hearts with exultation, announcing Jesus' victory over death. We make room in the pew for one more person, then another and another. We beam with joy as we listen to encouraging and promising sermons. The church swells with joyful celebration as we rejoice with our Risen Lord.

But for the disciples, joy is far from the way things were on the very first Easter Sunday. On *that* day, confusion, questions, and fear filled their hearts and their minds. The women who saw the angels are overcome with apprehension. Peter and John race to the tomb in disbelief. And Thomas doubts. They are shocked and bewildered, and once together, they huddle in an upper room in Jerusalem. Knowing the empty tomb causes the Jews' suspicion of who might have stolen His body, they wait with trepidation to hear the distant thunder of the soldiers' ominous footsteps coming up the stairs to arrest them, huddling together even more closely than they did at first. The fear that permeates *their* Easter Sunday stands in stark contrast to the joy of *ours*.

+++

This morning, we hear the story of two fearful disciples who, on Easter Sunday evening, leave the upper room in Jerusalem and walk to Emmaus seven miles away to one of their homes. It's not so much that they are going *to* Emmaus but that they are running *from* Jerusalem.

The two walk briskly, escaping the perceived danger and clinging to the safety of Emmaus. A crisp, refreshing spring breeze stands in contrast to the stuffy confines of the upper room, to the fearful disciples waiting there, and to the anxiety in their hearts. Filled with more questions than enlightened thoughts and as their jagged conversation continues, they desperately try to find meaning of the morning's events. They have not seen the empty tomb, but they accept the witnesses of the women and of Peter and John who have. They realize that the Jews and the Romans will certainly conduct an investigation, an interrogation. Some of their brothers and sisters in the faith will be arrested, even killed. This fear motivates their walk. The safety of Emmaus lies miles away. Leaving the others behind on the evening of the first Easter Sunday, Jesus' resurrection already causes division, even among His most faithful disciples.

On their way to Emmaus, a stranger approaches them. It is Jesus, but they do not recognize Him. Just as Mary Magdalene did not know Him at the tomb that same morning, Jesus' transformation after His resurrection makes it impossible for anyone to know Him.

So it is with us!

We too have been in the presence of Jesus Christ and not recognized Him!

As the stranger speaks the Word to them, the two disciples initially think they know more than Him. One of them abruptly interrupts, asking in a rather condescending voice, *"Are you the only stranger in Jerusalem who does not know the things which have taken place these past few days?"*

Aren't there times when our attitude is the same as theirs, when we consider ourselves above others, whether with our knowledge or our power or our status? And doesn't this demeanor portray us as having a holier-than-thou attitude? This is what happens on the road to Emmaus: The disciples think they know more than the Risen Christ. What holy irony!

On their walk, the disciples come to know this stranger as one of them, a faithful Jew well versed in the Scriptures who brings peace to their troubled souls and deepens their faith. The uniqueness of His understanding entices them to learn more. Once they reach the house in Emmaus, they beg Him to stay, and He graciously accepts their hospitality. A lantern and candles light the room as the sun quickly fades on the horizon.

They prepare a late dinner while still engaging in deep conversation with this stranger, now turned friend. Wine, goat cheese, fruits, nuts, and bread carried with them from Jerusalem are laid out on the small wooden table. They are enthralled by Him. It would take a lifetime of study by an elder to learn what this relatively young man reveals to them. To them, their questions seem elementary compared to His deeper understanding of the Scriptures. As He continues to draw parallels from the Hebrew Scriptures to the Messiah, the fulfillments of His ministry, the multiple predictions of His death, and His rising on the third day, their eyes slowly widen as the clarity of salvation history awakens them to more than they could have ever dreamt possible. Yet they still do not recognize salvation's fulfillment as He sips His wine and asks for another piece of bread.

The disciples peer deeply into the eyes of this friendly stranger. *He looks familiar. I have seen this man somewhere before. How can it be that he knows so much about the Scriptures, and we have never met him?*

Jesus understands their desperate desire to recognize Him, and so He continues to make eye contact with them as He takes the bread in His hands and lays it on the small wooden plate in front of Him. They peer even more deeply into His eyes, into His very soul.

In a flash, they are taken back to the Passover Meal they celebrated together three days earlier, to the feeding of the five thousand, to the number of times in the past three years they broke bread together, into the eyes of Moses as he prepares the people to celebrate the first Passover meal and their release from Egyptian captivity. In His eyes, they feel a connection to all life has held and to what it continues to hold.

Jesus breaks the vision as He lowers His head, pronounces a blessing over the bread, breaks the bread into three pieces, and offers a portion to each of them. *Oh, my God!* they proclaim. Instantly, the stranger is recognized! Bewildered, astonished, and amazed, they bury their heads in their hands, trying desperately to process this profound moment. Their hearts swell with overwhelming emotion as they suddenly realize that *He is with them! The things that the woman and the others report about the empty tomb are true. All of the scriptures this stranger cited along the road refer to Him, and He sits across from us!* The candles' light dims as the night's darkness deepens. Rubbing their eyes and wiping their tears, they look up, anxious to see Him, to speak to Him, to praise Him. But He is gone. With joyful and exuberant hearts, they rush back to Jerusalem to tell the others.

+++

Do you see what just happened? When the disciples are on their long arduous seven-mile walk, Jesus talks about the Scriptures. That is their Liturgy of the Word. When they reach Emmaus, He blesses, breaks, and distributes the bread. That is their Holy Communion. The Liturgy of the Word is followed by Holy Communion. Does this sound familiar? They recognize Him in the breaking of the bread as they recall His words at the Passover meal: *"Do this in remembrance of Me."* It is not until He breaks the bread that they realize the stranger as their Lord and Savior. In the breaking of the bread, they realize that in running, they are found; in their fear, they become joyful.

Similar to the disciples who felt isolated and confused, our fears and turmoil, our doubts and concerns, our stress and anxiety that we sometimes experience makes us feel as though we are walking alone on our journey of life. At these times, we are blind and cannot see Him; we are deaf and cannot hear Him. We are oblivious to His holy presence. Does Jesus disguise Himself, or is Satan preventing us from seeing Him? Either way, Jesus becomes a stranger in the midst of our chaos. For us, Emmaus represents the place where we go to escape the complexity of our lives.

Each time you come to church, you make the journey to Emmaus. Whether you travel seven miles or seven years, you bring with you long miles of fears and turmoil, doubts and concerns, stress and anxiety. Even though the Source of everything you need is always with you, you feel so alone. But you are never alone. He is always with you, even though you may not recognize Him.

So you come to Emmaus. You come to church. And you arrive at a place of comfort, unity, and peace. You hear the Word. *The bread is broken.* The Risen Lord is no longer a stranger. The Risen Lord finds you, even though you have lost track of Him. The Risen Lord knows the answers to your questions. Yet during difficult times, you call His Very Presence into question. However, just as the disciples who were with Him when He broke the bread, He makes His appearance in ways that are familiar to you. You consume Him, and you are consumed by Him.

+++

The only way to make sense of Easter is to encounter the Risen Christ. Only then is the resurrection believable. He wants you to invite Him into your life. He wants to visit, read the Word, and break bread with you. He wants a close, personal relationship with you. The holiest moments are when the two of you are one. There may be times during your week when you feel His closeness. Those times are to be treasured, for they too are holy. Those moments can sustain you during the week. They provide the assurance that He is near. But they cannot compare to the closeness between the two of you when you receive His body and blood in Holy Communion. *"The Father and I are one just as you and I are one"* (*John 10:29*). Nothing is holier than Holy Communion. *Nothing!*

+++

We are not told why Jesus suddenly vanishes after breaking bread with the two disciples in Emmaus. Like the other appearances on Easter Sunday, Jesus doesn't stay long nor is anyone allowed to touch Him because He has not yet been to the Father. There is something mysterious about Jesus' return to the Father on Easter Sunday. We can only say that our visits with Him are always too short. People are too anxious to leave a Sunday service. Instead of lingering after the service and relishing His presence, people become more concerned about the line at brunch. They become consumed with the plans they have for the day. The concerns of the world begin to take over. And Jesus feels cheated. Like the disciples in Emmaus, we catch a glimpse of Him and then lose sight of Him once again. He seems to vanish and disappear. And the business of the world surrounds us once again. Why not invite Jesus along with you? But the irony is that He is there already, but like the two disciples, you do not recognize Him.

We are the yo-yos in this relationship. Jesus is the constant One. We come and go. Jesus stays. He calls us by name. Jesus always reveals Himself in the simple, mundane events of daily life. Emmaus moments can happen not only in church but in moments throughout the day. However, because of the distractions of the world, we do not have the capacity to maintain a close relationship with Him for any length of time. Jesus always wants more out of our relationship with Him, but we are often preoccupied with our daily lives. And during those times, we push Him away. How hurtful for Him! Just when He feels as though the relationship is on the verge of a major breakthrough, we back off. There are always spiritual peaks and valleys. And our outside distractions sometimes plummet us back down into the valley.

But He never leaves us. We leave Him. At Emmaus, Jesus is the One who disappears, and although that is typical of Easter Sunday, that is uncharacteristic for Jesus. In our encounters with Jesus, He longs for more quality time with us. Jesus is constant. He isn't concerned about the line at brunch because there is always room at the heavenly banquet.

He walks with you every day. You can find Him if you look for Him. He's in the imploring eyes of someone in need. He's there in the laughter of a small child. He's present in charitable acts. He lives in your life during the week until you return to Emmaus the following Sunday.

In this way, the Eucharist gives you a little taste of the heavenly banquet. In the kingdom, there is no confusion or doubt or fear. There are no distractions or worldly concerns.

In the kingdom, there will be nothing that can come between you and Him. It will just be the two of you, and it will be more than enough, more than sufficient, more than fulfilling. The kingdom will be more than just a glimpse. It will be for eternity. In the kingdom, your relationship with Him will be all that He had hoped. And your heart will sing with joy!

+++

This week…
Linger after the Sunday service and spend some time in quiet meditation anticipating where Emmaus moments might happen in the week ahead. Invite Him to come along.

Directions

Jesus told his disciples, "Do not let your hearts be troubled. Believe in God, believe also in me. In my Father's house there are many dwelling places. If it were not so, would I have told you that I go to prepare a place for you? And if I go and prepare a place for you, I will come again and will take you myself, so that where I am, there you may be also. And you know the way to the place where I am going." Thomas said to him, "Lord, we do not know where you are going. How can we know the way?" Jesus said to him, "I am the way, and the truth, and the life. No one comes to the Father except through me. If you know me, you will know my Father also. From now on you do know Him and have seen Him." (John 14:1–7)

This Gospel passage overflows with compassion. Jesus senses that His disciples are lost, confused, and perplexed. On a few previous occasions, with similar circumstances, He told them that their lack of trust hinders their relationship with Him, and that their doubt overshadows their faith which, at times, contributes to their unbearable and overwhelming suffering. And it is during these times that He experiences frustration with them, and they, in turn, feel bewildered by Him.

But this time, Jesus shows empathy for them. After all, these are His disciples. They have left their homes, their jobs, and their loved ones to follow Him. For three years, they have devoted their lives to him; they have been His faithful companions, listening to Him preach in unorthodox ways about a kingdom which remains a mystery to them. And now Jesus says He is leaving them to be with His Father in a mysterious kingdom, one that they do not know, nor will they ever fully understand. He tells them to have trust, faith, and hope. And He reassures them, *"You know where I am going."* But they feel abandoned!

As much as the disciples feel abandoned, Thomas also believes that Jesus is forsaking him. What Thomas doesn't realize though is that Jesus is speaking from a spiritual level, and Thomas is speaking from a physical one. So what does doubting Thomas do? He asks Jesus for directions. Realizing Thomas' blindness, Jesus says to him, *"You do not need directions. Follow me. I am the Way, the Truth, and the Life."*

+++

What we must understand, though is that Jesus does not say "I am *one* way" to reach the kingdom. Quite the opposite. God did not give us His Son for us to have options. *There is no other option.* God gave us His Son because the redemptive act of His Son on the cross was absolutely necessary for our salvation. No one can come to the Father except through the cross. Jesus pays the bill for our sinfulness. And the cross becomes the instrument by which we are reunited with the Father. Jesus is the *only* Way to the Father. He goes ahead of his disciples to prepare a place for them so that one day they will be one with Him and the Father. *There is no other option! Not for His disciples, not for doubting Thomas, not for us!*

At times though, the gap between our faith and our temporal lives creates a chasm between us and Jesus, making us perplexed and leaving Jesus frustrated. Many times, when we make plans to go somewhere, someone will say, "I'll get there early and save you a seat." Or the receptionist at a hotel tells you, "Your room is ready." This is what Jesus means when He tells His disciples, *"I am going to prepare a place for you."* The preparatory work is a reference to His death and resurrection, which are necessary for the disciples to enter the kingdom. There is work to be done before the disciples join Him there. So he tells them, *"I am going ahead of you."*

On three previous occasions, Jesus informs His disciples that He must suffer, die, and rise on the third day, but they only hear that he will suffer and die, which prevents them from sharing in the anticipation and glory of His resurrection. But Jesus wants them to focus on His resurrection, and so He reassures them, *"I am going, but I will come back for you so that where I am, you may be also."* And even though He so desperately wants them to believe Him, to trust Him, and to have faith in Him, they hesitate.

Our catechism recognizes that Jesus' mission is the church's mission, and *"the Mission of the Church is to restore all people to unity with God and each other in Christ"* (*Book of Common Prayer*, 855). Thus, atonement with the Father comes only through atonement with the Son. It's like the formula: if A = B and B = C, then it follows that A = C. If we share in the life of the Son, and the Son shares in the life of the Father, then it follows that through the Son, we share in the life of the Father. Hence, there is only *one* Way to the Father, and that is through the Son.

Jesus is the only Way. In no other religion does A = B.

But the devil makes it easy for us to get lost. One wrong turn and, *boom*, you find yourself off course because Satan has deliberately led you down the wrong road. He has slowly and methodically convinced you that you are on a better road, a more direct and less confusing road to happiness and self-fulfillment than Jesus' road. Satan tells you that everyone else is wrong, and only you are right. And you begin to believe him a little more each day. Once in his grip, he infiltrates every aspect of your life, and eventually, you feel empowered by him, making you boast, "Why should I follow so many misguided people? I know better than they do. I should find my own path, go my own way." Before you know it, your life has completely gone awry, and you eventually disregard everyone who truly loves and cares about you. Jesus becomes a miniscule vision on the road you left behind. And the devil smiles.

Wow! These are alarming thoughts, indeed. Granted, individuality and self-development can foster a healthy self-esteem, but taken to the extreme, you may find yourself on a precarious tightrope where one wrong step can end in disaster. When you ignore Jesus and allow your egotism to overshadow His love for you, you may be on a parallel path to His, but you are not on *His* path. You are not following *the Way*.

+++

When Jesus says, "*I am the Truth,*" He does not mean that He is one of several ways of looking at the truth. Many people think that the truth lies in the eyes of the beholder, as if the truth can change depending on the person involved. If the truth does not have Jesus at its moral center, then it is not the truth.

However, it is easy to rationalize and create your own version of the truth. As our son was growing up, he would make up a story to divert the truth, and we would ask him, "What is the truth? If you were standing in the presence of Jesus, and He asked for the truth, what would you tell him?"

Our son could never avoid those questions. He would always come clean. And because Jesus was at the core of his moral center, he has matured into a very honest man today. And so it should be with you. The search for Jesus is the search for the truth. When you find the truth, you find Jesus. The two are synonymous. This is what the disciple John means when he says, *"If you say you have no sin, then you deceive yourself and the truth is not in you"* (*1 John 1:8*).

If you deceive yourself, think about those words. Self-deceit is the *"mother of all sin"* because all sin is born out of our ability to talk ourselves into thinking that we are not wrong. Self-righteousness, arrogance, hypocrisy, and pretentiousness are the children of self-deceit. It's a rather large family, and none of its members are ever truthful. Remember, the search for the truth is a search for Jesus. The search for Jesus is the search for the truth. On Good Friday, as Jesus stood before Pilate after He had been whipped, beaten, spat upon, and given a crown of thorns, Pilate asked Him, *"What is truth?"* (*John 18:38*). But Pilate had it all wrong. It's not, "*What* is the truth?" but "*Who* is the truth?" The truth is not open for interpretation. The Truth is a living person. Jesus is Truth.

+++

Jesus does not say, "I am *a* Life," as if life in the Holy Spirit is one of many ways to live, as if the breath of God is one of many ways to breathe, as if the child of God is one of many ways to be His, and as if being anointed by the Holy Spirit and marked as Christ's own forever is one of many ways to be blessed. Rather, Jesus says, "I am *the* Life." Jesus calls us to follow Him into the life of the resurrection. The life of the resurrection, which is the eternal life, comes only through Jesus. Jesus is *the* life.

The Episcopal Church teaches us that *we are in the world, not of the world.* You cannot live by a double standard. You cannot serve the world and serve Jesus, yet many people try to have a foot in both worlds: *"No one can serve two masters. He will either love the one and hate the other or hate the one and love the other. You cannot serve God and wealth" (Matthew 6:24).* When you allow temporal pleasures to motivate you, then you are being driven by worldly desires and not by Jesus. At these times, Satan will pounce on you and deliberately clutter your mind.

However, *"the fruit of the Spirit is love, joy, peace, patience, kindness, generosity, faithfulness, gentleness, and self-control. If we live by the Spirit, let us also be guided by the Spirit" (Galatians 5:22, 23, 25).* If your life is not producing these fruits, then you are not living the life that Jesus has to offer you. Examine your life. Are you producing the fruits of the Spirit, or are you producing the fruits of the world? Your heart must treasure one or the other. Which one will it be?

Jesus says, "I am the Way...the Truth and the Life. No one comes to the Father except through me."

Like you, Thomas is just as confused after his conversation with Jesus as he was before it. But you and Thomas must remember that Jesus does not come to condemn you but, rather, to save you. Thomas' confusion will end on Pentecost when he receives the Holy Spirit. But when will your confusion end? When will you travel on the road with Jesus? When will you make a conviction to nourish the fruits of the Spirit? When will you experience the Spirit of Pentecost? When will you declare that you will be with Jesus in a place beyond this earthly life? When will your doubt end?

God wants you to read this scripture. Jesus waits for you. He wants you to follow His Way. He wants you to be truthful to His Truth. He wants you to share in His Life. Jesus wants you to be with

Him in the kingdom. He came for you. All that He did, He did for you. Jesus is the Savior of the world. Jesus is your Savior.

But you must strive to be one with the Way, the Truth, and the Life. To become one with Jesus, you must change your priorities. You must not allow the temporal world to envelope you and prevent you from following Jesus to the kingdom. Resist Satan. Do not allow him to avert your eyes away from the kingdom. Do not allow his trickery to infiltrate your life. Do not fall prey to his cunning ways.

Open your eyes to the fruits of the Spirit. They are the keys to the life you should lead. Put the spiritual fruits on the front burner. Lock the temporal desires in a cabinet and throw away the keys. Look for opportunities that cultivate the fruits of the Spirit in your life. In a prayer, ask the Holy Spirit for help.

As you strive to be one with the fruits of the Spirit, ask yourself these questions:

- Love—Do you see each person as a child of God?
- Joy—Do you call on Jesus to help you find joy in your life?
- Peace—Do you strive for peace and harmony?
- Patience—Do you show patience under all circumstances?
- Kindness—Do you reach out with kindness and love?
- Generosity—Do you go the extra mile, especially for those in need?
- Faithfulness—Do you honor God by putting Him first in your life?
- Gentleness—Do you smooth over your rough edges?
- Self-control—Do you resist temptation by not allowing Satan to control your life?

> Producing the fruits of the Spirit will put you in touch with the Way, the Truth, and the Life.
> Jesus will send Thomas to give you directions.
> Jesus tells you, *"Do not let your heart be troubled. Believe. Trust. Have Faith."*

+++

This week...
Put the fruits of the Spirit on your refrigerator or
someplace where you will see them every day.
They are the keys to the life you should be leading.
Do more than memorize them; live your life by them!

Fallen Soldiers

This is my commandment, that you love one another as I have loved you. No one has greater love than this, to lay down one's life for one's friends. You are my friends if you do what I command you. I do not call you servants any longer, because the servant does not know what the master is doing; but I have called you friends, because I have made known to you everything that I have heard from my Father. You did not choose me but I chose you. And I appointed you to go and bear fruit, fruit that will last, so that the Father will give you whatever you ask him in my name. I am giving you these commands so that you may love one another. (John 15:12–17)

The guard at the Tomb of the Unknown Soldier takes twenty-one paces across the front of the tomb, performs an about-face, switches his rifle to his outside shoulder, and pauses twenty-one seconds.

The guard takes twenty-one paces across the front of the tomb to the other side, performs an about-face, switches his rifle to his outside shoulder, pauses twenty-one seconds, and takes twenty-one paces across the front of the tomb to the other side.

The guard repeats these exact movements for sixty minutes during the winter and the spring and for thirty minutes in the summer and the fall until the next guard takes his place at changing of the guard.

This continuous, precise, and disciplined maneuver occurs in the blazing sunshine, the drenching rain, the freezing snow, and the howling wind. Every minute of every day...twenty-four hours a day…365 days a year…since Veterans' Day, 1921, these distinguished sentinels faithfully honor *the Tomb of the Unknown Soldier* that serves as a symbol for all unidentified soldiers in each of America's wars.

The guards come from every walk of life and from every state in the United States of America. From their unparalleled physical conditions to their unblemished military records, these soldiers epitomize perfection. They perform their solemn duty and faithful commitment to the unknown soldier with "perseverance, diligence, and humble reverence" (The Sentinel's Creed).

The twenty-one paces and the twenty-one seconds represent a twenty-one-gun salute, the highest military honor. The rifle is placed on the outside shoulder of the guard to signify that the soldiers who are honored by the tomb are no longer at war. They have sacrificed enough. War for them marks their *final distant thunder*.

Once selected, guards commit to two years of service. During that time, they live in barracks under the tomb. For the first six months of their duty, they do not speak to anyone, watch any television, or have access to any electronic devices. For the rest of their lives, guards are not allowed to drink alcohol, smoke, or use profane language. When not on duty, they spend their time studying, reading, and learning about the brave men and women buried in Arlington National Cemetery, including memorizing each of their names and where each one is buried. After two years of service, the guards receive and wear on the lapel of their uniforms the *Guard, Tomb of the Unknown Soldier identification badge,* a heavy sterling-silver pin, etched with an inverted wreath, signifying mourning, and also etched with the east face of the tomb depicting the figures of peace, valor, and victory.

In September 2003, as Hurricane Isabel, the deadliest and most intense hurricane of that year, approached the East Coast of the United States and threatened Washington, DC, Congress took two days off in anticipation of the menacing storm. The guards assigned to the tomb were granted permission to suspend their duty. They responded unanimously, "With all due respect, we refuse to abandon our post." Facing pelting rain and extreme hurricane-force winds, they would not forsake their duty of guarding the tomb, the highest honor afforded to any service person. Once again, they demonstrated their steadfast commitment to those who have paid the ultimate price for our freedom.

+++

While Elizabeth and I both moved to Florida in the latter part of our childhood, I spent my early childhood in Kentucky. Down the street from my house, there was a large open cemetery where one section was surrounded by a black wrought-iron fence with a small gate leading to the gravesites reserved for local veterans who had died during war. Small American flags adorned each gravesite, waving gently in the breeze, as if each veteran softly whispered, "*God Bless America!*" The cemetery had the tallest flagpole and the largest American flag I had ever seen. It dwarfed me when I stood next to it. Straining my neck to see its striking old-glory-red and radiant-white stripes along with its grand and impressive fifty white stars set majestically against the old glory blue made a little tyke feel even smaller.

Every Memorial Day, our town held a 10:00 a.m. service inside the Veterans' Section of the cemetery. The service included distinguished guest speakers, some of whom were veterans, a twenty-one-gun salute, a band from our local high school, and ended with a glorious and grand parade which eventually passed right in front of our house on its way to Main Street. My entire family always attended this service because my dad knew several veterans who were killed in World War II, and it was his way of paying respect to his fallen comrades.

As soon as the service ended, my two older sisters and I would run home as fast as our little legs could carry us, yelling excitedly, "*Hurry up! Or we'll miss the parade.*" When we finally reached our front yard, out of breath, and with bright-red cheeks from our mad dash, we eagerly waved our small American flags as everyone in the parade passed by. In the midst of one of those parades, waving my flag, the *spirit of patriotism* surged through my veins for the very first time.

+++

Reverend Kenneth and Elizabeth Herzog

America is a vision deeply rooted in freedom, independence, equality, justice, and hope, given to our Founding Fathers by Almighty God. When we say *the United States of America,* we refer to a group of states formed by our Founding Fathers to make God's vision real. Unfortunately, aspiring to this vision for an entire country brings its own set of challenges which, at times, come with a tremendous cost. Brave and courageous men and women who fight for our country face these challenges as they carry out this vision every single day of their lives.

On Memorial Day, we honor those men and women who paid the ultimate price, the sacrifice of their lives for our country's vision. We remember these valiant and heroic men and women as we celebrate this national holiday by singing patriotic hymns, by flying our flags, by watching grand and glorious parades, and by the president laying a wreath on the Tomb of the Unknown Soldier.

Today, Elizabeth and I live next door to a retired marine whose faithful service and commitment to our country's vision lives deep in his heart. Two years ago, he and I went door-to-door in our neighborhood and offered to install a flag and holder on each mailbox for the price of the parts. Of the fifteen families we visited, all but one participated. To our surprise, however, on the Fourth of July, the one nonparticipant succumbed to the patriotic pressure and had us install a flag on his mailbox. Since then, on each national holiday, everyone in our neighborhood proudly flies the flag, a display that makes an incredible sight. And the patriotism I felt as a child swells once again in my heart. I can just imagine one of the little tykes in our neighborhood feeling the *spirit of patriotism* surging through his/her veins for the very first time.

+++

Amid the awe-inspiring glory of patriotism Americans experience on Memorial Day, we must pause to remember its purpose: the enormous number of Americans who lost their lives in battle for our freedom.

A Distant Thunder

The Revolutionary War—25,278 American soldiers died.
The Civil War—623,026 American soldiers died.
World War I—116,708 American soldiers died.
World War II—407,316 American soldiers died.
The Korean Conflict—36,914 American soldiers died.
Vietnam War—58,169 American soldiers died.
El Salvador Conflict—20 American soldiers died.
Invasion of Beirut—266 American soldiers died.
First Gulf War—39 American soldiers died.
Invasion of Grenada—19 American soldiers died.
Invasion of Panama—40 American soldiers died.
Second Gulf War—269 American soldiers died.
Somalian War—43 American soldiers died.
Bosnian War—12 American soldiers died.
The War in Afghanistan—1,423 American soldiers died.
The War in Iraq—4,430 American soldiers died.

When you add up the American soldiers who have died in these wars, what do you get? You get an American flag with its old-glory-red stripes standing out just a little more than its radiant white ones. You get broken hearts. You get veterans *who did come home* remembering those *who did not*. You get single-parent families. You get children left behind. When you add up all of these fatalities…you get 1,317,588 Americans who paid the ultimate sacrifice for our freedom! How can we *not* honor these fallen soldiers on Memorial Day!

This past week, I heard an announcer enthusiastically boast during a radio commercial, *"We have all of your needs for this weekend's cookout as we salute those brave men and women who are serving our country."* Excuse me, but that would be Veteran's Day, November 11. This is Memorial Day. And while we should honor all of our veterans, Memorial Day is for honoring and remembering those veterans who *did not come home.*

Reverend Kenneth and Elizabeth Herzog

Memorial Day originated in 1868 as an event to honor those soldiers killed in the Civil War. During the early years of that war, a pious clergyman remarked to Abraham Lincoln, "Let us have faith, Mr. President, that the Lord is on our side during this great struggle." Lincoln quickly retorted, "I am not at all concerned about that, for I know that the Lord is always on the side of what is right. But it is my constant anxiety and prayer that I and this nation be on the Lord's side."

+++

In the Gospel that opens this reflection, Jesus tells us to love one another. Imagine that! Calling war an act of love seems absurd and self-contradictory.

Thinking love sends a soldier into the pits of hell poses even more confusion. Yet love of freedom, love of justice, love of country, and love of righteousness serve as our motives for war. Even the Father sending His only Son to His violent death in the grip of hell revealed the greatest act of love known to mankind.

Each of our patriotic hymns is a tribute not only to our country and those who serve Her but also to our God as well. The second verse of "America, the Beautiful" proclaims the following:

O beautiful for heroes proved in liberating strife,
who more than self their country loved, and mercy more than life!
America! America!
God mend thine every flaw, confirm thy soul in self-control,
thy liberty in law.

The Founders of our country mirror the Founders of our Faith: Abraham, Isaac, and Jacob…Washington, Jefferson, and Lincoln. As we remember the soldiers who died during the time we celebrate Jesus' resurrection, it is by divine design that Memorial Day usually falls during the Easter Season.

Without the Lord God, our country loses its foundation. Without the Lord God, our country's soldiers have served and died in vain. Each time we refuse to obey Jesus' command to love one another, we grant the devil a stronger foothold in the world. Each time we refuse to love one another, we empower another dictator with an even louder voice in the world. Each time we refuse to follow Jesus' law of love, we desecrate the cross and the flag, and we witness another crime against God and our country. Each time we refuse to love, we belittle another soldier's commitment to our country's vision. Those Americans who actively pursue the removal of God from the fabric of our country should try living in an occupied country ruled by tyranny!

The end of war begins in our hearts; therefore, we must always love one another and stand up for the truth and the righteousness of God. Not all foreign nations have our spiritual foundation. For some of those countries, freedom, equality, and justice are granted only to a select few. The majority live in constant fear and oppression. *God, help these nations see the Light!*

If the freest, wealthiest nation in the world does not defend the freedom of those who are incapable of defending themselves, who will? If a nation abundantly blessed by God's love does not commit itself to God, who will? If an American soldier fighting for justice and truth and who places him/herself in harms' way isn't the imitation of Christ's love for us, who is? Who will fight the war against evil if America doesn't?

America's vision of a nation living together with peace, justice, and equality will never be completed in this life. The nations of the world living together with peace, justice, and equality will never be accomplished in this life. Peace, justice, and equality will remain elusive visions until the Second Coming when they are finally fulfilled in the kingdom. Only Jesus' return at the Second Coming will attain these visions and will destroy the obstacles that now prevent them. Only then will everyone follow Jesus' command to love one another.

The evil must be destroyed for love to prevail. The battle of war between nations is a reflection of the spiritual warfare between God and Satan. Why do we send our soldiers into the chaos of war if love were not the end result! Why did God send His Son into the pits of hell if love were not the end result! War is orchestrated by Satan. Love is orchestrated by God. Satan may win the battle, but at the Second Coming, God will win the war. The ultimate victory will be His. Out of the atrocities of war, God's love will prevail!

+++

We gather to celebrate Memorial Day weekend in the context of the Eucharist by worshiping the One who laid down His life for our spiritual freedom. *"Do this in remembrance of me."* Each time we gather to celebrate the Eucharist, it is another Memorial Day. One million three hundred seventeen thousand five hundred eighty-eight American soldiers died for our country's freedom. *One Savior died for our spiritual freedom.*

It is an honor and a privilege to be an American Christian. As American Christians, we are doubly blessed. We experience God's love through His sacrifice for our spiritual freedom, and we also experience our American soldiers' love through their sacrifice for our country's freedom: *"No greater love does one have than to lay down his life for his friends" (John 15:13)*. But we often take this too much for granted. We need to celebrate and feel the love of both. We must honor our fallen soldiers for their service to our country, *and* we must delight in the sacrifice of our Savior.

The *Episcopal Eucharistic Prayer A* proclaims the relationship among Memorial Day, the Lord Christ, and the kingdom. It prays the following:

> *We celebrate the memorial of our redemption, O Father, in this sacrifice of praise and thanksgiving. Recalling his death, resurrection, and ascension, we offer you these gifts. Sanctify them by your Holy Spirit.*
>
> *Sanctify us also that we may faithfully receive this holy Sacrament, and serve you in unity, constancy, and peace; and at the last day bring us with all your saints into the joy of your eternal kingdom.* (*BCP,* 363)

The remembrance of this weekend runs deeper than our national patriotism. The fallen soldiers we honor are a reflection of the Communion of the saints. We may eat hamburgers and hot dogs on Memorial Day, but our lasting nourishment is found in the body and blood of the Holy Eucharist. The patriotic hymns we sing are church hymns as well.

You cannot pray for world peace unless the love of Jesus reigns in your heart. You cannot pray for the end of evil dictators unless the love for freedom reigns in your heart. You cannot pray for universal healing unless the love for equality reigns in your heart. Love one another. And let it begin with you.

+++

This week…
As you celebrate Memorial Day, take time to worship and praise God for giving our country His vision of love, equality, and freedom. Memorial Day…yes, we do remember!

Jesus Prays for You

Holy Father, protect them in your name that you have given me, so that they may be one as we are one. But now I am coming to you, and I speak these things in the world so that they may have my joy made complete in themselves. I have given them your word, and the world has hated them because they do not belong to the world, just as I do not belong to the world. I am not asking you to take them out of the world, but I ask you to protect them from the evil one. Sanctify them in your truth; your word is truth. I ask not only on behalf of these, but also on behalf of those who will believe in me through their word, that they may all be one. As you, Father, are in me and I am in you, may they also be in us, so that the world may believe that you have sent me. The glory that you have given me I have given them, so that they may be one, as we are one. Father, I desire that those also, whom you have given me, may be with me where I am, to see my glory, which you have given me because you loved me before the foundation of the world.

Righteous Father, the world does not know you, but I know you; and these know that you have sent me. I made your name known to them, and I will make it known, so that the love with which you have loved me may be in them, and I in them. (John 17:11, 13–15, 17–26)

Do you know that Jesus prays for you? Constantly, fervently, and compassionately, Jesus prays for you. He actively listens to your prayers and petitions them on your behalf to His Father. As He sits at His Father's feet, He gently tilts His head upward, and with His tender and compassionate eyes, He gazes deeply and benevolently begins His prayer, "*Holy Father, protect them in your name that you have given me, so that they may be one as we are one,*" which continues as a pure and loving supplication to His Father on our behalf.

In his book, *The Sacred Ways of a Lakota Indian*, Chief Black Elk describes a ritual of his tribe which served as a rite of passage from boyhood into manhood.

After proving that he could hunt, scout, and fish, a young boy was put through one final test to prove himself. On the eve of his thirteenth birthday, the young brave was blindfolded and led into a dense forest to spend the night alone. He was told that when he felt the warmth of the morning sun, he could remove his blindfold and find his way back home.

Chief Black Elk recalls how frightening an experience it was even for him when he was a young boy. "Every time a twig snapped," he said, "I pictured a wild animal ready to pounce on me." After what seemed to be an eternity, Black Elk finally felt the warmth of the dawn. He then removed his blindfold only to see that a stone's throw away, his father was sitting with a bow and arrow. He had been there all night protecting his son. In the same way, your heavenly Father is right there to protect you. And like the young boy, you don't always see Him, nor do you always sense His presence, but He is there, and Jesus prays to Him for you.

If only we would pray this way: "Listen, Father, I have many thoughts and concerns to speak to You about, so bear with me because this is going to take some time." This is the way you should pray. Don't allow the demands of your life to interfere with your prayers. Jesus wants to spend time with you, at any time, at any place, at any moment, on any day.

John, chapter 17, is a long prayer Jesus makes for you. It is a great chapter to read when the world is closing in on you. Jesus makes this prayer while He is on Earth, but His prayers for you continue even when He is in the kingdom. In this passage, Jesus is having a simple conversation with His Father, and He knows that His Father is listening. While our prayers are typically short and to the point, Jesus takes advantage of bending His Father's ear and holding the Father's attention until He says everything He wants to say. Oh, that we would pray this way, "Listen Father, I have some things to say, so bear with me..." This is the way you should pray. And those of you who are parents need to have long conversations with your children. Do not cut them short. These conversations are a reflection of your own connection of your prayers with theirs, remembering that His prayers are forever present tense.

The main emphasis of praying is for you to be one with the Son so you can be one with the Father, *"so that they may be one as we are one... As you, Father, are in me and I am in you, may they also be in us...so that they may be one, as we are one."*

Unity with the Father through the Son is the entire, total, whole, complete, comprehensive, all-inclusive purpose of the history of salvation. Abraham, Isaac, and Jacob, Moses, the promised land, King David and his son King Solomon, the age of the prophets, John the Baptist, Jesus, Peter, James and John, Paul and the Epistles, Pentecost Sunday and the Holy Spirit, the totality of church history, and the Second Coming—everything and everyone who ever participated in

God's plan did so for the purpose of uniting us to the Father through the Son.

The catechism of the Episcopal Church states, "*The mission of the Church is to restore all people to unity with God and each other in Christ*" (*Book of Common Prayer,* 836). All the Father wants is for us to be with Him in the kingdom. That is His passion. That is His eternal longing. How many movies have you seen about a child who is kidnapped, and the parent will sacrifice everything to find the lost child? We have been kidnapped by the world, and the Father is sacrificing everything to get us back.

We have been kidnapped by the world. We have been kidnapped by the evil one. *"I ask that you protect them from the evil one."* Jesus uses His name to pray to the Father to protect us from the evil one so that all obstacles preventing unity may be broken down. Only the name of Jesus Christ can drive the evil one away. Only Jesus has power over Satan. And the evil one is out to kidnap you. *"Discipline yourselves; keep alert. Like a roaring lion your adversary the devil prowls around, looking for someone to devour"* (*1 Peter 5:8*).

Spiritual author Robert McCheyne wrote, "If I could hear Christ praying for me in the next room, I would not fear 1,000 enemies. Yet even though I cannot hear Him, I am confident that He is praying for me." Even now He is willing to protect you. He stands watch over you. He continues to pray for you. And when the enemy attacks, He will fight for you. Jesus is the first one to coin the phrase "No one left behind."

The psalmist proclaims:

> *Let God arise, and let his enemies be scattered; let those who hate him flee before him. Let them vanish like smoke when the wind drives it away; as the wax melts at the fire, so let the wicked perish at the presence of God. But let the righteous be glad and rejoice before God; let them also be merry and joyful. (Psalm 68:1–3)*

Jesus' prayer is not of this world. He does not pray that we win the lottery or gain any other means of worldly success. He does not even pray for our good health. His prayer goes far beyond the physical world and into the spiritual world. He prays for our spiritual well-being. This is where our true treasure lies. This fulfills the will of our heavenly Father. How often we pray for those things that will make our life here on earth more comfortable. But this is not Jesus' prayer. Jesus sees the bigger picture. Jesus understands that unity with the Father through Him, the Son, will leave earthly concerns behind. Unity with the Father makes our earthly concerns so trivial. Jesus is telling us that our prayers are too limited and narrow in scope. We need to see the bigger picture as well. *"For what will it profit a man to gain the whole world and lose his soul"* (Mark 8:36)?

Success in the material world may bring happiness, but life in Jesus brings joy. As Jesus prays, *"I speak these things in the world so that they may have my joy made complete in themselves."* Jesus is joyful because He is one with the Father. Complete joy is life in Jesus. Happiness will fade. Joy is eternal. Happiness is the ocean's wave. Joy lives on the ocean's floor where there is very little disturbance. When we reach the kingdom, there will be no happiness, only pure joy. Our hearts will be so alive that worldly happiness will no longer be desired, as if it were not even a passing thought.

Jesus prays that we are sanctified in the truth. In other words, the truth will make us holy, *"Sanctify them in your truth; your word is truth."* When we stand in the presence of Jesus, we will be forced to face the truth, the whole truth, and nothing but the truth, so help us, God. Jesus is the Word of God, and the Word is truth. Through human eyes, this can be frightening. Everything will be revealed. We will see that our innermost secrets are common knowledge to God. Our Collect for Purity prays, *"Almighty God, to you all hearts are open, all desires known, and from you no secrets are hid."* Our biggest fear is that the wrath of God will be hanging over our heads. But if we look with divine eyes, the truth will finally prevail, and hiding is no longer necessary. The truth will shatter the darkness of lies, deceit, excuses, arrogance, sham, pretense, and fraud. We will finally be free from the cunning ways of the evil one! In the presence of Jesus, there is no other way to be. The presence of Jesus will bring us eternal joy.

The Easter season is quickly coming to a close. It will soon be Pentecost. And yet the crescendo of the resurrection lingers in our hearts. The rolling away of the stone is the *distant thunder* of our memory. We are in the midst of three powerful and glorious events: Easter, the Ascension, and Pentecost Sunday. They are like a trilogy of incredible spiritual fireworks which explode in the heavens. Yet even in His almightiness, even in His eternal glory with the Father in heaven, even in the divine worship which we attribute to Him, Jesus does not forget you. He knows you by name. He prays to the Father to protect you so that one day, you will be one with Him. What else does He have to say to convince you? What else does He have to do?

+++

Abraham Lincoln's youngest son, Tad, was rather rambunctious, but his antics were warmly welcomed by White House staff. Tad had severe learning disabilities and had won a soft spot in his father's heart. The president and his wife, Mary, gave Tad free reign of the White House.

One day, Tad came across a Union soldier standing in one of the rear corridors. Tad engaged in a conversation with the soldier and learned that he was seeking the president's permission to return to his home to care for his dying mother. He was her only surviving child. Tad took the soldier by the hand and said, "Come with me." He led the soldier through the kitchen, down some hallways, and finally entered the Oval Office where the president was meeting with some of his generals. Tad went up to his father, tugged on his coat, and said, "Daddy, this man wants to talk to you." Out of love for his son, Lincoln stopped what he was doing, listened to the soldier, gave his permission, signed the order, and then resumed the meeting.

Just as Tad had access to his father, we have access to our Father through the Son. In fact, the only access we have to our Father is through the Son. Out of love for His Son, our Father listens. How this plays out with God is a mystery beyond our understanding.

Mystery begins where knowledge leaves off. To whom is the Father attending when the Son interrupts? How are prayer requests prioritized? Are prayers for healing more important than a student who says a prayer prior to a major exam?

We don't know, and we can't even begin to answer these questions. We often think of God in human terms, like a deli where you take a number, stand in line, and wait your turn. But this is not God. Somehow and someway, God has the capacity to listen to all of His children at once. *He is God, by god!* And He is a personal God. He has the capacity to be one Being and yet to be for each of us, as if we are the only one in line.

And for each of us, there is Tad who runs to the Father on our behalf. His name is Jesus. Any resulting doubt or mistrust on our part is coming from the evil one. The last thing that Satan wants you to do is pray. *But pray, we must!*

+++

This week...
Recite the following prayer slowly...
Dear Jesus, I need Your help.
There are things in my life that are troubling me.
When I try to handle them alone, they only get worse.
Please ask the Father to ease my burden,
so that You and I can be one with You.
Amen.

Coming Full Circle

As he was speaking to them, as they were watching, he was lifted up, and a cloud took him out of their sight. While he was going and they were gazing up toward heaven, suddenly two men in white robes stood by them. They said, "Men of Galilee, why do you stand looking up toward heaven? Jesus, who has

> *been taken up from you into heaven, will come in the same way as you saw him go into heaven." (Acts 1:9–11)*

We often think of life as linear. We often think that the events in our lives have a starting point and an ending point measured on a line to demonstrate time. For example, as a way to document times in your life, you might say, "I worked at my first job from this date to that one," or "I lived in my childhood home until I moved away to live on my own." Often, spiritual retreats ask participants to create a timeline, indicating different phases and events that helped shape them as individuals. Even on a tombstone, the date of birth and the date of death are connected by a line.

However, the Ascension of Jesus points to a new way of thinking: one that is circular, not linear. At the Ascension, the Son of God returns to the right hand of His heavenly Father after He comes to us at Christmas. While His earthly life *could* be measured on a line—He lived thirty-three years—His spiritual life creates a circle, coming from His Father and returning to Him, completing His earthly ministry. This creates the circle of life by which all spiritual time is now measured.

Ash Wednesday reminds us *we are dust and to dust we shall return:* ashes to ashes, dust to dust. In Genesis, God formed Adam from the dirt, from the clay, and from the mud of the earth. Coming from dirt and returning to dirt, Adam completes the first circle of earthly living. Similarly, our mortal bodies come into the world with God's blessing from the act of procreation by our earthly parents. Thus, our earthly bodies have an earthly circle, coming from the earth and returning to the earth at death. But our spirits have a heavenly one, originating from God and returning to Him. Thus, all life comes from God and will eventually return to Him.

The circle of our mortal bodies coming from the earth and returning to the earth and the circle of our souls coming from the kingdom and returning to the kingdom is demonstrated in the diagram below. The intersecting portion indicates when the two are together during our earthly life, no matter how long or short.

A Distant Thunder

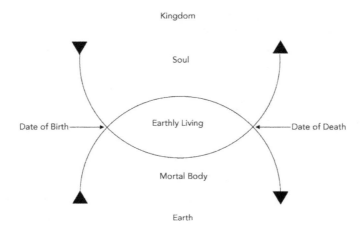

Jesus' circle of life mirrors ours with one exceptional difference: On Easter Sunday, He rises body and soul because He is sinless, unlike our bodies that return to the earth. As our sinful mortal bodies decay and return to the earth, our God-given spirit, the source of our eternal life coming from God, will return to Him. Thus, the Ascension powerfully reveals the profound circle of faith.

+++

The Ascension takes place on Mount Olivet, a familiar location to Jesus and His disciples. It is a sprawling ledge of limestone, rock, and dirt with the city of Jerusalem to the south and the countryside to the north, leading to cities and villages in the northern parts of Israel. Jesus crosses Mt. Olivet three times during the final week of His earthly life: during His triumphal entry into Jerusalem on Palm Sunday, at His Olivet Discourse when He explains the apocalypse, and in the garden of Gethsemane at the foot of the mountain the night before He dies.

The scene of the Ascension opens with Jesus and His disciples climbing for the last time to the top of the limestone ledge overlooking the city of Jerusalem. The disciples are in utter amazement and absolute awe of the Risen Christ. For the past forty days since His resurrection, Jesus' appearances to His disciples have been spotty and unpredictable. At times, He appears to all of them at once. At other times, He appears only to a few. But He never reveals to them when His next visit will occur. On their way to the top of the mountain, none of them linger behind; instead, they follow Him closely, nudging each other as they try to maneuver their way to the center of the fold where Jesus walks, stepping on each other's sandals and on His as well. To the people below, a cloud of limestone and dust marks the location of their walk. It will be their last walk with Him.

The conversation among them is as familiar as the walk they are taking. As usual, they speak on two levels: Jesus on the spiritual and the disciples on the physical. The disciples fall back on their Jewish expectations of the Messiah, and they want to know if this will be the time when He raises an army to overthrow the Romans. Still struggling with the nature and the purpose of the resurrection, the disciples ask probing questions, anxiously searching for details of the revolt against the Romans, hoping the release from their torment will come soon. But Jesus speaks of the apocalypse, a time when all of creation will complete the eternal circle of life, when every fiber of life will return to the Father. The disciples are ready to fight. Jesus is ready for peace.

Reaching the top of the limestone ledge, Jesus pauses and stares down at the city of Jerusalem. He remembers the countless times He has visited the Holy City, especially during His childhood when He was enthralled with the vastness of the city and the enormity of the temple. He recalls the scene in the marketplace: people bartering with eager merchants, the fragrant aroma of lamb, goat, fish, and vegetables grilling on an open fire, and the intricately woven baskets filled with figs, grapes, pomegranates, and olives. He remembers the incredible and the life-giving services at Passover and other Jewish feast days. The disciples remain curiously patient as He slowly scans the rooftops, the outline of the temple, and the garden of Gethsemane. His eyes well up from the emotional goodbye taking place in His heart. The moment, *for the moment*, is bittersweet. One of the disciples softly clears his throat to get Jesus' attention, suggesting they have been standing motionless long enough. Reentering the present moment, His melancholy suddenly transforms into incredible anticipation of reentering the kingdom where He will be reunited with His Father. He has longed for this moment for quite some time. It's time to go.

He slowly turns toward them, and one by one, He peers into the eyes of His beloved disciples, making each one feel slightly uncomfortable, raising their curiosity even more. His heart swells for them. His confidence in them is the highest it has ever been. He knows that in ten days, this small band of disciples will encounter the Holy Spirit who will set their hearts on fire to forever change the world. "I love you," He assures them. "I bless you, and I will be with you until the end of time. Believe in me. Trust in me. This is not the end, only the beginning." As He speaks to them and as they lovingly gaze at Him, yearning for understanding, a radiant white cloud glowing with rays of brilliant sunlight sent by His Father suddenly appears in the crystal-blue sky and slowly engulfs Him as it mysteriously lifts Him out of their sight.

+++

What an incredible and fascinating scene! The disciples have witnessed some absolutely astonishing events during Jesus' ministry, but next to the resurrection, this is, by far, the most incomprehensible one. Bewildered, the disciples ask each other, "Did you just see what I saw?" In a short forty-day span, Jesus completely overwhelms them. The magnitude of God, the power of God, the gravity-defying, creative renewal of God shocks the disciples far beyond their ability to understand and imagine.

This scene is amazing on three different levels. On one level, the Ascension is the completion and fulfillment of Jesus' ministry: It is the circle of life. It is the circle of faith. What meaning would the birth of Christ have if not for the resurrection to renew it? And what meaning would His resurrection have if not for the Ascension to free it? At His birth, the Son of God becomes human, occupying one small space in one small span of time. The Ascension, however, is like a spiritual cosmic firecracker that launches skyward, explodes like an opened umbrella, and shines on every particle of existence. Jesus now has the ability to enter into each cosmic particle and redeem it.

Jesus' return to the kingdom initiates a heavenly welcome home party *with all of the angels, archangels, and all the company of heaven.* The heavenly banquet table is set. The spirits who passed through the tomb while He lay in state on Good Friday greeted and embraced Him. It is an exuberant scene. The kingdom is once again completed after thirty-three earthly years of His absence.

After greeting the heavenly hosts, the Son eventually makes His way to the throne of His Father who embraces Him with His tender love. "I am very proud of You, Son," proclaims the Father. "You were obedient to death, even death on the cross. I could not have asked any more from You. Well done, good and faithful servant. Welcome home!"

The Son responds, "It was my good pleasure to serve You, Father. You are the Master not only of creation but recreation as well. There were many trying times, especially in the garden of Gethsemane, but the thought of Your love, protection, and eternal presence sustained me through each difficult moment. I am joyful to be home!"

Even at this tender moment with His Father, Jesus still worries about His disciples left on Earth. Knowing His Son's inner thoughts, the Father comforts Him, "Rest assured, my Son, they will remain fearful for only a short time until they are filled with our Holy Spirit on Pentecost. Then their fear will be transformed to overwhelming joy."

The Son responds, "I understand, Father, once filled with the power of Our Holy Spirit, they will proclaim Your love for the world."

As they speak, the Holy Spirit anxiously stands by the Father and the Son with eager anticipation. Relishing the presence of His Son, the Father tenderly tells Him, "Come. The banquet is ready, and You have many guests to greet."

On another level, this scene is amazing because the cloud represents the mystery of God. The cloud of God appears at Jesus' Transfiguration *(Matthew 17:5)*, and from the cloud comes a voice proclaiming, *"This is my Beloved Son in Whom I am well pleased."* The same mysterious cloud and the same words from the heavens are also heard at His baptism *(Matthew 3:17)*. In this way, God connects His baptism, resurrection, and ascension. As He ascends in the cloud, the humanness of Jesus dissipates, and He returns to His Father as the pure Son of God.

The two men in white robes who stand by the disciples make this scene amazing on a third level. We are reminded of the two men in white robes who appear to the women as they peer into the empty tomb on Easter Sunday morning, making another connection between the resurrection and the ascension. The question, *"Why do you stand looking up toward heaven?"* that the two white-robed men ask the disciples at the Ascension is similar to the question, *"Why do you look for the living among the dead?"* that the two white-robed men ask the women at the tomb. These questions challenge them to ponder God's unlimited almighty acts. They require spiritual contemplation in order to reach a deeper understanding. As you witness the activity of God in your life, He asks you a similar question, *"Do you understand what I am doing?"* It is now your turn to ponder.

Unlike the question to the women at the tomb, the question asked by the two men in white robes to the disciples at the Ascension is followed by a statement pointing to Jesus' return at the Second Coming: *"Jesus, who has been taken up from you into heaven, will come in the same way as you saw him go into heaven"* (Acts 1:9–11). Jesus will return in glory the same way He ascended. This awe-inspiring scene will be reversed for those who are alive to witness it. Thus, the Ascension carries unparalleled significance in the scope of Christ's life. From it, we not only look backward on the fulfillment of His earthly life, but we also look forward to it until His coming again.

+++

The Ascension occurs forty days after Easter. Counting forty days forward from Easter Sunday always brings us to a Thursday, the day we celebrate the Ascension. Prior to Easter, we have forty days of Lent, a time of penitence and reflection and sacrifice, leading us to a change of heart away from our sinfulness. After Easter, we celebrate forty days with the Risen Christ, leading us to a change of heart away from our mortality.

The disciples first begin to make sense of the totality of Jesus' purpose on Earth when the Holy Spirit appears on Pentecost Sunday, ten days after the Ascension and fifty days after Easter:

Jesus ascended so His Spirit could descend.
Jesus left so His Spirit could stay.
Jesus separated so His Spirit could unite.

The Ascension frees the resurrection so that Jesus can be present in each human heart. Jesus tells His disciples, *"It's to your advantage that I go"* (*John 16:6*). The Ascension is for us. Through His final triumph, Jesus transcends His ministry in Palestine and comes to each of us as the Resurrected Lord. The One who preached and ate meals with His disciples two thousand years ago is now preaching and eating meals with His friends everywhere, in all periods of time, in all spaces of the earth. The Ascension allows the Son of God to be in heaven, and at the same time, it allows His Spirit to be with His brothers and sisters everywhere:

- He is with us when we pray.
- He is with us when we celebrate the Eucharist.
- He is with the church in Uganda.
- He is with the plight of the migrant workers.
- He is with the hungry souls of those in prison.
- He is with the people who work for peace in the Middle East.
- He is with the broken and sinful.
- He is with us to restore the perfect peace of the Father.

The Ascension leaves the foot of the cross firmly planted in Calvary, but it hurls the cross-member splintering across the atmosphere. The Ascension allows Jesus to transcend Jerusalem and to embrace the entire globe, the entire universe. *He has the whole world in His hands!*

+++

The Cosmic Christ
A Theory by Fr. Ken

Somewhere, in a far quadrant of the universe not yet detected by humans, is a planet unfamiliar to stellar maps, undetected by any space probe, and unknown in any constellation. There exists the planet *Orbis*. On *Orbis*, the God of all creation purposely places life. Through the process of evolution over billions of years and guided by the hand of God, intelligent life has evolved. This intelligent life has been created in the image of God: free, loving, and filled with the breath of God's Spirit. If the inhabitants of *Orbis* never sin, then *Orbis* would be an extension of heaven, and its inhabitants would be living in the fullness of God's eternal love.

However, should the inhabitants of *Orbis* abuse their free will, if they rebel against God, if Satan discovers this planet and infiltrates their lives with his evil, and if they sin, resulting in their separation from God, it would be necessary for the Father to send His Son not only to become one of them and express His love for them but also to die for them in order to pay for their sins, as He did on Earth with His beloved Son, Jesus. After His death, the Son would resurrect on *Orbis*, and after His resurrection, the Son would ascend and return to His Father in the kingdom. *Yes, He ascends.* The Son must ascend in order to make all of this possible. *"O inhabitants of Orbis, why do you stand here looking up at the sky? Jesus, who has been taken up from you into heaven, will come back in the same way you saw him go up."*

It is the Circle of Life.
It is the Circle of Faith.
There is far too much to understand.
There is far too much to discover.

Perhaps hundreds, maybe even thousands, of planets like *Orbis* exist in our universe. Perhaps on one, a Moses-like leader is being called forth right now to lead a modest band of slaves into a new land. Maybe on one of these uncharted planets, right this very minute, there are prophets being called to remind the Chosen Ones of the covenant. Maybe on one of these distant planets, right now, the Son is with them, in all of God's resurrected brilliance, preparing the followers for the indwelling of God's Spirit at Pentecost. And maybe, just maybe, on one of these remote planets, the Second Coming has already taken place, and the planet has been reshaped, recreated, and given rebirth with its new inhabitants. Thus, a new circle of life begins.

This *Cosmic Christ* could be a continual outpouring of God's infinite love across the vastness of the infinite universe. The *Cosmic Christ* does not diminish one ounce of God's love for the people on Earth, for we are reminded that even in the vastness of the universe, God has not forgotten us. By examining God's infinite love, we realize the immensity of the universe. By examining the immensity of the universe, we realize God's infinite love. The Ascension allows all of this to take place.

The circle of life moves us from despair to hope, from doubt to faith, from loneliness to love. Once we have hope, faith, and love, we will encounter the absolute joy of the never-ending circle of life, the never-ending circle of faith. God loves you!

+++

This week...
Go outside on a clear night, look at the stars, and ponder the vastness of the universe. Then consider the vastness of God's love and rejoice that He has included you in the enormity of His created works.

The Season of Pentecost

The world cries for hope, for love, for peace. But how do we bring peace, love, and hope to a broken world? The season of Pentecost, one the most least celebrated times in our lives, should be one of the most important. It is a time of harvest, to harvest not only our crops but also our lives: to cultivate our lives by preparing ourselves to grow with God, to receive the fruits of His love, and to celebrate His blessings in our lives.

Wildfires

> *When the day of Pentecost had come, the disciples were all together in one place for fear of the Jews. And suddenly from heaven there came a sound like the rush of a violent wind, and it filled the entire house where they were sitting. Divided tongues, as of fire, appeared among them, and a tongue rested on each of them. All of them were filled with the Holy Spirit and began to speak in other languages as the Spirit gave them ability.*
>
> *Now there were devout Jews from every nation under heaven living in Jerusalem. And at this sound the crowd gathered and was bewildered, because each one heard them speaking in their own native language. All were amazed and perplexed, saying to one another, "What does this mean?" But others sneered and said, "They are filled with new wine."*
>
> *But Peter, standing with the eleven, raised his voice and addressed them, "Men of Judea and all*

who live in Jerusalem, let this be known to you, and listen to what I have to say. Indeed, these are not drunk, as you suppose, for it is only nine o'clock in the morning. God raised Jesus from the dead and we are all witnesses. Therefore, let the entire house of Israel know with certainty that God has made him both Lord and Messiah, this Jesus whom you crucified."

Now when they heard this, they were cut to the heart and said to Peter and the other disciples, "Brothers, what should we do?" Peter said to them, "Repent and be baptized every one of you in the name of Jesus Christ so that your sins may be forgiven; and you will receive the gift of the Holy Spirit." So those who welcomed his message were baptized, and that day about three thousand were added. They devoted themselves to the apostles' teaching and fellowship, to the breaking of the bread and the prayers. (Acts 2:1–6, 14, 15, 32, 33, 37, 38, and 40–42)

Pentecost Sunday always falls in late May or early June. Depending on the date of Easter, the season of Pentecost can last anywhere between twenty-two and twenty-eight weeks, taking it well into summer and fall. The April showers that bring May flowers have come and gone. The crisp cool air of spring slowly fades and is replaced by the long hot days of summer. As the summer heat intensifies, conditions for wildfires gradually increase. Sweltering heat, strong gusty winds, extremely dry air, and powerful cloud-to-ground lightning bolts make conditions ripe for wildfires. From just a spark, a fire can suddenly spread and quickly ravage a large area of land. Its raging and menacing blaze can be seen for miles around, causing panic, confusion, and fear to those who are nearby.

The above passage from *the book of Acts* describes a spiritual wildfire that swept through the city of Jerusalem on the first Pentecost Sunday two thousand years ago. The passage opens with the eleven disciples in the upper room. Fearing their arrest, one of the disciples discreetly peers through a draped window looking for Roman soldiers and Jewish officials while the others huddle in prayer. In the midst of their watch, they suddenly hear a sound like a strong driving wind, making them even more apprehensive. However, their perceived fear comes not from the outside but from the inside. The sound of the wind is actually the Holy Spirit zealously rushing from heaven and powerfully engulfing the entire room. The disciples sense a presence they cannot identify and unlike any they have felt before. Unexpectedly, the presence calms their anxiety and fear. Even though they don't understand what has just happened, peace fills their hearts.

The Holy Spirit slowly reveals Himself like divided tongues of fire and gently rests one tongue on each of their heads. This is the moment when the Holy Spirit connects their faith from their heads to their hearts. In a matter of an instant, everything the disciples cognitively knew about Jesus is passionately placed in their hearts. The disciples now share the fullness of the Spirit's revelation. *This is the moment of their enlightenment; this is the moment of the Holy Spirit.* By nine o'clock that morning, the Holy Spirit's tongues of fire enable each disciple to speak in a language other than his native tongue, preparing them to proclaim the good news of Jesus' resurrection to the multitude waiting in the street. *This is the moment the world is changed.*

The Holy Spirit ignites an awe-inspiring spiritual wildfire within them. Jesus' faithful disciples who have traveled extensively with Him and who have witnessed, firsthand, His miraculous acts of compassion, healing, mercy, and forgiveness now *know Him in His fullness*. But it is not until the Holy Spirit connects the knowledge of Him in their heads to the love for Him in their hearts that they *boldly proclaim His name*. And once their love for Him moves into their hearts, their faith spreads through the entire city, causing the three thousand newly baptized to become *"on fire with the Lord."*

Imagine three thousand people repenting their sins, proclaiming their faith in Jesus Christ, and receiving the Sacrament of Baptism. *Wow! What an incredible and magnificent moment that must have been! That must have been one long service!* Three thousand people affirmed their faith on that first Pentecost Sunday, which Christians refer to as the birthday of the church.

+++

The Holy Spirit wants to ignite a revival in your heart just as He did with the eleven disciples. He knows that sometimes we become too complacent in our faith, sometimes our secular lives overwhelm our spiritual ones, sometimes we become reluctant about proclaiming Jesus as our Lord and Savior, sometimes we take Him for granted, sometimes we lack adoration for Him. Sometimes, *we know* the wildfire for Him in our hearts is an inconsequential flicker. *He knows this too! But the Holy Spirit wants us back!*

The spark of our love for Jesus Christ needs reigniting. Jesus must once again be the focus of our attention. We need to start a spiritual wildfire in our hearts. We shouldn't be *firefighters*. We should be *fire starters for Jesus*. We need a revival of our faith. We need to put the fire of Jesus' love in our hearts and set it ablaze.

How do you become a *fire starter?* It's easy. *Attend fire-starter school.*

Attend a weekend retreat, offered periodically in many churches. The Episcopal Church offers Cursillo, a three-day weekend when participants share a profound experience of Christian life through songs, witnesses, and worship. If you have already attended a retreat in your church, sign up to work on a team at a new retreat, or refuel your faith by attending a small group spiritual reunion. Teenagers could attend a weekend retreat especially designed for their age group, or they could join Young Life, a program that helps teenagers grow in their faith.

Whatever you decide, don't limit yourself! Read your Bible every day. Join a Bible study. Listen to a spiritual radio station. Pray more often and more deliberately. Speak openly about Jesus Christ. Make bold proclamations of Jesus' love to people you encounter throughout your day. Say a prayer before a meeting at the office. Talk to your children or grandchildren about God. Hum a spiritual hymn as you travel through your day. Surround yourself with God, and He will send His Holy Spirit directly into your heart. *Start a spiritual wildfire for the Lord!*

The most important way to start a spiritual wildfire is to acknowledge your sin, repent, and ask for forgiveness. Sin is the root of spiritual apathy. Sin pours guilt into your heart! Sin drowns your life with sorrow! Sin engulfs you with anxiety, doubt, and fear. Sin wages war with your spiritual life! Sin places you tightly in the devil's grip. Sin makes it impossible to turn to Jesus until you acknowledge your sin and repent. With sin, the spiritual wildfire never sparks. Without it, your heart burns with love for Him!

+++

In the above passage from *the book of Acts*, Peter tells the people, *"Repent and be baptized every one of you in the name of Jesus Christ so that your sins may be forgiven; and you will receive the gift of the Holy Spirit."* Peter directly connects repentance, forgiveness, and receiving the Holy Spirit. Jesus does the same in His first appearance to the disciples after the resurrection on Easter Sunday evening:

> *Jesus stood among them and said, "Peace be with you. As the Father has sent me, so I send you." When he had said this, he breathed on them and said to them, "Receive the Holy Spirit. If you forgive the sins of any, they are forgiven; if you retain the sins of any, they are retained." (John 20:21–23)*

Repentance and forgiveness, the resurrection and new life in Jesus, and the breath of the Holy Spirit closely connect with one another.

+++

One of the great joys of ordained ministry is witnessing someone undergoing a conversion experience. While the most powerful time is through the *reconciliation* of a *penitent*, a conversion experience can come at any time: at worship, during a sermon, singing a hymn, hearing a single verse from Scripture, during a counseling session, at a retreat weekend, or receiving a card or a note from a family member, just to name a few.

Some years ago, a woman told me that her relationship with Jesus had faded terribly over the course of several years. She and her husband and their friends were on vacation in Europe. While they were enjoying a meal and each other's company, a song came on the jukebox sung in English by an American artist. That secular song reminded her of fond memories from her youth. Realizing how far she had strayed from Jesus, she burst into tears. Her husband and friends had no idea what was wrong. How could she go from laughing one moment to crying the next? She simply said, "I must find a church!" One song at the right time and in the right place invited the Holy Spirit to ignite her spiritual wildfire for Jesus. Another heart was turned. *God is amazing!*

Conversion experiences are typically accompanied with tears, lots of them. If you were to run a spiritual DNA test on one of these tears, you would find traces of guilt, remorse, forgiveness, release, grace, love, rebirth, surrender, passion, joy, and peace, all in a single tear. Ironically, these tears are the *fire starters* used by the Holy Spirit to rekindle the desire of a spiritual wildfire in our hearts, our desire for Jesus. Peter is speaking to you, *"Repent of your sins so that you may be forgiven; and you will receive the gift of the Holy Spirit."*

Looking back on your life, there was probably a conversion experience you went through. I'm sure the woman vacationing in Europe will look back on that moment as a mile marker in her relationship with Jesus. But conversion experiences happen all the time because we continually sin, and we are always in need of repentance. While some are major events, most are rather minor. Once we eliminate our sinfulness, we give the Holy Spirit room to work. He needs the clutter removed and the garbage taken out of our lives. It is only by burning our sins that we can live with a fire in our hearts for Jesus. If you want a Spirit-filled life, then you must repent. Whatever you are holding onto must be released. Face the truth. The search for the truth is the search for Jesus. When you find the truth, you will find

Jesus. And when you find Jesus, you will be in the truth. He waits for you. He will use the truth to start a fire within you.

+++

On the first Pentecost Sunday, we are told of the sound of mighty wind and tongues of fire coming to rest on the disciples' heads. All of this is true. But our suspicion is that Peter is the first of the eleven to be overcome by the Spirit. After the resurrection, after Jesus asks Peter three times if he loves Him, after forty days of Jesus' appearance to the disciples, and after witnessing the Ascension, those moments shook Peter to his very core, infusing his heart with the fire of the Holy Spirit. Peter repented for all of the times he doubted, denied, and turned away from Jesus. And Peter's repentance ignited the fire in the upper room. The disciples fell to their knees, covered their faces with their hands, while tears streamed down their cheeks as they begged for forgiveness.

+++

This week…
Be a fire starter by choosing one or more of the following suggested activities:

- *Read your Bible every day.*
- *Join a Bible study.*
- *Listen to spiritual music.*
- *Pray more often and more deliberately.*
- *Speak openly about Jesus Christ.*
- *Make bold proclamations of Jesus' love.*
- *Say a prayer before a meeting at the office.*
- *Read a Bible story to your children or grandchildren.*
- *Hum a spiritual hymn as you go about your daily routine.*
- Start a "fire" in your heart for Jesus!

Reverend Kenneth and Elizabeth Herzog

Roots and Wings

Rejoice with Jerusalem, and be glad for her, all you who love her; Rejoice with her in joy, all you who mourn over her,
That you may nurse and be satisfied from her consoling breast;
That you may drink deeply with delight from her glorious bosom. (Isaiah 66:10, 11)

Under a clear, crisp, starry sky, the intense cries of labor pains shatter the first silent night. Joseph carefully lays out hay and blankets, providing warmth for Mary from the cold dirt floor. The soothing herbal tea can do little more than provide temporary solace to the pain that lies within her. Mary's piercing shrieks echo throughout the stillness of the night, reaching the radiant stars. The donkey is annoyed. The attentive angels hover over the manger, waiting patiently for His emerging birth, and God affectionately waits to give His people His most precious gift.

The Son of God comes to us, and the angels joyfully announce the birth of our long-awaited Messiah. Seeing His newborn Son, the Father longs to embrace Him as tightly as the embrace they shared months earlier prior to the Son's departure for the womb. As heaven rejoices His birth, the newborn Son is oblivious to His empty throne at the right hand of the Father and to the emptiness in His Father's heart.

Mary lies nestled in the corner of the manger. The mysterious announcement she received nine months earlier from the Archangel Gabriel is now cradled in her arms. God's Son takes His first breath and cries His first cry. Some of the blood from the new birth trickles through her fingers. She wipes His delicate head with her meager clothing and gently presses His tiny body to her breast. He sucks the nourishing milk only she can provide. She feels His heart beating with intensity. Tears of joy flow from her cheeks as she bows her head to give Him the first of a million kisses on His forehead. Tenderness surrounds this awesome moment. As she watches and listens to her

Son drink, she ponders His future life. She ponders what God may have in store for Him, for her, for the world. Judea is now God's home. The earth has adopted His Son. It is the first Christmas. The Incarnation is minutes old. God, the Eternal Creator of the universe, enters human history in the Person of His Son and is given the human name Jesus, a name meaning "God saves."

+++

In the above Scripture passage, the Prophet Isaiah captures this tender moment between mother and child. Isaiah, one of the most compassionate and hopeful Old Testament prophets, provides an image of Jerusalem as a mother who cradles and nestles in her bosom those who are nurtured and fed by her. Isaiah creates this image to describe God's motherly love for Israel. The profound love between mother and child reflects God's profound love and yearning for His people. Isaiah shows God's soft, tender, and motherly side, a side of God that His Son will reveal to the world locked in almighty fear of Him. Through His Son, the world will experience God's compassion, forgiveness, mercy, grace, and unconditional love.

Perhaps Isaiah's metaphor of Jerusalem as a mother stems from his understanding of this maternal relationship. The great Prophet Isaiah must have had a special bond with his mother.

Thus, he extends this relationship to describe the bond between God and His people. God loves, protects, and nurtures us much the same way a mother loves, protects, and nurtures her child.

+++

With the first kiss on her Son's forehead, Mary initiates the *first of two* most important gifts parents give their children…*roots*. Roots form the foundation of our identity, including our personality. Nature and nurture influence the development of our roots, which help determine who we are and from where we come. Roots powerfully influence every facet of a child's life, including the child's relationship with God. Throughout life, especially during troubled times, a child often reverts to the security of the fetal position. Strong roots develop strong identities. Strong identities develop strong lives. Therefore, it is crucial that parents provide a solid foundation during the early developmental years.

Joseph and Mary provide deep, nourishing roots during Jesus' childhood. Visited by the Angel Gabriel, both parents are divinely appointed and entrusted with the overwhelming responsibility of raising God's Son. It is no wonder they panic when they lose track of Him after a Passover pilgrimage to Jerusalem during His twelfth year (*Luke 2:41–47*). Mary, Jesus' biological mother, and Joseph, His adopting father, further demonstrate that roots are partially genetic and partially environmental. *Did I tell you He has His mother's eyes? Did I tell you He has His father's temperament?* Because of their humility, God chooses Mary and Joseph for the most glorious and the most difficult role ever given to any human. How could the Son of the Almighty, Eternal, and Infinite God grow up to be anything other than humble?

The pain of childbirth usually foreshadows the challenges of raising a child. But not in this case. Even though Jesus shares the moral ignorance of humanity, He refrains from the sinfulness of rebellion: *"For we do not have a high priest who is unable to empathize with our weaknesses, but we have one who has been tempted in every way, just as we are—yet he did not sin"* (*Hebrews 4:15*).

At some point in Jesus' childhood, especially as other children are born into their family, Mary must have had a special and private conversation with Jesus about His unique, eternal, mysterious, and Spirit-filled conception. As Jesus progressed through His childhood, His roots were further influenced by His younger siblings. Luke summarizes Jesus' early years in two simple verses:

> *He went down to Nazareth and stayed with Mary and Joseph and was obedient to them. His mother meanwhile treasured all these things in her heart. Jesus, for his part, progressed steadily in wisdom and age and grace before God.* (*Luke 2:51, 52*)

Raising the Son of God, Mary and Joseph faced different challenges than other parents. They were aware of the delicate responsibility of raising God's Son. But they also realized the responsibility of teaching Him the lessons and values they would teach all of their children, without favoring their Firstborn. What a difficult challenge that must have been!

As a child, Ken thought Jesus sat in the back of the classroom and knew the answer before the teacher even asked the question. But Jesus does not possess extraordinary intelligence. Actually, He fully and humbly shared in human ignorance, growing in wisdom and knowledge as any child would under the careful eye of His holy and faithful parents. With daily school in the synagogue and weekly worship on the Sabbath, Jesus slowly, gradually, and practically became aware of the struggle with His divinity that would challenge Him until His baptism.

+++

There comes a time in our lives when we must leave the security of our homes. There comes a time when the child matures, reaches independence, and ventures out into the world. Every animal species undergoes this transition, but none as dramatic as the human species. More than any other, the mature human can rationalize the security of the home and the fears faced by leaving.

During His adolescent and early adult years, Jesus lived with His family in Nazareth. The Scriptures do not reveal any insight about this time of His life, but after formal Jewish schooling around the age of thirteen, adolescents typically continue living at home, learning important life skills from their parents. Daughters learn homemaking skills from their mothers, and sons learn occupational skills from their fathers. Jesus and His brothers learned carpentry skills from Joseph, and might have even opened a family business building houses and making tables, chairs, and other household items. Eventually, each of their children leave home, perhaps because of marriage, perhaps because of the challenge of opening their own business in another town, or perhaps because of their desire to *chart their own course*. This is the point when the foundation of their *roots* supported the strength of their *wings*.

There comes a time in Jesus' life when He must leave home. And as much as she loves Him, Mary must let Him go. There is a great foreshadowing of His departure when, after being lost for three days in the temple at the age of twelve, Jesus tells His parents, *"Do you not know that I must be about My Father's business?" (Luke 2:49)*. When it is time for Him to leave, Mary learns firsthand *the second* of the most important gifts parents give to their children…*wings*.

When the time comes, children must go, and parents must be willing to let them go.

Ken's Uncle John and Aunt Dorothy had thirteen children. When they turned eighteen, they were immediately given *wings*. They had a little ceremony. Uncle John would open the front door of the house and proclaim, "Fly thee out into the world and *chart thine own course*." In other words, "Get the heck out of my house!" (Maybe not as dramatic as that!) Some left willingly. Some left reluctantly. It didn't matter, as long as they left.

I don't suspect that Jesus' departure is as dramatic. The fire of the Holy Spirit that consumes His baptism at age thirty gives Him purpose, not as a carpenter but as the Son of God. The Spirit gives *wings* to His public ministry, which calls Him far beyond the walls of His childhood home, far beyond the boundaries of His hometown of Nazareth. And by leaving, Jesus changes the course of human history. This has been His mission from the very beginning. The good news of a loving, compassionate, grace-filled God must be proclaimed to a world in dire need of salvation, and He cannot proclaim it from the comforts of His home. The people will not come to Him. He must go to the people. But in doing so, He carries in His heart the love of His parents, the security of His home, and the *roots* of His childhood.

+++

There comes a time in the disciples' relationship with Jesus when He moves them from *roots* to *wings*. After three years of spiritually nourishing and feeding them, teaching them the Word, and training them in the Way, their faith reaches a point of maturity, and they are expected to go. Their *roots* must now be turned into *wings*:

> *The harvest is plentiful, but the laborers are few, therefore, ask the Lord of the harvest to send out laborers into the harvest. Go on your way. See, I am sending you out like lambs into the midst of wolves. Carry no purse, no bag, no sandals, and greet no one on the road. (Luke 10:2–4)*

This passage comes right after Jesus predicts His own death for a second time. He is very aware of the evils that His disciples will encounter. He sends them out into a world that will mock them, hate them, and destroy them. Isaiah's image of the mother's succulent bosom suddenly changes. Now they are lambs in the midst of wolves. He tells them to take nothing for their journey. Giving them *wings*, Jesus tells them to *depend* on their faith for their provisions. This perplexes them. But they obey Him, and they are absolutely amazed at the results: curing, healing, and casting out demons:

> *The disciples return with joy, saying, "Lord, in your name, even the demons submit to us!" He said to them, "I saw Satan fall from heaven like a flash of lightning! See, I have given you authority to tread on snakes and scorpions, and over all the power of the enemy; and nothing will hurt you. Nevertheless, do not rejoice at this, that the spirits submit to you, but rejoice that your names are written in heaven." (Luke 10:17–20)*

By leaving their earthly home, the disciples are promised a heavenly one because they were not afraid of giving *wings* to their faith.

+++

The same challenge is presented to you. It is not enough to rest on your religious roots and never leave the bosom of your childhood faith. Hopefully, you have been attending church. Hopefully, you have been involved in the life of your parish. Hopefully, you have been drinking the succulent milk of the sacraments. But now, Jesus is sending you out. Your faith must reach a maturity level that compels you to spread the good news of Jesus' love: in your family, in your neighborhood, in your workplace, in your town or city, or perhaps in another part of the world. This is the mission of the church. The Gospel calls you to get out of your comfort zone and extend yourself to further enhance the ministry of Jesus Christ:

> *All authority on heaven and on earth has been given to me. Therefore, go and make disciples of all nations, baptizing them in the name of the Father and of the Son and of the Holy Spirit, and teaching them to obey everything I have commanded you. And surely I am with you always, to the very end of the age. (The Great Commission: Matthew 28:18–20)*

Every Sunday at the dismissal of the Episcopal service, the people are sent out into the world with the command: *"Go in peace to love and serve the Lord"* (*BCP,* 366). These are not just words. With this command, Jesus tells us to get on with His work in the world. It is admirable that you go to church, but church must extend beyond your childhood faith, beyond the walls of the church building, beyond your comfort zone. The world is filled with a bountiful harvest, and you are being called to work it. However, you may face an alarmingly hostile world that is ready to devour you when you mention the name of Jesus Christ. But that is further proof you need to go. Overcome your fears and hesitation and *just go.* "Go where?" you might ask. Go where God is sending you. Get involved in one of your church's ministries. *"The harvest is plentiful, but the laborers are few."* Be one of the few. You can ill afford to rest in the bosom of your faith. It is your turn. It is time to do your part. Jesus is sending you. Your salvation and the salvation of the world depend on your *wings*.

+++

The woman cradles her Son in her arms and presses His lifeless body close to her bosom. She feels no heartbeat. Some of His blood from the cross trickles between her fingers. She wipes His precious head with her meager clothing. The woman is Mary; her son is Jesus. It is not Bethlehem but Calvary. It is not the manger but the garbage dump. It is not the crèche but the cross.

As Mary holds her son, she reflects on the *roots* and the *wings* she has given Him. This awesome moment is wrapped in tenderness. Tears of sorrow flow from her cheeks onto her son as she bows her head to give Him the last of a million kisses on His forehead. As she does, it occurs to her that through His death, His life has been given *wings*. Wings that allow Him to fly into eternity, to the heavenly paradise from where He came. Go! Go and spread this word of God's eternal love.

+++

This week…
Reflect on the influences of your roots and how
you can give wings to your faith.

Who Is My Neighbor?

Just then a lawyer stood up to test Jesus. "Teacher," he said. "What must I do to inherit eternal life?" He said to him, "What is written in the law? What do you read there?" He answered, "You shall love the Lord your God with all your heart, and with all your soul, and with all your strength, and your neighbor as yourself." And he answered

> him, "You have given the right answer; do this, and you will live."
>
> But wanting to justify himself, he asked Jesus, "And who is my neighbor?" Jesus replied, "A man was traveling from Jerusalem to Jericho, and fell into the hands of robbers, who stripped him, beat him, and went away, leaving him half dead. Now by chance a priest was going down that same road; and when he saw him, he passed by on the other side. So likewise a Levite, when he came to the place and saw him, passed by on the other side. But a Samaritan while traveling came near him; and when he saw him, he was moved with pity. He went to him and bandaged his wounds, having poured oil and wine on them. Then he put him on his own animal, brought him to an inn, and took care of him. The next day he took out two denarii, gave them to the innkeeper, and said, 'Take care of him; and when I come back, I will repay whatever more you spend.'
>
> Which of these three, do you think, was a neighbor to the man who fell into the hands of the robbers?" He said, "The one who showed him mercy." Jesus said to him, "Go and do likewise."
> (Luke 10:25–37)

Jews and Samaritans border each other geographically, and their countrymen have fought for centuries like rival siblings who seldom get along. A profound animosity exists between them; consequently, their children grow up with roots of deep-seated prejudices. By the time Jesus is a young man, both countries have lost a multitude of soldiers at the hands of the other.

Their disregard for the welfare of one another is the reason Jesus tells the Jewish lawyer the parable of the good Samaritan that demonstrates the importance of showing compassion to those in need, including one's adversary.

There is a difference between sympathy and compassion. Sympathy means you recognize what the person feels. Compassion, however, brings empathy, a fuller understanding of the situation because you're to action. Neel Burton, MD, in his article "Empathy vs. Sympathy" published in the May 22, 2015, issue of *Psychology Today*, offers this explanation:

> When you experience compassion for another person in need, you not only understand their feelings but you also feel called to help. Compassion, or "suffering alongside" someone, is more engaged…and is associated with an active desire to alleviate the suffering of its object. With compassion I not only share your emotions but also elevate them into a universal and transcending experience.

Jesus' entire ministry centers around healing and acts of compassion. He not only shows sympathy for people who are struggling, but He also stops what He is doing to help them. For example, after learning that His cousin and best friend John the Baptist has been beheaded and wanting to mourn by Himself, *"He withdrew from there in a boat to a deserted place by Himself. But the people followed Him on foot. When He saw a great crowd, He had compassion for them and cured their sick"* (Matthew 14:13–14).

Another act of compassion occurs as He leaves Jericho, and two blind men cry out to Him, pleading for His mercy to cure their sight. Hearing their cries and overcome with compassion, *"Jesus touched their eyes. Immediately, they regained their sight and followed Him"* (Matthew 20:29–34). Ephesians 4:32 tells us to *"be kind and compassionate to one another, forgiving each other, just as Christ God forgave you."* The Bible abounds with similar incidents of Jesus' compassion.

+++

In the parable of the good Samaritan, Jesus teaches the Jewish lawyer and us that compassion rises above prejudices, biases, and stereotypes. Compassion even rises above enemies. To fully understand the parable, we must understand that during biblical times, Jewish lawyers and rabbis questioned each other to discern the other's astuteness of the law. When questioned, the lawyer often presented a hypothetical situation to support his interpretation of the written law. This practice, also known as the Socratic Method, served as an excellent learning opportunity for the lawyer asking the question. These questions or "tests" took place all the time: in the temple, in the marketplace, in each other's homes, whenever they were together.

The Jewish lawyer challenges Jesus' interpretation of the law, but he also wants to back Jesus into a corner, hoping to discredit His claim of being the Messiah. However, by this time in His ministry, Jesus quickly discerns the lawyer's twofold motive. When the lawyer asks his first question, *"What must I do to inherit eternal life?"* Jesus responds by asking him, *"What does the law state?"* Citing Leviticus 19:18, the lawyer responds, *"Love God with all your heart, mind and soul, and love your neighbor as yourself."*

Still *wishing to justify* his interpretation out of a sense of self-righteousness, the lawyer asks a second question, *"And who is my neighbor?"* Jesus answers with the hypothetical situation of the Good Samaritan and then asks the lawyer, *"Which of these three, do you think, was a neighbor to the man who fell into the hands of the robbers?"* By this time, the lawyer realizes that the Samaritan was the only one who acted with compassion, so he responds, *"The one who showed him mercy."* Thus, Jesus brings the lawyer to a higher level of moral reasoning by illustrating that his neighbor is not limited by nationality, ethnic background, or cultural identity but is anyone who needs compassion. And the lawyer's moral foundation rooted in written law is now shaken.

Like the lawyer, we often establish parameters and boundaries around our willingness to help others. We often ask, *"Who is my neighbor?"* When we come across someone in need, we may help the person for a few minutes but probably not an hour. We may donate a dollar but maybe not five. If we have extra time, we may stop to help someone whose car won't start, but if we are in a hurry, there's a good chance we'll rationalize that someone else will help. If we know the person who needs our help, we're all in. If the person is a stranger, then we are less likely to offer our help. Sometimes, our willingness to help others even depends on what they will do for us.

> *"But the lawyer, wishing to justify himself, asks 'Who is my neighbor?'"*

Ask Michelle. A newspaper in Florida reported a story about Michelle, a senior in high school and a member of her school's cross-country team. During one of the last meets of their season, Michelle was running along a narrow stretch of the course that bordered a small canal when she heard a desperate cry for help coming from the tall grass at the water's edge. She stopped and found a runner from an opposing school who had twisted her ankle and had fallen off the path into the reeds and the shallow, mucky water.

> *Now a priest happened to be going down the same road. He saw her but passed by on the other side. And a lawyer did the same.*

Michelle helped the girl up the bank to the side of the path. With a shaky voice and tears streaming down her face, the runner told Michelle that she had been lying in the muddy water for what seemed like forever, crying for help to the runners who passed by, but no one stopped. She thanked Michelle over and over again for stopping to help her. As they waited for help, none of the runners who passed by stopped to help them. Finally, one of the coaches driving a golf cart spotted them. He stopped and brought both girls to a medical tent.

It seems as if the race was more important to the runners who didn't stop than showing compassion to someone in need. It seems as if their priorities were not aligned correctly.

But Michelle's were. It didn't matter to Michelle that the girl was from an opposing school. It didn't matter that she wouldn't finish the race. It didn't matter that she may have put her team's standing in jeopardy. It didn't matter; she just stopped. Later, when a reporter asked her why she decided to stop instead of continuing the race, Michelle said that she didn't even think about it; *she just stopped!*

+++

Jesus comes to us with the purpose of establishing a community of individual journeys of faith to further the work of the kingdom. Certainly, a personal relationship with Jesus Christ is extremely important, but our journey can't stop there. He wants us to embrace a sense of community that shows compassion for those in need. He wants us to live in harmony, not in opposition. Jesus commands us to *"love your neighbor as yourself."* He teaches us that our neighbor is anyone in need. Compassion forms the foundation of the community Jesus wants us to establish. A community rooted in compassion willingly accepts and actively affirms its responsibility to help those in need.

The early church best exemplifies the meaning of a Christian community soon after the indwelling of the Holy Spirit on Pentecost Sunday:

> *Those who believed shared all things in common; they would sell their property and goods, dividing everything on the basis of each one's need. They went to the temple area together every day, while in their homes they broke bread. With exultant and sincere hearts, they took their meals in common, praising God and winning the approval of all the people. Day by day the Lord added to their number those who were being saved.* (Acts 2:44–47)

Four major revelations about the community Jesus establishes are included in this passage from Acts: People filled with the Holy Spirit naturally form a community. In a pure Christian community, earthly possessions are sacrificed for the common good. Most people want to live in a harmonious community. And we are saved by living for others.

+++

Created in the image of God, humans are called to love one another. The natural flow of love is outward, beyond ourselves. Unlike gravity that pulls everything down, love pushes itself out toward others. Temporal love is self-centered. Christian love is other-centered. Humans are most alive when we give ourselves away. We receive the most when we give the most. The gift is in the giving, which is the paradox of humanity.

Humans are not autonomous; our dependence on others completes us. We have an insatiable, unquenchable desire to feel needed. We have an insatiable, unquenchable desire to extend ourselves. Through our relationship with others, we learn the most about ourselves. When we exist for others, we find the presence of Jesus Christ. When love inspires us, we are the perfect image of our Creator. When love motivates us, love of God and love of neighbor are inseparable. If you look into the heart of a person in need, you will find Jesus.

+++

In this parable, a priest and a lawyer both pass by the beaten victim without helping him. They justify not helping because no one sees them. From their perspective, right is right only when someone is watching. The Samaritan, however, shows compassion, even though no one is watching. The parable teaches us that compassion breaks down the barriers that keep us from loving one another.

> But the lawyer, wishing to justify himself, asked, "Who is my neighbor"'

Ask Patrick, a ticket agent for a major airline. The last flight had already left, and the airport would soon shut down for the night. While Patrick attended to his work, he noticed a young woman sitting near his ticket window cuddling a small infant. She seemed nervous, frightened, and lost. The tears welling up in her eyes prompted Patrick's decision to speak to her.

> *Now a priest happened to be in the same airport. He saw the woman but walked by on the other side. And a lawyer did the same.*

But not Patrick. Patrick understood compassion. He stepped out from behind his counter and approached the woman. "Have you nowhere to go?" he asked. In a trembling voice, the woman explained that she had only been in the United States for a little over a year and had no immediate family or friends to help her. She also told him that her husband had recently taken a job in another city, and she was supposed to fly out that night to meet him, but she missed her connecting flight. She was stranded. She was low on baby formula. And she was unsure of what to do.

Patrick realized he needed to help her. He could not just walk away from the woman. He knew she was looking for some sign of hope. Compassion for the woman moved him to action. The woman later told me that if Patrick had not offered his help, she would have become frantic.

"Come with me," Patrick said to the stranded woman. He walked behind his counter, called his wife, and explained the situation. He then turned to the woman and said, "You can spend the night with us." Before they left, Patrick exchanged the ticket so the woman and her baby would leave on a flight early the next day.

Since this happened long before the days of cell phones, Patrick also called the airport where her husband was waiting, explained the situation to him, and arranged for him to speak to his wife. He also assured her husband that everything would be fine.

On the way home, Patrick stopped and bought baby formula. When they arrived at his house, his wife embraced her, offered her a cup of tea and something to eat. Instead of spending the night on an uncomfortable chair in a cold deserted airport, the woman and her infant spent the night in a cozy bed in their warm and inviting guest room. The woman told me that she couldn't believe Patrick and his wife were so kind, giving, and compassionate.

> *Do not neglect to show hospitality to strangers, for by doing so, some people have entertained angels without knowing it. (Hebrews 13:2)*

The next day, Patrick brought the young woman and her baby to the airport in time to make the flight, and she was eventually reunited with her husband. The woman told me that she has always thought of Patrick as her guardian angel, and she thanked God for his and his wife's generosity and compassion.

+++

I think Jesus sometimes disguises Himself to catch our attention. He could be an elderly lady in the parking lot struggling with her grocery bags, or He could be a call for help when you are in the middle of doing something "important," or He could be someone asking you for a ride, taking you miles out of your way. I think Jesus does these things not so much to test us but to present opportunities to expand our faith, to tear down our parameters and boundaries, to open our hearts, to live not for ourselves but for others, and to teach us what it is like to be Him. The story of Patrick and the young woman has a very special meaning to me because, years later, the young woman becomes my mother-in-law and the waiting husband, my father-in-law. *And that little baby…well…she's my loving wife.*

+++

This week…
Reach out to someone in need with a reassuring smile or a gentle hug or a kind word. Your gesture doesn't have to be grandiose, just sincere. In other words, think of someone other than yourself, knowing that your compassion may prompt someone to show compassion to someone they know.

*Ask Jesus to tear down your boundaries, to open your heart, knowing that He will be with you.
Who knows, you may be helping your future spouse or your future best friend.
But above all, love God with all of your heart, mind, and soul, and love your neighbor as yourself.*

The Maggie Principle

For we know that the law is spiritual; but I am of the flesh, sold into slavery under sin. I do not understand my own actions. For I do not do what I want, but I do the very thing I hate. Now if I do what I do not want, I agree that the law is good. But in fact, it is no longer I that do it, but the sin that dwells within me. For I know that nothing good dwells within me, that is, in my flesh. I can will what is right, but I cannot do it. For I do not do the good I want, but the evil I do not want is what I do. Now if I do what I do not want, it is no longer I that do it, but the sin that dwells within me.

So, I find it to be a law that when I want to do what is good, evil lies close at hand. For I delight in the law of God in my innermost self, but I see in my members another law at war with the law of my mind, making me captive to the law of sin that dwells in my members. Wretched man that I am! Who will rescue me from this body of death? Thanks be to God through Jesus Christ our Lord!

So then, with my mind I am a slave to the law of God, but with my flesh I am a slave to the law of sin. (Romans 7:14–26)

Without revealing his specific sin, Paul does, however, explain the internal dynamics of spiritual warfare: the battle between the flesh and the spirit. His spirit quests for truth, righteousness, honesty, love, and other noble and altruistic virtues. His flesh craves for anything that will satisfy his physical desires, whether right or wrong. The flesh cares not for morality, only for satisfaction. While the spirit lives eternally, the flesh eventually dies and decays. Satan knows the flesh is our weakness, and by disguising himself as righteous and good, he uses the flesh as the key to unlock the door to the spirit's sacred chamber. Once inside, he can do his most devious work. Paul understands this dynamic, and by revealing his sinful self, he cautions us about the presence of spiritual warfare in our lives.

+++

Prior to my ordination, my wife, Elizabeth, and I taught at the same parochial high school. Elizabeth taught English, and I taught religion. Maggie, one of our most memorable and favorite students, was a quiet young lady in her junior year. Her lanky frame, round freckled face, dark-brown eyes, and curly red hair that she often wore in two long braids reminded us of a Raggedy Ann Doll without the stuffing. She was not the most outgoing student in her class; in fact, if Maggie spoke two consecutive sentences, it was like hearing a dissertation. But she was highly intelligent and, for the most part, comfortable in her own skin.

One day as she was leaving class, Maggie passed by my desk, stopped briefly, and excitedly announced, "I'm going for my driver's license this afternoon. Wish me luck!"

"Best of luck, Maggie!" And I assured her that she would pass the test, but I also joked that I was happy that my wife and I lived twenty miles away from school. Maggie slightly raised her eyebrows, gave me her mysterious Mona Lisa smile, gently shook her long red braids, and chuckled ever so quietly as she left the room.

The next day, as Elizabeth and I were finishing our lunch in her room, Maggie walked in early for English class. She came in with downcast eyes, and her distinctive smile had been reduced to a serious frown.

"Well?" we asked.

After a few moments of awkward silence and noticeable hesitation, she sheepishly told us what had happened during her driving test.

"Well," she started, "I got an A on the written exam."

"We wouldn't expect anything less from you, Maggie," we exclaimed!

"I did very well on the road test. I stopped at the red lights and stop signs. I yielded at the yield signs. I obeyed the speed limit, and I left the appropriate distance between my car and the car in front of me. I even avoided hitting a man on his bicycle."

"That's very important," we remarked.

She added, "I used my blinkers every time I turned. And the officer was very pleased with my driving skills."

"See, I told you that you'd be just fine," I reminded her.

"Then came the parallel parking." She sighed with downcast eyes. "You know," Maggie continued in a despondent voice, "I must have practiced parallel parking at least twenty times with my dad. I got to where I could do it blindfolded and even dreamt about it in my sleep. So when I turned my head around to look out the back window, I said to myself, *Whatever you do, Maggie, don't knock over the cone.* Well, guess what? I not only knocked it over, but I also proceeded to run it over!"

By now her voice quivered, and we could tell something had gone terribly awry.

"The officer got out of the car, put the cone back in place, got back into the car, and politely asked me to try again. So I did. And I knocked it over again. By the third try, I not only knocked over the back cone, but as I was pulling forward, I accidentally hit the brake, which jerked the car. Without even thinking, I quickly stepped on the gas and proceeded to knock over the front cone as well. I got to the point where I was having trouble telling the difference between the gas and the brake! I was angry, frustrated, and upset with myself, and I felt like a complete failure!"

By this time, Maggie's usual calm demeanor suddenly transformed into an unrecognizable and somewhat startling being. Her round face tightened, her dark-brown eyes flared, and her dimpled

A Distant Thunder

cheeks became as bright as her long red braids. Her fists clenched so tightly that she looked like she was ready for a fistfight, but only with herself. We couldn't believe our eyes! Our unassuming and even-tempered student dramatically changed into this uncontrollable and distraught person we had never seen before.

"I didn't understand what was happening to me!" she bellowed. "It was like I didn't have a brain. First, I screamed, then came the flood of tears. I could hardly breathe. The officer told me that we had enough for one day, and I could try another time. I felt completely defeated!" Somehow it was difficult picturing Maggie being so desperately angry with herself and even more difficult picturing her without her astute reasoning skills, but that seemed to be the case. Now every time we see someone struggling to parallel park, we think of Maggie.

+++

Most of us have fallen prey to *the Maggie Principle*, a time when our brains disconnect from our bodies, and we end up doing the very thing we don't want to do or say the very thing we don't want to say. Paul experiences a similar disconnect; however, his involves a battle between the flesh and the spirit. We too may experience the same battle, a time when our judgment becomes distorted, our values become blurred, and our virtues become tarnished, and we know what is wrong, but we do it anyway! We don't listen to our spirit warning us of the perils we are about to face. Our desires outweigh our reasoning, and we eventually give in to a temptation that we initially wanted to avoid.

Two hundred years before Paul, the Greek philosopher Plato wrote a discourse in his notable work, the *Republic*, about the nature of justice as it relates to a community and to an individual's soul. In the section "The Middle Period Dialogues: Moral Psychology," Plato discusses his theory of the soul as having at least three parts:

1. A *rational* part (the part that loves truth, which should rule over the other parts of the soul through the use of reason),
2. A *spirited* part (which loves honor and victory),
3. An *appetitive* part (which desires food, drink, and sex).

And justice will be that condition of the soul in which each of these three parts "does its own work," and does not interfere in the workings of the other parts (see esp. *Republic* IV:435b–445b).

Plato then describes what can go wrong in one's soul...when the appetitive simply overrules reason's judgments. He speculates that we may suffer, in this "moral weakness"—"[when] one finds oneself doing something that one actually believes is not the right thing to do" (see especially *Republic* IV:439e–440b, *Internet Encyclopedia of Philosophy*).

When we apply Plato's theory to Paul's internal conflict, we recognize that Paul's struggle results from his inability to fight his sinful desires. Sometimes our lives have become so uncertain that, like Maggie, we have trouble discerning the difference between the gas and the brake. Other times, our lives have become so unstable that, like Paul, we experience a battle between the flesh and the spirit. When this occurs, the appetitive part of our soul rules the rational part, heightens our vulnerability, leaves us open to "moral weakness," and propels us into our sinful act. Like Paul, we may *"do not do the good [we] want, but the evil [we] do not want is what [we] do."* But how much do we enjoy the evil we do?

In many cases, the sinner finds pleasure and benefit in his sin, which only increases his desire for it. This is the internal struggle Paul describes. However, sin also has a communal effect. The more we sin, the more emotionally isolated we become from the people in our lives, especially those who are most negatively affected by it. Ironically, those people may actually suffer even more than the sinners themselves as they may face their own self-doubt, despair, and defeat. Once we hurt someone who loves us, then whom do they trust?

This is the meltdown Paul relates to us in his Epistle: *"I do not understand my own actions. For I do, not what I want to do, but I do the very thing I hate. What a wretched man I am."* For Paul, the explanation rests not in some psychological analysis but in the very fact that evil has infiltrated his life and is waging war with his good intentions. Without a lifetime of spiritual conflict and without a recognition of the evil one, Paul never could have written this passage.

It's difficult not to feel sympathy for Paul. He continues to struggle with a sin he knows is wrong but cannot stop. It's also difficult not to feel sympathy for those who struggle like Paul. Yet it's hard to comprehend how Paul and people like him continuously open the door to temptation, allowing the appetitive part of their souls to powerfully grip their lives.

Paul loves Jesus, and many of those who struggle like him also love Jesus. They know Jesus went to the cross for the sins they battle, yet they continually allow those sins in their lives, which only widens the gap between their faith and their sinful acts. When faced with a rational decision between Jesus and Satan, they will choose Jesus every time, but Satan preys on their vulnerabilities and uses their weaknesses to infiltrate their lives and to eventually trap them in his powerful web of sin.

+++

Satan knows the brain has to disconnect from the body in order for the flesh to rule the spirit. He gives power to the flesh because he knows the flesh is our weakness. If Satan can unplug the body from the brain, the advantage becomes his. Instead of the brain controlling the body, Satan uses the body to convince the brain that it needs what is sinful. However, Jesus realizes that Satan is the instrument of this disconnect, and anticipating Satan's ploy, Jesus wakes His sleeping disciples on the night He is betrayed and warns them that *"the spirit is indeed willing, but the flesh is weak"* (Matthew 26:41).

While Maggie's parallel parking episode was not sinful, Satan wanted her to fail and become frustrated. And while the disciples' sleep was not sinful, Satan did not want them with Jesus during His time of desperate prayer. Satan's strategy is to win over the appetitive part of our soul and then wait for the rational and the spirited parts to either join or disconnect from it. Thus, we see *the Maggie Principle*, Plato's theory, and Paul's struggle in action.

+++

There is hope, however. Humans are created in the image of God, which is everything good and pure and holy. In the original design of creation and in a perfect world, the brain, the spirit, and the body work in harmony. This is the natural order God intends for us.

Humans do not have a sinful nature but a fallen one. Our pure nature will always be identified with the image of God. The struggle Paul experiences is a struggle we all experience. It is a struggle between God's vision for us and what we have become. Sin only widens this gap. Thus, we must never settle for sin. We must never allow Satan to control us. We must never embrace Satan's temptations. Satan's presence in our hearts should always be a point of contention. What we must remember is God's vision for us.

Jesus is the only remedy for *the Maggie Principle*. Paul asks, *"Who will rescue me from this body of death?"* And he immediately answers his own question: *"Thanks be to God through our Lord Jesus Christ."* Paul knows Jesus is the answer. Two thousand years before Maggie was born, Paul already had it figured out. Only Jesus outsmarts Satan. Only Jesus forces Satan out. Only Jesus prevents the disconnect. Only Jesus defeats evil. Only Jesus proclaims, *"I will cast out demons by the Spirit of God"* (Matthew 12:26). Only Jesus provides the hope we need.

Only by realizing his sinfulness, suffering because of it, confessing his sin to God, and asking for forgiveness from the people he has hurt will the sinner's burden be lifted. And only by Jesus' grace will the sinner experience peace and work toward living a virtuous life.

Some people think that in order to have a relationship with Jesus, they must live a life void of conflict and sin. Some people think that Jesus only wants people who are spiritually mature. These people claim that if you have problems, flaws, or sin, Jesus will turn away from you.

However, the Scriptures proclaim the opposite. The Scriptures speak of a myriad of sinners crying out to Jesus. These people want Jesus to get rid of the evil in their lives and put them on a path to righteousness. The Gospels also speak about people crying out to Jesus. Jesus assures them and us that when we cry out to Him, He listens. Jesus hears the cry of the afflicted and *"come[s] only for the lost sheep of Israel" (Matthew 15:24)*. He wants to free those people who struggle with *the Maggie Principle*. He wants to free those people who are battling a war against the desires of the flesh. His desire is so passionate that He sends His disciples to help them *(Matthew 10:6)*.

Jesus wants us to come to Him when temptation overwhelms us, when sin consumes our lives, and when the flesh conquers our reasoning. During these times, Jesus tugs at our hearts and whispers in our ears: "Come to me when you are lost and confused and lonely and depressed. *'Come to me all you who travail and are heavy laden, and I will refresh you' (Matthew 11:28)*. Come to me, and I will take care of you. Come to me, and I will provide the strength you need to turn away from your sinful acts. Come to me, and I will heal you and give you peace." Go to Him! Jesus is the answer, the only answer.

+++

Elizabeth and I struggled to write this section. We knew what we wanted to say, but the words were difficult to find. The entire section did not flow very well. Ideas became jumbled. Thoughts were random. We had to read and reread, edit and edit again. We wrestled with this section more than any of the others. It took weeks to write. And then it dawned on us. We were writing about Satan, and he was putting up one roadblock after another. *Duh!* While we pray every time we sit down to write, we began to pray specifically for Jesus to take Satan out of the mix and let us say what He wants us to say. In other words, we prayed to become the instrument of Jesus' voice, not Satan's.

As much as Satan nags you, you must be just as persistent when you ask Jesus for His help. As much as Satan wears you down, you must pray to Jesus to build you up. If Satan is constantly at work in you, then you must be constantly in prayer. But be aware of Satan's vicious cycle. The more you pray, the more Satan attacks. The more Satan attacks, the more you should pray.

When Satan comes knocking on the door to your spirit, you must say, "Hey, Jesus, will you get that?" Only then will you stay connected. Only then will you say what you want to say. Only then will you go where you want to go. Only then will you do what you want to do. And only then will you look in the mirror and find Jesus saying to you, *"What a righteous person you are!"*

+++

This week...

Every morning, look in the mirror and say to yourself, "I am a righteous person." Say this sentence with conviction in your heart and honor in your spirit.

At the end of your day, look in the mirror and say, "I was a righteous person today." Say this sentence with conviction in your heart and honor in your spirit.

And every chance you have, practice your parallel parking!

An Act of Forgiveness

Then Peter came and said to Jesus, "Lord, if another member of the church sins against me, how often shall I forgive? As many as seven times?" Jesus said to him, "Not seven times, but I tell you, seventy-seven times.

For this reason, the kingdom of heaven may be compared to a king who wished to settle accounts with his slaves. When he began the reckoning, one who owed him ten thousand talents was brought to him; and, as he could not pay, his lord ordered him to be sold, together with his wife and children and all his possessions, and payment to be made. So, the slave fell on his knees before him, saying, 'Have patience with me, and I will pay you everything.' And out of pity for him, the lord of that slave released him and forgave him the debt.

But that same slave, as he went out, came upon one of his fellow slaves who owed him only a

> *hundred denarii, and seizing him by the throat, he said, 'Pay what you owe.' Then his fellow slave fell down and pleaded with him, 'Have patience with me, and I will pay you.' But he refused; then went out and threw him into prison until he would pay the debt. When his fellow slaves saw what had happened, they were greatly distressed, and they went and reported to their lord all that had taken place.*
>
> *Then his lord summoned him and said to him, 'You wicked slave! I forgave you all that debt because you pleaded with me. Should you not have had mercy on your fellow slave as I had mercy on you?' And in anger his lord handed him over to be tortured until he would pay his entire debt. So, my heavenly Father will also do to every one of you, if you do not forgive your brother or sister from your heart."* (Matthew 18:21–35)

The last line of this Gospel stings. Jesus tells us that unless we forgive others, our heavenly Father will not forgive us. *Ouch, Jesus, that hurts!* We are also told to forgive sincerely from the heart. Do not just speak words of forgiveness and then continue to harbor feelings of resentment. Rather, forgive with the heartfelt intention of seeking healing and reconciliation, no matter how difficult this may be.

Peter is being facetious when he asks Jesus if forgiving someone seven times is enough. For Peter, forgiving someone seven times seems absurd, but Jesus thinks otherwise and tells Peter to forgive *"not seven times, but...seventy-seven times,"* symbolizing the boundlessness, limitlessness, and immeasurableness of forgiveness. Then Jesus teaches Peter the parable of the unforgiving servant, which discloses a mixed bag of theological tricks.

Knowing that most stories have a hero and a villain, we initially identify the king as the hero. After all, the king's compassion to the servant who could never repay him wins us over. The king's only request, however, is that the servant who received mercy becomes a minister of mercy. And when the servant refuses to forgive a fellow slave for a far less amount owed to him, he becomes our villain. The hero and the villain have been identified, and all is well with the story.

In the beginning, we want the king to forgive the servant. But by the end, we are pleased that the servant is in jail, yet we aren't too happy with the king either. Just when we think the story is about forgiveness and mercy and just when we think we have the story figured out, the king takes back his forgiveness, reinstates the servant's huge debt, and orders his extreme punishment. Now we're stuck with a king who first forgave but then rescinded his forgiveness and with a servant who was forgiven but then failed to forgive.

Nothing is as we expected. The parable runs around in a circle and ends without reconciliation and compassion, leaving us bewildered and perplexed. The ending traps us in a labyrinth of confusion. And herein lies the moral: Without forgiveness, everything remains a vicious cycle.

+++

In *the Our Father* we pray, *"Forgive us our trespasses as we forgive those who trespass against us."* We ask God to forgive us to the extent that we forgive others. But how often do we ponder the full meaning of this request? How often do we consider the reciprocal nature of God's forgiveness? And more importantly, how often do we recognize the offense we commit against God when we refuse to forgive others? The analogy of the debt forgiven, the debt not forgiven, and the offense Peter encounters relates directly to the offense God experiences through our refusal to forgive. *Ouch, Jesus, that hurts!*

Because of our arrogance and self-righteousness, we maximize the seriousness of the offense committed against us, but when *we don't forgive*, we minimize the seriousness of our offense against God. When we refuse to forgive, we offend God and remain unforgiven in His eyes.

+++

Years ago, Ken and I had very close friends whose daughter became engaged to the love of her life. At the engagement party, excitement filled the air, and both families were overjoyed. Although the couple had a year to plan and prepare for their wedding, the weeks zipped by much too quickly. When it was time to choose the wedding party, the couple asked their best friend if her two children could be included. Their friend enthusiastically agreed, and the couple expressed their excitement about their friend's children's participation as junior bridesmaids.

At first, their friend cooperated with the couple's decisions about her children's participation. As time passed, however, the friend's increasing demands caused unnecessary stress for the couple. As tensions intensified and emotions escalated, the couple's relationship with their friend eventually unraveled.

After the rehearsal dinner, the couple finally confronted her, which resulted in a terrible shouting match of one insult being thrown after the next. Despite the hurt, anger, and frustration felt by the couple, their friend, and other friends and family, the wedding went on as planned.

The newlyweds and the friend eventually wrote letters of apology to each other, but it became painfully obvious that their friend still harbored ill feelings. According to the newlyweds, their friend's "apology" seemed more defensive than heartfelt. The couple reached out to her several times after receiving her letter, but she completely ignored their calls and emails.

Fast-forward four years. While shopping in a crowded department store one Saturday afternoon, the couple saw their friend in the distance. They started to walk toward her, calling her name. At first, their friend didn't hear them, but as the couple came closer and called out to her again, she finally turned and saw them. When the couple walked up to her, they reached out for a hug. But the friend turned around and walked away, leaving them sad and bewildered.

+++

Refusing to forgive someone gives us satisfaction because we control the situation. We dictate the terms of the relationship. We demean the worthiness of the other person. We dishonor the sacrifice on the cross. However, if refusing to forgive didn't give us pleasure, we wouldn't hold on to it. *Right?*

In his article "Why You Secretly Enjoy Getting Angry," published in a 2018 issue of *Psychology Today,* Leon F. Seltzer, PhD, offers an explanation of why our anger brings us pleasure:

> *Your anger, essentially retaliatory in nature, agreeably serves the function of restoring to you a sense of righteousness and control, even dignity and respect. Added to this, the energizing surge of adrenaline accompanying your eruption further accentuates your sense of "wronged virtue." So naturally, you feel morally superior to whoever or whatever provoked you in the first place.*

Satan lures us into his perpetual trap, gives us a reason not to forgive, helps us justify it, and convinces us to feel good about it. Initially, our mind tells us that we must forgive, but our heart yearns for retaliation. As explained in *the Maggie Principle*, Satan disconnects the rational part of our soul from the appetitive, reminding us of Paul's dilemma: *"I do not understand my own actions. For I do not do what I want, but I do the very thing I hate"* (Romans 7:15). Satan tricks us into loving what we hate and traps us in his vicious cycle of anger and unforgiveness. Thus, the parable that Jesus taught two thousand years ago and Paul's dilemma remain relevant today.

+++

As often as we find reasons not to forgive those who offend us, we also find reasons not to ask for forgiveness to those whom we offend. The table turns, but the disconnect remains the same. Luring us, once again, into Satan's evil trap. Over the years, Ken and I have had numerous conversations about the danger of falling into Satan's pit of evil.

This is exactly what happened to me a few years ago. As an English department chair with more than twenty successful years teaching advanced placement English language and composition, I felt justified when I told a less experienced colleague who taught another AP English class that she must change her current policies and follow the same policies that I require for my AP class. I expected her to assign one in-class AP essay a week and give a minimum of nine in-class AP multiple-choice quizzes per quarter. In other words, I wanted her requirements to mirror mine.

When I made these demands, I never realized how unreasonable I was being. I not only disregarded her autonomy as a professional, but I also demeaned her previous experience. I completely disregarded my offense against her, and I completely ignored my offense against God.

Needless to say, my colleague became so upset with my demands that she requested a meeting with me and our head of school. A week before the meeting, I turned to Jesus and asked Him for guidance. After many prayers and long talks with Ken, I felt prepared to explain and defend myself. Little did I know what God had planned for me.

At the beginning of the meeting, our head of school asked my colleague to speak first. As she spoke, I slowly began to feel her pain, her frustration, and her anxiety. As she continued speaking, the Holy Spirit slowly softened my heart and drove Satan out. Once Satan left, I suddenly realized how unreasonable and unfair I had been to her. I immediately asked for her forgiveness and told her how extremely sorry I was for causing her so much pain and frustration. I also said that I respected her as a professional, as a colleague, and as a member of our department. I asked for her forgiveness again and promised her that I would not interfere with her goals and expectations for her AP class. She not only graciously accepted my apology, but she also completely forgave me. And we gave each other a really big hug! *Thanks be to God!*

The day after the meeting, our head of school told me that she had never seen anyone in a similar situation humble themselves as I did. I thanked her for her support, but I also told her that God entered my heart during the meeting and that He spoke with me and through me. What I didn't tell her though was that Satan lost, and God won! In retrospect, I wish I had!

As often as we justify our reaction when someone offends us, we must forgive. And as often as we justify our action when we offend someone else, we must ask for forgiveness. Not to forgive or not to ask for forgiveness is sinful and hurtful to God who has forgiven us through the sacrifice of His Son. The unwillingness to forgive or ask for forgiveness disgraces God and reinstates the debt that Jesus paid in full for us once and for all. Those who refuse to forgive or ask for forgiveness put themselves in serious spiritual jeopardy. But by asking for forgiveness or forgiving someone, we put ourselves on the road to salvation.

+++

The psalmist writes, *"As far as the east is from the west, so far has He removed our sins from us"* (*Psalm 103:12*). While God's forgiveness is immeasurable, we often keep the sin of a person who has offended us close at hand, like we are playing the card game of hearts. Then just at the right time, we lay down the card of resentment, which negates any possible act of forgiveness. But if we cannot forgive those who trespass against us, how can we expect God to forgive our trespasses?

In the New Testament, the Greek words *aphiemi* and *aphesis* refer to God's forgiveness of our sins. In other words, in God's eyes, the sin never took place; it never happened. God forgives us when we repent; He forgives us as though we never offended Him. If there is anything that God cannot do, it is to remember a sin that has been repented. Here's the catch though: If we want *that kind of forgiveness* from God, then we must extend *that kind of forgiveness* to another.

Jesus declares, "You must forgive another person as though the action never took place."

But you say, "I can't do that."

And God tells you, "Well then, neither can I."

But you exclaim, "Lord, forgive my unforgiveness!"

And the Lord responds, "I will, but only if you forgive. 'Vengeance is Mine,' saith the Lord. And it belongs to no one else" (*Deuteronomy 32:35*).

But you insist, "That person truly offended me and hurt me deeply."

And the Lord exclaims, "Now you know how it feels when you offend Me! Why don't you pray *the Our Father,* and this time, pay close attention to the words!"

+++

In 1958, a Korean graduate student at the University of Pennsylvania left his apartment one evening and went to the corner mailbox to send a letter to his parents. On his way back, he crossed paths with some angry teenage gang members who attacked him and beat him with a lead pipe. By the time the police arrived, he was dead. The people of Pennsylvania cried out for vengeance. The district attorney secured legal authority to try the boys as adults so they would receive the death penalty.

In the midst of the chaos, a letter arrived from Korea, signed by his parents and twenty relatives, expressing the family's decision

> *to petition for the most generous treatment possible within your laws of government be given to those who have committed this criminal action. In order to give evidence of our sincerity in this petition, we have decided to save money to start a fund to be used for the religious, educational, vocational, and social guidance of the boys when they are released. We have dared to express our hope with the spirit received from the Gospel of Jesus Christ who died for our sins and in doing so prayed for His offenders, "Forgive them, Father, for they know not what they do." The only way to stop irrational anger is by an act of equally irrational forgiveness.* (qtd. in an NBC news article by Emil Guillermo, 29 July 2016)

When we find ourselves unable to forgive or ask for forgiveness, go to the cross, the perfection of forgiveness. There, Jesus endures the excruciating pain from the nails of your sin.

No matter how much you hurt, your hurt can't compare to His.

Turn your pride into humility. Turn retribution into reconciliation. Turn revenge into mercy. Change the culture, break the cycle, and forgive the past. Claim a new light by forgiving others or by asking for their forgiveness. When we forgive or ask for forgiveness, we are freed from the chains of evil. Once we do this, we can proclaim Dr. Martin Luther King's esteemed words for ourselves: *"Free at last! Free at last! Thank God Almighty, I am free at last!"*

+++

And so we return to the parable of the unforgiving servant. Our hero remains unidentified. Perhaps we *cannot* go back and write a new beginning, but we can begin again and write a new ending that breaks the vicious cycle of retribution. It may sound something like this:

> *There once was a king who forgave a tremendous debt that had been incurred by one of his servants. While settling his own accounts, the servant imitated the king by forgiving his fellow servant of a lesser debt. When the king learned that the servant he forgave had offered forgiveness to another, the king invited the servant to come and live in his castle.*

"The king invited the servant to come and live in his castle!" Get it?

+++

This week…
Think of someone you need to forgive. You're saying, "Which person?"…Right? Choose a family member or a friend or a colleague. Close

your eyes for one minute and think of that person. After a minute, open your eyes and say this prayer:

"Lord God, I am struggling. I have been holding a grudge, and I am very sorry. It has been long enough. I know that it has formed a barrier between me and You, and I am extremely sorry. Free me from my burden. Release me from my bondage. Unlock the chains around my heart. Let me forgive in the same way that You have forgiven me."

Close your eyes again. Take a deep breath, exhale, and let go of your grudge. It's gone...like it never happened. Reach out to the person who offended you and say, I forgive you!

The Tapestry of the Living Bread

"Very truly, I tell you, whoever believes in me has eternal life. I am the bread of life. Your ancestors ate manna in the wilderness, and they died. This is the bread that comes down from heaven, so that one may eat of it and not die. I am the living bread that came down from heaven. Whoever eats of this bread will live forever; and the bread that I will give for the life of the world is my flesh."

The Jews then disputed among themselves saying, "How can this man give us his flesh to eat?" So, Jesus said to them, "Very truly, I tell you, unless you eat the flesh of the Son of Man and drink his blood, you have no life in you. Those who eat my flesh and drink my blood have eternal life, and I will raise them up on the last day, for my flesh is true food and my blood is true drink. Those who eat my flesh and drink my blood abide in me, and I in them." (John 6:47–56)

Christianity draws its faith from both the Old and the New Testaments, and together, these Testaments make up the Holy Bible. The New Testament fulfills the law, prophecies, and promises of the Old Testament. And this fulfillment dominates the

Scriptures: *the book of Genesis* describes the creation of the world; *the book of Revelation* describes the new heaven and the new earth; Adam sins, so God recreates the spiritual world through Jesus, the Second Adam, who saves us from our sins; circumcision, the sign of the old covenant, becomes baptism, the sign of the new covenant; the Ten Commandments become the Eight Beatitudes; the lamb of the Passover meal becomes the Lamb of God; the promised land of Canaan becomes the kingdom; the altar of sacrifice becomes the altar of celebration; the Sabbath becomes Sunday; shepherds become bishops; rabbis become priests; faithful followers become disciples.

Jesus explains this fulfillment early in His ministry during *the Sermon on the Mount*: *"Do not think that I have come to abolish the law or the prophets; I have not come to abolish them but to fulfill them"* (*Matthew 5:17*). Like the narrow neck of an hourglass, everything from the Old Testament flows into Jesus, and everything in the New Testament flows from Him.

+++

When Jesus proclaims He is *"the bread of life,"* He becomes the essential thread in the *tapestry of the Living Bread*, woven by God for our salvation. This tapestry begins around 1300 BC when Moses leads the Israelites out of slavery in Egypt to freedom in the promised land. During the first Passover meal, God instructs the Israelites to take *"some of the [lamb's] blood and put it on the sides and tops of the door frames of the houses where they eat the lamb. They shall eat the lamb that same night; they shall eat it roasted over the fire with unleavened bread and bitter herbs"* (*Exodus 12:7, 8*). By following God's instructions, the Angel of Death will *pass over* their homes during *the tenth plague: death of the firstborn*.

After each of the previous nine plagues, the Pharaoh did not allow the Israelites to leave Egypt, which makes them wonder if they will obtain their freedom this time. God gives the Israelites specific instructions for eating the Passover meal: *"And thus you shall eat it: with a belt on your waist, your sandals on your feet, and your staff in your hand. So, you shall eat it in haste. It is the Lord's Passover"* (*Exodus

12:11). With heightened anticipation, they obey God and eat the Passover meal, hoping He will overcome the Pharaoh's obstinacy so they can begin their journey to freedom.

The scent of freshly roasted lamb and warm unleavened bread calls them to the table. As they bow their heads, they pray fervently that this meal will be their last one in captivity. However, the bitter herbs remind them of their ancestors' 430 years of misery in Egypt, which increases their urgency for freedom. Their quiet and subdued table conversations stand in stark contrast to the piercing and terrifying screams that will soon emerge from the Egyptians' homes.

At midnight, Moses gives God's people the word: It is time to go, and God's people must go quickly! The Israelites abandon their homes and all of their possessions as they begin their journey. Although they are aware that this night will be the turning point of their history, they are unaware that this night will be the turning point of salvation history. Thus, their Passover meal leads us to our Eucharist. And their journey to freedom becomes our journey to salvation.

As part of the Passover ritual, God instructs Moses to tell the Israelites that they must celebrate the Passover meal every year: *"This day shall be a day of remembrance for you. You shall celebrate it as a festival to the Lord; throughout your generations you shall observe it as a perpetual ordinance"* (*Exodus 12:14*).

+++

Having celebrated the Passover meal every year of His life, Jesus longs to celebrate His last Passover meal with His disciples in Jerusalem. They, however, are unaware that this meal is their last one with Him. Anticipating this night for several weeks, Jesus smiles when He learns that the disciples have secured the upper room.

On the night of this Passover, the scent of freshly roasted lamb and warm unleavened bread calls them to the table. However, the bitter herbs remind them of their ancestors' misery in Egypt. As they bow their heads in prayer, Jesus fully understands what they do not. Judas, one of the twelve disciples, eats among them; however, no one but Jesus knows Judas' real intentions. As Jesus scans His disciples' eyes, all but one speak of joy, friendship, and innocence. Judas' eyes tell the story of greed, deceit, and conspiracy, which ends with Jesus' arrest later that night. In the midst of this tension,

> *while they were eating, Jesus took a loaf of bread, and after blessing it he broke it, gave it to his disciples, and said, "Take, eat; this is my body." Then he took a cup, and after giving thanks he gave it to them, saying, "Drink from it, all of you; for this is my blood of the new covenant, which is poured out for many for the forgiveness of sins."* (Matthew 26:26–28)

That night, Jesus brings the *tapestry of the Living Bread* to its fulfillment: The bread becomes His body, the wine becomes His blood, the Last Supper becomes the first Eucharist. The Catholic community believes in the real presence of Jesus Christ in Holy Communion. We believe that the bread and the wine are not symbols but are the body and blood of Jesus Christ.

And even though this mystery transcends our understanding, we accept it by faith.

As soon as you consume the body and blood of Jesus, the Eternal One touches each particle of you, and you become one with Him. You carry the Spirit of the Risen Christ back to your pew the way Mary carried the unborn Child to Bethlehem. His eternal presence remains within you, even as you return to the temporal world. If you could see what happens when you receive Holy Communion, you would be awestruck! You consume Him, and He consumes you. Nothing would be more important than receiving the body and blood of Jesus Christ.

+++

While Ken willingly attended church with his family, attending church wasn't high on my list of priorities as a teenager. I thought my

Sunday mornings would be more productive if I completed a school project, studied for an upcoming test, or finished my reading assignments. I even tried to convince my parents that God wouldn't love me any less if I missed church every once in a while. But they insisted that I attend church with the family. *So I went.*

    My self-centered attitude slowly changed after I graduated from college and started my professional career as an English teacher. I remember the *very* day that God called me to church. That Sunday started like most weekend mornings: a brisk jog, a cup of soothing tea, and an intriguing book. At some point between my sips and my reading, I realized that way too much time had slipped away, making me very late for church. Knowing that I would arrive during the middle of the service, I rationalized that God would understand if I didn't attend church that morning. As I wrestled with my thoughts, the Holy Spirit whispered, "Just go. Late or not, go." *So I went.*

    By the time I arrived, the Eucharist had already begun. Consumed with embarrassment, I tried to find an open pew at the back of the church, but the only one available was in front of the altar. When I reached the pew, I slipped in very quietly, went immediately on my knees, and gently closed my eyes. I listened with a heavy heart as the priest continued the service:

> *On the night He was handed over to suffering and death, our Lord Jesus Christ took bread; and when He had given thanks to you, He broke it, and gave it to His disciples, and said, "Take, eat: This is my Body, which is given for you. Do this for the remembrance of me." After supper He took the cup of wine; and when he had given thanks, He gave it to them, and said, "Drink this, all of you: This is my Blood of the new Covenant, which is shed for you and for many for the forgiveness of sins. Whenever you drink it, do this for the remembrance of me."* (*The Book of Common Prayer*, 368)

As the priest spoke Jesus' words, I pictured Jesus at His very Last Supper, with His very faithful disciples, on His very last night. My eyes filled with tears, my heart swelled with emotion, and my mind raced with repentance. That morning, I heard Jesus, I saw Jesus, I felt Jesus. And I finally realized that *Jesus is the bread of life*—mine and yours.

Today, a brisk jog, a cup of soothing tea, and an intriguing book pale in comparison to Holy Communion with our Lord and Savior.

God weaves Jesus' last thread in the *tapestry of the Living Bread* when Jesus promises His disciples: *"I will not drink from this fruit of the vine from now on until that day when I drink it new with you in my Father's kingdom"* (Matthew 26:29). The *tapestry of the Living Bread* becomes one of Scripture's greatest fulfillments in salvation history: The Passover meal leads to the manna in the desert, to the feeding of the five thousand, to the Last Supper, to Holy Communion and, finally, to the heavenly banquet. When you receive Holy Communion, you also become a thread in the *tapestry of the Living Bread*.

+++

Being raised Roman Catholic, I found the Episcopal Church through my wife Elizabeth, a cradle Episcopalian. In the Roman Church, children do not receive Holy Communion until they complete proper instruction, beginning at the age of six. However, all baptized Christians of any age can receive Holy Communion in the Episcopal Church. Clinging to my Roman roots, I didn't allow our three-year-old son to receive Communion. When we went to the Communion rail, I instinctively crossed his arms so he would only receive a blessing. Even though Elizabeth and I disagreed and had long conversations about this, I insisted.

During Communion one Sunday, our small but determined son quickly extended his hands as the priest came by with the bread. In one swift motion, the priest placed the host in our son's tiny hands, and he immediately ate it. Surprised and startled, I turned to Elizabeth, who gave me a slight smile. The priest, who was also a good friend of ours, looked at me and quietly chuckled. I thought to myself: *Was this prearranged? Did our priest decide to give our son the host? Did Elizabeth give him permission?* Right before the chalice bearer arrived with the consecrated wine, I quickly crossed our son's hands on his chest.

After the service, the priest asked me why I was displeased when our son received the bread. I said that our son didn't understand the Eucharist, so he shouldn't be allowed to receive Communion until he does.

After a short pause, he asked me, "Does your son understand the human digestive system?"

I responded, "Well, of course not."

He asked, "Do you withhold food from him because he doesn't understand?" As I started to answer him, he quickly added, "Your son's lack of understanding doesn't invalidate the Eucharist. Your son needs spiritual food as much as he needs physical food."

I responded, "Okay, you've given me something to think about."

After thinking about his analogy and discussing it with Elizabeth as we drove home, I realized that his reasoning made sense.

When we arrived home, I asked him, "Son, what did you do during church today?"

He said, "I ate the bread."

I asked him, "What is the bread?"

And he responded, "The bread is Jesus."

At that moment, I looked into my son's deep brown eyes and felt a reciprocated love between us. Jesus strengthened my relationship with my son that morning, and I suddenly realized that the Holy Spirit had extended his small hands during Communion.

"From now on," I told him, "you can take the bread every time we go to church as long as you remember it is Jesus."

As a priest, when I give the host to a toddler during Communion, I often think about my simple yet meaningful conversation with my son over thirty years ago. Could it be that our son was longing to receive Holy Communion for some time, but his blind and narrow-minded dad denied it? Could it be that our son had to quickly sneak Jesus before his dad stopped him? Could it be that Jesus was saying to me, *"Let the little children come to me, and do not hinder them, for the kingdom of heaven belongs to such as these"* (Matthew 19:14)?

+++

Jesus on the Moon

Neil Armstrong, the first person to walk on the moon, is a household name, not only nationally but also internationally. But it is Buzz Aldrin, Armstrong's copilot in the lunar lander, who takes his place in the *tapestry of the Living Bread*. Aldrin, a deeply spiritual man, initiated something very holy soon after he and Armstrong landed at Tranquility Base. *Something very holy!* When asked about the landing, Aldrin replied,

> *As we made our way toward the lunar surface, we realized our flight trajectory was long. We had overshot the original point of touchdown. The computer was taking us into a crater the size of a football field with moguls the size of cars. That is when Neil decided to go for manual control and switched off the auto-pilot. We had 40 seconds of fuel. We chose a point to the right of the crater. Tranquility Base became wherever we could land safely.*
>
> *When we finally set down, we were seconds away from running out of fuel. I was calm but anxious, and I could hear the gasp from Houston. After all of our training, this was for real. After we checked all of our onboard computers, I asked for a moment to pray in our own way; to take a deep breath, to give thanks to God for a safe journey thus far, and to ponder the magnitude of the event.*
>
> *For me, this meant Holy Communion. I reached for the stow away bag above the Abort Systems Manual Indicator. Inside were the con-*

secrated elements given to me by my parish back home...the Body and Blood of Jesus Christ.

In the 12 % gravity, the wine swirled around the small chalice and settled at the bottom half floating in the air. The host was too delicate to handle with my gloves so I plucked it out of the air with my tongue. I drank the wine. We were about to step out onto the lunar surface and I was completely at peace. It was very satisfying to know that Holy Communion was the first food consumed on the moon. ("Apollo11," foxnews.com)

At that moment, Buzz Aldrin turned the lunar lander into a small church. Even though Neil Armstrong claimed the moon for the United States, Buzz Aldrin claimed it for Jesus!

+++

So here we sit...

Three thousand five hundred years from the first Passover meal, two thousand years from Jesus' Last Supper, and 240,000 miles from the moon.

The body and the blood of Christ in Holy Communion connects us to these events. Receiving Holy Communion gives a new meaning to "put your hands together." When you receive Holy Communion, your hands become the hands of the Israelites who ate the first Passover meal. Your hands become the hands of those who collected the manna in the desert. Your hands become the hands of the five thousand who were fed with the loaves of bread and fish. Your hands become the hands of the eleven faithful disciples at Jesus' Last Supper. Your hands become the hands of Buzz Aldrin on the moon. Your hands become a thread in the *tapestry of the Living Bread*. The body of Christ, the Bread of Heaven, rests peacefully in your hands.

+++

Reverend Kenneth and Elizabeth Herzog

This week...
Go to church and take your place in the tapestry of the Living Bread. And when you see children extending their hands during Communion, know that they too are a thread in the tapestry of the Living Bread.

A Lowly Widow

Jesus sat down opposite the treasury, and watched the crowd putting money into the treasury. Many rich people put in large sums. A poor widow came and put in two small copper coins, which are worth a penny. Then he called his disciples and said to them, "Truly I tell you; this poor widow has put in more than all those who are contributing to the treasury. For all of them have contributed out of their abundance; but she out of her poverty has put in everything she had, all she had to live on." (Mark 12:40–44)

A widow
whose abandonment is forever remembered,
whose widowhood is forever embraced,
whose poverty is forever rich,
whose lowliness is forever exalted,
whose sacrifice is forever rewarded,
and whose anonymity is forever enshrined...

This Gospel tells the story of a nameless widow, not as a parable or as an illustration but as a real-life lesson. Her story calls us to look in the mirror and find our place in salvation history.

During biblical times, a widow's oldest son inherited the family's wealth. In their male-dominated culture, most sons felt no financial responsibility for their mothers, leaving the widows begging for money and selling their arts and crafts in the marketplace. People generally shunned and disrespected widows because they thought that a widow's sin caused her dire situation.

On this Sabbath, Jesus and His disciples sit opposite the treasury, watching people as they arrive. Before people enter the temple, they stop at the treasury and deposit their temple tax into silver and gold vessels that resemble large tubas with their mouths wide open. Jewish shekels, the only acceptable currency at that time, were coins about the size of a quarter, only much heavier. When wealthy people deposited their temple tax, the numerous coins made a continuous clunking noise, which attracted people's attention. Some of them even turned around, straining to see the person who put so many coins in the vessel.

While Jesus watches people deposit their coins, He notices an old woman wearing a tattered woolen tunic tied at the waist by a thin rope that holds her small cloth pouch, well-worn leather sandals that barely protect her swollen feet, and a frayed cotton veil that partially covers her unkempt hair. As she approaches, Jesus watches her. But she is unaware that He sees her.

Stopping in front of one of the vessels, she slowly unties her pouch, carefully empties it into her palm, and thoughtfully stares at her money, two small copper coins worth about a penny. She has three options: If she gives nothing, she can buy enough barley to make two small loaves of bread. If she gives one coin, she can buy a small bag of lentils. Or she can give everything. Looking at her coins, she deposits both…clink…clink, making almost no sound. And not even one person cares enough to notice, except Jesus.

The widow understands that her meager donation will not offset the temple's expenses. She knows that her two small copper coins will barely cover the cost of one cube of incense used to mask the repugnant smell of a burnt animal, sacrificed as another person's offering. She realizes that no one notices how much she gives. However, her obedience, her trust, and her sacrifice do not go by unnoticed. In fact, her humble act becomes a lesson Jesus teaches His disciples and us. And she is forever remembered.

Obedience… Trust… Sacrifice…

+++

A widow
whose abandonment is forever remembered,
whose widowhood is forever embraced,
whose poverty is forever rich,
whose lowliness is forever exalted,
whose sacrifice is forever rewarded,
and whose anonymity is forever enshrined…

The widow's sacrifice in this Gospel is similar to a widow's sacrifice six hundred years earlier when she became the Prophet Elijah's servant (*1 Kings 17:8–16*). As instructed by the Lord, the Prophet Elijah commands her to bring him food and water during a time when there was a devastating drought. But she doubts that she can fulfill his demands. She tells him that she is gathering firewood to make her last loaf of bread for her and her son before they die of starvation. Realizing her dilemma and anguish, Elijah reassures her:

> *Do not be afraid; go and do as you have said; but first make me a little cake of it and bring it to me, and afterwards make something for yourself and your son. For thus says the Lord the God of Israel:* "*The jar of meal will not be emptied and the jug of oil will not fail until the day that the Lord sends rain on the earth.*" *The widow did as Elijah instructed.* (*1 Kings 17:13, 14*)

Trusting the Lord, this lowly widow doesn't give *a small* portion of what she owns. She doesn't give *half.* She gives *everything.* Like the widow in the temple precinct, this widow's obedience, trust, and sacrifice become an integral part of the good news. And she is forever remembered.

Obedience… Trust… Sacrifice…

+++

*A revered widow
whose abandonment is forever remembered,
whose widowhood is forever embraced,
whose poverty is forever rich,
whose lowliness is forever exalted,
whose sacrifice is forever rewarded,
and whose holiness is forever enshrined.*

We do not know how or when this widow's husband dies. However, we do know that she suffers tremendous agony without her husband's support:

*she watches her Son being tortured and whipped,
she watches Him carry His cross to Calvary,
she watches the soldiers drive the nails,
and she watches Him die before her eyes.*

Obedience… Trust… Sacrifice…

These three widows foreshadow God who gives Himself to us. God does not give a *small* portion of Himself. God does not give *half* of Himself. God gives *all* of Himself, including His *greatest* sacrifice: His Son on the cross for our salvation. Because of His incredible passion for us, God yearns for a personal relationship with us. And our relationship with Him depends on our obedience to Him, our trust in Him, and our sacrifice for Him.

+++

Soon after I was ordained a priest, my favorite pastoral calls were with Mary and Everett, a frail couple in their late eighties whose undying love and affection for each other brought me joy during each visit. Always wrapped in a sweater, Mary parted her grayish-silver hair in the middle and let it fall at will, which accompanied her warm, radiant smile. Tall and lanky, Everett walked bent at the hip and wore a scruffy beard. He was hard of hearing and had suffered a mild stroke, leaving him with a slight speech impediment.

Reverend Kenneth and Elizabeth Herzog

They lived in a cramped one-bedroom apartment at an assisted-living facility. The scent of the day depended on which aromatic candle Mary lit. She often told me that she liked to burn candles to keep their home from smelling stuffy, "like old people." We always sat at their small kitchen table, laughing and sharing our stories, and Mary usually served me a purple drink that tastes like tepid watered-down Kool-Aid because, according to her, *cold drinks are not good for anyone who has been out in the sun.* Before I left, we always shared Holy Communion. On their sixtieth wedding anniversary, they asked me to pray over them and lead them through the renewal of wedding vows. I had never been in a room where so much love swirled around.

Everett's health was much worse than Mary's, and I always expected him to die before her. When Mary suddenly became seriously ill, I was very surprised. Their daughter and the hospice nurses became Mary's primary caregivers. Their daughter's tender and loving care for her mother reflected her parents' love for each other. At Mary's request, she died at home, and her service was as simple as the life she led.

After Mary's death, Everett lived in a quiet, reflective world, so I visited him more often. The room's once swirling love now held a stagnant stillness of grief and loneliness, and it began to smell stuffy, "like old people."

On one visit, Everett said that he wanted to make a donation to the church. I immediately told him, "Everett, you don't have to do that," as if to imply that he needed his money more than the church did.

Suddenly, there was a stillness in the room; Everett leaned back in his chair and, for a brief moment, became very quiet. *The widow in the temple precinct whispered to him: "Put your trust in the Lord, Everett."* He took a long breath, smiled, and said to me, "But I want to."

He walked over to his desk, sat down, opened the top drawer, and took out his checkbook. Shaking as he wrote, he entered the date, wrote the name of the church, filled in the amount of $2,000, and signed his name. He carefully removed the check from his checkbook and handed it to me with the warmth of Mary's smile. I sat embarrassed and humbled. I stared at his check as if it were a sacred document.

I soon realized that those few moments were *so holy*. I realized that his gift had nothing to do with me or the church. Rather, Everett's gift had everything to do with his relationship with the Lord. He did not give from his abundance; he gave from his poverty. Everett wrote his check with great joy and discovered that joyful giving releases God's abundant goodness:

> *The one who sows sparingly will also reap sparingly, and the one who sows bountifully will also reap bountifully. Each of you must give as you have made up your mind, not reluctantly or under compulsion, for God loves a cheerful giver. And God is able to provide you with every blessing in abundance, so that by always having enough of everything, you may share abundantly in every good work.* (2 Corinthians 9:6–8)

Our relationship with the Lord is often backward. We say, "Lord, if you bless me, then I promise to follow you."

But the Lord says, "No! You follow me, then I will bless you."

The Lord says this because He knows the human heart. He knows that if He blesses us first, we will have a tendency not to give to Him.

+++

One lowly widow who sacrifices her last two coins in the treasury,
One lowly widow who sacrifices her last morsel
of food for the Prophet Elijah,
One revered widow who sacrifices her Son,
One lowly widower who sacrifices from his life's savings…

When we finally fulfill our relationship with God, we will meet the three widows and Everett and his wife, Mary. By God's grace, we will take our seat with them at the heavenly banquet. We will feast on the fatted calf from the prodigal son. We will share the roasted lamb

Reverend Kenneth and Elizabeth Herzog

with bitter herbs from the Passover meal. We will eat the fish from the nets that did not break. We will receive the consecrated unleavened bread and wine. And for dessert, we will enjoy the delicacy of angel food cake served with heavenly roasted coffee.

In this glorious setting, the three widows and the one widower will dance happily with their spouses around the Lord's table as they have never danced before. They will cheerfully sing His praises and joyfully glorify His holy name, so enthusiastically that all of creation will hear them. *And the angels and archangels and all the company of heaven will give them a standing ovation!*

+++

This week…
Listen to the hymn, "Trust and Obey" by John H. Sammis.

The Royal Wedding

Once more Jesus spoke to them in parables, saying, "The kingdom of heaven may be compared to a king who gave a wedding banquet for his son. He sent his slaves to call those who had been invited to the wedding banquet, but they would not come. Again, he sent other slaves, saying, 'Tell those who have been invited: Look, I have prepared my dinner, my oxen and my fat calves have been slaughtered, and everything is ready; come to the wedding banquet.' But they made light of it and went away, one to his farm, another to his business, while the rest seized his slaves, mistreated them, and killed them. The king was enraged. He sent his troops, destroyed those murderers, and burned their city. Then he said to his slaves, 'The wedding is ready, but those invited were not worthy. Go therefore into the main streets, and invite everyone you find to the wedding banquet. Those slaves went out into the streets and gathered all whom they found, both good and bad; so the wedding hall was filled with guests.

But when the king came in to see the guests, he noticed a man there who was not wearing a wedding robe, and he said to him, 'Friend, how did you get in here without a wedding robe?' And the man was speechless. Then the king said to attendants, 'Bind him hand and foot, and throw him into the outer darkness, where there will be weeping and gnashing of teeth.' For many are called, but few are chosen."
(Matthew 22:1–14)

+++

Writers experience a unique challenge when they describe the unimaginable. They may create a metaphor, a simile, an analogy, or even a parable, hoping that the reader will find some clarity and understanding in their comparisons. Even so, they still face a daunting task. Imagine explaining the space shuttle to Orville and Wilbur Wright or describing self-driving cars to Henry Ford. Imagine explaining cell phone technology to Alexander Graham Bell. *So how do we describe something unimaginable?*

When Jesus describes the kingdom, He teaches us different parables that capture the kingdom's unimaginable glory. One of the most memorable relates the story of a woman who loses a precious coin: The joy she experiences when she finds the coin is like the joy in heaven when one sinner is found *(Luke 15:8–10)*. He then gives us the parable of a man who finds a buried treasure in a field and sacrifices everything he owns to buy the field. Thus, the joy of owning the treasure is similar to the joy of finding the kingdom *(Matthew 13:44)*. Jesus also teaches us another lesson: The kingdom of heaven is like a mustard seed, the smallest seed that grows into a tree. Similarly, the smallest amount of faith can blossom into the greatest joy *(Matthew 13:31–32)*. Striving for even greater clarity, He teaches us *the parable of the wedding banquet*, which captures the joy of the kingdom more effectively than any other parable. Even so, Jesus still faces the unique challenge of fitting the kingdom into our human perspective.

+++

Ken and I grew up in the Palm Beaches, an area that hugs the Atlantic coastline in Southeast Florida. Palm Beach, a barrier island nestled between the Atlantic Ocean and the Intracoastal Waterway, is one of our wealthiest communities. Beginning in mid-November, our part-time residents return to Palm Beach from their summer homes in the Northeast and open their stately winter mansions on the island until they leave again in mid-April. Full-time residents call this part of the year *the season*, a time when Palm Beach blossoms with one social gathering after the next.

One of Palm Beach's oldest and most historic resorts is the Breakers, a five-diamond Italian Renaissance-style hotel built by Henry Flagler during the late 1800s. The Breakers offers its guests "an experience, *exclusivity redefined*, room to roam and *reconnect*, restaurants that *raise the bar*, and *grand spaces* for grand events" (The Breakers). *And grand it is!* Even Gatsby's lavish mansion can't compare to the beauty, the splendor, and the grandeur of this magnificent resort.

When the son of one of our dearest friends from our church became engaged, he and his fiancée asked Ken to officiate at their wedding in Palm Beach during the height of the season, and of course, Ken graciously accepted. When we received our invitation, which included two nights at the Breakers with all expenses paid, Ken and I instinctively knew that this wedding would be comparable *"to a king who gave a wedding banquet for his son" (Matthew 22:1–14)*.

The ceremony took place on the resort's Ocean Lawn, a perfectly manicured, luscious emerald-green area, lined on both sides with impressive coconut palm trees that stand guard over the Atlantic Ocean. As the waves gently broke against the shoreline and the seagulls gracefully speckled the sky's delicate hues of gentle orange and pale pink, God's glorious golden rays peeked through wispy clouds, just as the couple exchanged their vows at sunset. Over two hundred guests witnessed love personified.

After the newly wedded couple retreated to their suite, we walked up the travertine staircase from the Ocean Lawn to the Mediterranean Courtyard. Once upstairs, waiters dressed in black tuxedos offered us signature cocktails and canapés, elegantly placed on silver platters. A five-person string ensemble softly strummed classical music that floated gracefully in the gentle breeze, serenading not only the guests but also the twinkling stars that illuminated the night's sky.

After almost an hour, three trumpets joyfully announced the couple as they appeared at the top of the courtyard's expansive marble staircase. The couple invited their guests to greet them and their wedding party inside the 200-foot-long lobby. The lobby's elegant furniture, exquisite art, distinctive chandeliers, and impressive Italian vases, filled with delicate white orchids, enhanced its floor-to-ceiling windows, intricately designed vaulted ceiling, and beautifully woven carpets. The string ensemble now accompanied the gently flowing water from the grand marble fountain. And as Ken and I waited to greet the couple, we felt as if God had given us a glimpse of the glory and the splendor of His kingdom.

From the receiving line, Ken and I strolled hand in hand down the luxurious lobby to the sumptuous and elegant Venetian Ballroom, "a 9,600-square-foot ballroom, with 25-foot-high ceilings, six exquisite crystal chandeliers, and furniture dressed in fabrics of golden hues" (The Breakers). As we entered this exquisite room, waiters served us French champagne that sparkled like dazzling diamonds swirling gracefully to the top of each long-stemmed crystal champagne flute.

A waiter escorted us to our table, covered with an embroidered white linen tablecloth and set with gold-rimmed bone china, crystal stemware, and silver flatware. The soft light from the crystal chandeliers flooded the room with a rainbow of dancing colors that accentuated the table's towering crystal centerpiece, filled with white roses, hydrangeas, and orchids. Music from a chamber orchestra floated gently throughout the room, providing peace, serenity, and tranquility for everyone who entered.

Reverend Kenneth and Elizabeth Herzog

After a sumptuous seven-course dinner, the couple danced their first dance as husband and wife. When they finished, they invited their guests to join them on the dance floor and rejoice with them as they started their life together as one. And as Ken and I danced the night away, we felt as if God had showered His never-ending love on us and on everyone who entered this magnificent room.

To this day, Ken and I still can't believe that we experienced what most people can only imagine. But we also believe that what we experienced can't even begin to compare with the beauty and the glory and the majesty of God's kingdom, in which we will all share: *"The twelve gates were twelve pearls, each gate made of a single pearl. The great street of the city was of gold, as pure as transparent glass" (Revelation 21:21).* Once in the kingdom, the Holy Spirit will fill our souls with the joy of everlasting glory. Once in the kingdom, we will attend a feast unlike any other!

+++

Why would anyone even consider not accepting God's invitation to His kingdom? Even so, there were some who declined the invitation: *"They made light of it and went away, one to his farm, another to his business" (Matthew 22:5).* For them, worldly concerns took precedence over attending the wedding banquet, taking their eyes off eternity.

It's no wonder the King becomes enraged; he takes their declined invitation personally. His preparation for the eternal Wedding Banquet includes the entire history of salvation, which takes Him thousands of years to piece together. And in holy irony, the Father pays for the heavenly banquet with His Son's life. In return, the Father demands repentance for their insulting behavior.

The King then orders his slaves to fill the wedding hall with anyone they find in the streets, referencing Jesus' ministry to the poor, the outcasts, and the downtrodden: *"The Lord has a heart for the poor" (Psalm 34:6).* They come for food but find hope in their Savior.

Using the world as his playground, the devil entices us to focus on the temporal world to increase the profit from our labor. However, the King invites us to focus on the spiritual world to increase the joy within our souls. A successful day in the secular world provides enough pleasure to briefly touch our souls, but a day filled with the Holy Spirit provides enough joy from our souls to engulf our secular world.

+++

In biblical times, when a king hosted a wedding banquet, he required his guests to wear beautiful robes, ensuring everyone was dressed properly. Since the poor would not have owned one of these robes, the servants gave them one to wear as they arrived, reminding us of our salvation:

> *I delight greatly in the garment of salvation in the Lord; my soul rejoices in my God. For he has clothed me with the garment of salvation and arrayed me in a robe of his righteousness, as a bridegroom adorns his head like a priest, and as a bride adorns herself with her jewels. (Isaiah 61:10)*

In the Gospels, Jesus refers to himself as the bridegroom and the church as His bride. Because the wedding gown and jewelry reflect the garment of salvation given to us by God the Father and through His Son's crucifixion, they are the costliest attire the bride will ever wear. However, unlike a bride's gown and jewelry, we wear the garment of salvation for eternity.

Unlike the poor who were taken off the streets to attend the King's Wedding Banquet, we do not inherit the kingdom simply because we are poor. We must all repent. And those who turn their backs on God's grace will be cast out into utter darkness and denied a place at His table.

+++

You have been invited to a Royal Wedding. Do not ignore your invitation. Do not allow daily distractions to prevent your attendance. Do not miss an eternity of unimaginable joy. Do not turn your back on God's grace.

This week:
Repent! Receive! Rejoice!
And by all means, accept His invitation!

Arrows and Targets

Jesus left that place and went away to the district of Tyre and Sidon. Just then a Canaanite woman from that region came out and started shouting, "Have mercy on me, Lord, Son of David; my daughter is tormented by a demon." But he did not answer her at all. And his disciples came and urged him, "Send her away, for she keeps shouting after us." He answered, "I was sent only to the lost sheep of the house of Israel." But she came and knelt before him, saying, "Lord, help me." He answered, "It is not fair to take the children's food and throw it to the dogs." She said, "Yes, Lord, yet even the dogs eat the crumbs that fall from their master's table." Then Jesus answered her, "Woman, great is your faith! Let it be done for you as you wish." And her daughter was healed instantly. (Matthew 15:21–28)

Elizabeth and I once saw a Peanuts cartoon with Charlie Brown practicing archery in his backyard. His arrows had little rubber suction cups on the ends, and instead of aiming at a target, he just shot at the fence. Wherever the arrow stuck, he went over and drew a bull's-eye around it.

After watching him for a few minutes, Lucy asked, "Charlie Brown, why are you doing this?" Charlie Brown's strategy is not new.

Jesus uses the same approach throughout His ministry. He indiscriminately shoots arrows that sometimes land on the fences of undesirable neighbors, and then he draws targets around them. He not only eats meals with known sinners, but he also associates with other unacceptable people. When He does this, He receives severe criticism from the Pharisees and the scribes who represent the *Jewish Homeowners Association* that strictly follows the proverb, "Good fences make good neighbors" (Frost).

Each time Jesus takes His disciples outside of Israel, they reluctantly follow Him, even though being in a foreign land causes them a tremendous amount of stress. They believe Jesus creates enough disturbance in Israel without causing more in foreign lands. For example, the disciples did not like going to Samaria because of the bitterness between the two nations. While there, Jesus engages in an in-depth conversation with a woman at the well *(John 4:1–26)*. According to Jewish custom, He should not be talking to this foreign woman. As His faithful disciples watch and wait, they grow more and more anxious. *Let's go, Jesus. Let's wrap this up and be on our way.*

Jesus raises the most eyebrows when He and His disciples arrive in the district of Tyre and Sidon. Of all the undesirable people living in this district, the Jews consider the Canaanites the worst. Many of their forefathers died at the hands of Canaanite warriors, which resulted in their bitter hatred and deep-seated prejudices against these people. Cautious Jews would walk miles out of their way to avoid this area for fear of being seen with the Canaanites who were considered unclean, pagans, and abandoned by God. No wonder His disciples are anxious.

Knowing it's not a good place to shoot arrows, they ask Jesus, "*Why are we here?*"

When they arrive in the city center, a Canaanite woman approaches them, petitioning and shouting out to Jesus on behalf of her daughter. Her emphatic pleas get His attention. As she approaches, her trembling hands reach out to Him for compassion, and He sees the overwhelming anxiety in her tightly wrinkled forehead and the intense anguish in her dark, deep-set eyes.

The scene couldn't be worse. Tensions are high. If the woman touches Jesus, He would be considered unclean and would have to undergo the Jewish purification rite. Undergoing this rite would demean His claim of being the Messiah. *Whatever you do, Jesus, do not pull an arrow out of your quiver. Let's lay low and be on our way.*

The woman's desperate pleas fall on deaf ears, which not only shocks His disciples but also delights them. They urge Him to send her away. Jesus agrees and tells the woman, *"I have come only for the lost sheep of Israel"* (Matthew 15:24).

But the woman persists, provoking an insult from Him when he refers to her people as dogs. Even so, she does not back down. Pleading with Him again, her bewildered dark eyes welled up with tears, but His cold, piercing stare sparks a fiery exchange between the two: the woman, crying for mercy; Jesus, refusing to give it.

At this moment, she has no concern about the past wars between their two nations. She doesn't care about the Jews' hatred toward her people. And she doesn't back down when He insults them. She cares only about her child. For her, mercy crosses all borders, eliminates all restraints, removes all fences. She continues to beg for His mercy as He is the only One who can offer her hope. But He still ignores her.

After being ignored and offended by the Messiah, some people might have felt too defeated to persist, too embarrassed to beg, or too humiliated to stay. Some people might have even given up hope. But when we lose hope, we lose ourselves.

However, this woman does not lose hope. She is not too defeated to persist, not too embarrassed to beg, and not too humiliated to stay. She places even more demands on Him, hoping His heart will soften, hoping He will cure her daughter.

She comes closer, drops to her knees, and bows her head. Her long black hair drapes over His feet, and her sobbing drowns her voice, the voice of desperation. Almost at the point of sheer exhaustion, she slowly lifts her throbbing head. Staring at Him with tears streaming from her swollen dark eyes, she begs, "Please, Jesus. Please have mercy. Please!"

As He peers into her blurry, tear-filled eyes, His eyes slowly and gently soften, giving her a glimmer of hope. "Please, Jesus, please!"

Filled with compassion, Jesus finally answers her, *"'Woman, great is your faith! Let it be done for you as you wish.' And her daughter was healed instantly"* (Matthew 15:28).

+++

It's almost impossible to read this passage without being moved. A mother crying over her child is one of the most heartbreaking scenes imaginable. Most parents would do anything to help their children: beg, plead, pray, and sacrifice everything they have. Sick children, lost children, abducted children, abused children, strays, runaways are all heart-wrenching situations that move most parents to take extreme measures. If you have ever begged for someone you love, you can empathize with the Canaanite woman's anguish in this poignant scene.

However, as touching as this scene is, it is also one of the most misunderstood passages in the Gospels. Why does Jesus become the antithesis of Himself, of everything He teaches, and of everything He believes? Why does it take Him so long to show compassion? Why does He turn a blind eye to this woman who desperately needs Him to heal her child? It doesn't make any sense, yet it makes perfect sense.

The passage teaches His disciples a valuable lesson about the narrow-minded boundaries of prejudices. Jesus turns the table on them, taking them from the fireball of hatred and bigotry and moving them to the light of love and compassion. He douses them with God's mercy, and we learn how not to live our lives.

+++

Prejudices, biases, and racism still plague us today. The more things change, the more they stay the same. Two thousand years! Two thousand years! *And have we not learned anything from this Canaanite woman?*

Satan loves to play the narrow-minded game of prejudices and then watch all hell break loose. And it does each time he plays.

Prejudices make us walk on eggs and hold our breath, hoping that another act of violence doesn't erupt. But that's the problem: We hope, but we forget to pray. Unfortunately, our prejudices will never heal until Satan is no longer in our lives; in other words, until the Second Coming: *"Come, Lord Jesus, come" (Revelation 22:20).*

Some people claim they aren't prejudiced. That's hard to believe. Most everyone is prejudiced in some way: race, political beliefs, sexual orientation, ethnicity, socio-economic status, etc. Denying you are prejudiced inhibits your spiritual and moral growth.

Let the light of truth shine on the darkness of your judgments. Recognize that the evil one is at work within you. And realize this is spiritual warfare. Be honest with yourself and with God. Do not stand with Satan and self-deceit. Admit your prejudices and then ask God to heal you: *"If we say we have no sin, we deceive ourselves and the truth is not in us; but if we confess our sins, God is faithful and just to forgive us our sins, and cleanse us from all unrighteousness" (1 John 1:8, 9).*

Prejudices are not a political issue. Prejudices are not a social issue. *Prejudices are a deep-seated spiritual issue!* A distorted ego not only ignores the spiritual but also judges others by its own self-serving standards that do not accept diversity. But we must realize that all people are children of God. It's not whom we see but how we see them.

Relying on our political leaders to provide a solution will bring even more disappointment and anguish. Passing laws, taking down statues, removing offensive flags, or giving hollow speeches will not turn a hardened heart. While many of our country's leaders express their positions on these deep-seated issues, few of them are calling us to pray.

Our country is starving for spiritual leadership. Prayer is our only hope. Jesus is our only answer. The wideness of God's mercy must be lived daily. The events of 9/11 put our country on its knees. Apparently, we have gotten up. Prayers for peace and for the removal of Satan must remain strong. As the disciple Paul tells us, *"Our battle is not against flesh and blood, but against the rulers of darkness and the evil forces of the world" (Ephesians 6:12).*

We must not pretend that our prejudices don't exist and that we are immune to Satan's attacks. Our struggle is within us. We must examine our hearts, recognize Satan's grip, and ask Jesus to dispel him. We must repent. We must pray. We must hope.

Our prayers for healing should be as desperate, as passionate, and as persistent as the Canaanite woman's. Does the Canaanite woman change Jesus' mind? Hardly! Jesus never sways from the compassion He has for her.

The question is not, can you change Jesus' mind, but can He change yours?

The question is not, how much of Jesus do you have, but how much of you does He have? The question is not, does Jesus have compassion for those who are different from you, but does your lack of compassion make you different from Jesus?

+++

Beth and I once saw a Peanuts cartoon with Charlie Brown practicing archery in his backyard. His arrows had little rubber suction cups on the ends, and instead of aiming at a target, he just shot at the fence. Wherever the arrow stuck, he went over and drew a bull's-eye around it.

After watching him for a few minutes, Lucy asked, "Charlie Brown, why are you doing this?"

Without hesitating, he replied, "This way I never miss."

Funny thing, Charlie Brown, there's a Bible story like that!

+++

This week...

Search your heart, identify your prejudices, and ask Jesus for healing. Instead of judging people, put yourself in their shoes.

Humility and compassion hold the key to empathy.

And empathy holds the key to accepting and loving others for who they are...people with thoughts and feelings and needs, just like you!

Reverend Kenneth and Elizabeth Herzog

The Golf Ball Analogy

I looked and there was a great multitude that no one could count, from every nation, from all tribes and peoples and languages, standing before the throne and before the Lamb, robed in white, with palm branches in their hands. They cried out in a loud voice, "Salvation belongs to our God who is seated on the throne, and to the Lamb!"

And all the angels stood around the throne and around the elders and the four living creatures, and they fell on their faces before the throne and worshiped God, singing, "Amen! Blessing and glory and wisdom and thanksgiving and honor and power and might be to our God forever and ever! Amen!"

Then one of the elders addressed me, saying, "Who are these, robed in white, and where have they come from?" I said to him, "Sir, you are the one that knows." Then he said to me, "These are they who have come out of the great ordeal; they have washed their robes and made them white in the blood of the Lamb. For this reason, they are before the throne of God, and worship him day and night within his temple, and the one who is seated on the throne will shelter them.

They will hunger no more; the sun will not strike them, nor any scorching heat; for the Lamb at the center of the throne will be their shepherd, and he will guide them to springs of the water of life, and God will wipe away every tear from their eyes."
(Revelation 7:9–17)

+++

Do you know us?
Do you believe in us?
Do you recognize us?

You ask, "Who are you and from where do you come? Identify yourselves and speak to me!"

One of the most emotional weddings Ken and I ever attended was the wedding of my colleague's son. Years before, her son was engaged to a young woman who was his childhood sweetheart. The love and bond between them grew stronger throughout high school and college. After they graduated from college, he asked her to marry him, which was not surprising to their parents and close friends who always felt they would marry one day. A few months after their engagement party, she died in a horrific accident that devastated him. For a few years, he didn't date anyone, lost contact with his closest friends, and had no desire to socialize. It took him years for his heart to mend and even longer to find true love once again. But he finally did.

On his wedding day, as his bride walked down the aisle with her father, a brilliant stream of light broke through an overcast sky, poured through the stained-glass window above the altar, and shone only on him. Everyone who knew his first fiancée gasped and looked at each other with tears in their eyes. He turned toward the stained-glass window and, for a brief moment, felt the presence of his first fiancée who wanted him to know that she was in the kingdom, celebrating with him and his bride on their wedding day. *Strange? Not at all. Not to us. Believe it or not…it happened.*

If you could believe, you would realize that the people in your life who have died are now in the kingdom watching over you. They are timeless and can live in the hearts of their loved ones simultaneously.

+++

John wrote this passage from *the book of Revelation* when the Roman persecution of Christians was more intense than ever. During the reign of Emperor Nero in the middle of the first century, the Romans initiated the elimination of the Christian faith from the empire. It was the Roman version of the Holocaust. The disciples Peter, Andrew, Paul, James, Philip, Bartholomew, Matthias, and Matthew were martyred along with countless others: *"Blessed are you when people revile you and persecute you and utter all kinds of evil against you falsely on my account. Rejoice and be glad, for your reward is great in heaven" (Matthew 5:11).*

Today is their day. Today is All Saints' Day.

When we think of All Saints' Day, we think of the well-known saints of the church: the disciples, Saint Theresa, Saint Patrick, Saint Joseph, Saint Francis, and countless others. Each of these "Major League" saints has an individual feast day on the liturgical calendar.

However, we should also celebrate the lesser-known saints from Scripture, church history, and our own lives with equal solemnity:

> *There are some of them who have left a name, so that others declare their praise. And there are some who have no memorial, who have perished as though they have not lived. Their posterity will continue forever, and their glory will not be blotted out. (Ecclesiastes 44:13, 14)*

All Saints' Day is the spiritual version of the Tomb of the Unknown Soldier, those who contributed to the kingdom on Earth but who are not well-known to the vast majority of Christians. They did charitable acts without being recognized. They led others to Christ without taking any credit. They lived the vision of the heavenly kingdom without being identified:

> *They will hunger no more; the sun will not strike them, nor any scorching heat; for the Lamb at the center of the throne will be their shepherd, and he will guide them to springs of the water of life,*

> *and God will wipe away every tear from their eyes.*
> *(Revelation 7:17)*

We know these people are in the kingdom, but there are times when we wonder if others are there.

+++

After Ken met with a parishioner who was having a difficult time coping with her father's sudden death, he asked me to reach out to her, hoping she might open up to me since my dad had died the year before. Having been through the shock of my dad's unexpected death, I not only empathized with her grief, but I also sympathized with her struggle.

When we met for coffee one morning, she was reluctant to speak about her father. However, after we talked for a while, she slowly opened up to me about him and their relationship. She said he was a mean-spirited man who lived his life in constant anger. He disconnected himself from the faith, which troubled her because she didn't understand his unwillingness to accept Jesus as his Lord and Savior. When she tried to talk to him about this, his anger flared, which upset her even more. Their relationship eventually developed into an angry cycle with no resolution. When he died, she questioned if he was in the kingdom. Even though she didn't think he deserved a Christian burial, she finally went along with her family's decision for him to have one.

The more she told me about her father, the more I wondered about the source of his anger. Though not a psychologist, I am a teacher of classic literature, and I have learned from our literary masters that our deepest pain is often the root of our most intense anger.

To help her better understand the pain often associated with anger, I asked her the same questions that I ask my students before we read and analyze Shakespeare's *Hamlet*: Why do we experience anger? Why does our anger sometimes become uncontrollable? Why does our anger sometimes make us feel powerless? And even though she started to understand her father's anger, I sensed that she still needed clarity. So I told her my golf ball analogy, which I often tell my students:

> *The two-piece modern golf ball is formed by surrounding a spherical molded core made of rubber with a hard covering. The core is then placed in an injection mold. Hot plastic is injected and forms a hard dimpled coating around the hard rubber core. ("How Are Golf Balls Made?" by Brian Hill)*

> *Our anger is not only the ball's hard dimpled coating but also the rubber core's hard covering. Our pain is buried deep inside the rubber core. Before we can confront our pain, we must remove the layers of anger that cover it. However, the more anger we remove and the more pain we expose, the more our vulnerability increases. But once we face our vulnerability, work through our pain, and release it, we can finally find peace. ("The Golf Ball Analogy" by Elizabeth Herzog)*

Even though she said my simple analogy gave her some clarity, she still wondered if her father's intense anger covered his pain, if her bitter frustration covered her anguish, and if their overwhelming doubt covered their faith.

I told her it's not our place to question. It's not our place to judge; it's God's. *Thanks be to Him!*

+++

God's grace is more powerful than doubt. God's mercy is more powerful than judgment. God's forgiveness is more powerful than sin. The sacrifice of His Son has plenteous redemption for all. The nature of God's abundant love judges differently than we do, which gives everyone the opportunity to dance and sing before the throne. Then our voices will blend with the Communion of the saints:

> *Come meet this motley crew of misfits, these liars and these thieves, There's no one unwelcomed here.*
> *The sin and shame that you brought with you, you can leave it at the door, And let mercy draw you near.*
> *He said, "Come to the table. Come join the sinners who have been redeemed.*
> *Take your place beside the Savior. Sit down and be set free. Come to the table."* ("Come to the Table," Warner Chappell Music, Inc., 2015)

Jesus' sacrifice on the cross transcends time and provides the necessary grace and mercy to forgive the sins of the whole world. The source of God's grace and mercy is from Jesus' blood on the cross. As Jesus' blood flows from His wounds, His grace and mercy flow through time and are not only available to everyone who lived after His sacrifice but also to everyone who lived before it.

For example, God forgives Moses' murder of an Egyptian taskmaster because the grace and mercy flowing from the blood of Jesus' crucifixion thirteen hundred years later were already available to Him. Moses' appearance with the Prophet Elijah at Jesus' Transfiguration can only happen because of Jesus' blood on the cross (*Matthew 17:3*).

+++

The Catechism of the Episcopal Church defines the Communion of the saints as "the whole family of God, living and dead, those whom we love and those whom we hurt, who are bound together in Christ by sacrament, prayer, and praise" (*BCP,* 862). This powerful definition explains how Christ unites all mortals to the angels and the saints: *"What is mankind that you are mindful of them, human beings that you care for them? You have made them a little lower than the angels and crown them with glory and honor"* (Psalm 8:4, 5).

While angels have never been mortal, saints are mortals who died and who are now in the kingdom. Humans accept the hierarchy of heaven with the Trinity first, followed by angels, then the saints and, lastly, mortals. But Christ's transformational love unifies all four in the activities of sacrament, prayer, and praise because His holy presence unifies "the whole family of God."

Our union with Christ connects us to the Communion of the saints. Receiving baptism connects us to John in the Jordan River. Celebrating the Eucharist connects us to the apostles at the Last Supper. Confessing our sins connects us to the repentant criminal who hung on the cross next to Jesus. Attending a wedding connects us to the bride and the groom who drank the water that Jesus turned into wine at their wedding feast in Cana of Galilee. Receiving Last Rites connects us to the women at Jesus' tomb on Easter Sunday morning. Praying connects us to Jesus in the garden of Gethsemane. Praising the Lord connects us to the heavenly chorus. Through Christ, our mortal humanity and God's saintly community become one family. United by Christ, the living and the dead are no longer separated and are both alive.

United by Christ, they are one.

+++

When people we know die, they hear everything we wish we would have said, and they know everything we wish we would have done. Even though we have a limited understanding of them, they have a perfect understanding of us. They know our deepest thoughts, they know our deepest regrets, they know our deepest concerns. Christ's transformational love allows them to see us through His grace and mercy and forgiveness. All animosity vanishes; all guilt disappears. Our knowledge on earth is limited compared to our knowledge in the kingdom: *"Now we see in a mirror, dimly, but then we will see face to face. Now I know only in part; then I will know fully, even as I have been fully known" (1 Corinthians 13:12)*. We must believe that they know what we do not.

After a loved one's death, the restlessness in our hearts is often calmed by signs from God that our loved one is with Him in the kingdom. But only through our faith can we recognize these signs: *"Faith shows the reality of what we hope for; it is the evidence of things we cannot see" (Hebrews 11:1).* Things we cannot see yet hope for are made real through faith.

In his article "Lesson by Faith: Hebrews 11:1–3," Steven Cole explains that *"such faith takes the future promises of God and makes them real in the present. It proves the reality of the unseen world. It gains God's approval. It understands the origins of all that is"* (Bible.org, 2004). Through our faith, God gives us the capacity to experience the kingdom and catch a glimpse of it while still on earth. Our eternal souls have no restrictions, except for what we put on them, through the depth of our faith or the lack thereof. Our faith allows us to communicate and have a relationship with those who have gone before us.

Strange? Not at all. Not to us. Believe it or not, it happens.

+++

Elizabeth's dad was an avid golfer who played at least three times a week and never missed watching or going to a PGA tournament. Elizabeth and I watched many golf tournaments with him on Sunday afternoons, which gave us as much pleasure as it did him.

One Sunday afternoon soon after he died, Elizabeth and I were watching the final round of a PGA tournament when an obnoxious crane flew on the green and pranced around as if he wanted everyone to notice him. Players, caddies, and officials tried to chase the crane off the green but to no avail. He was so insistent that the television commentators even joked about his antics. After watching for a few moments, Elizabeth looked at me and said, "That's Dad!" We both chuckled and said lightheartedly, "Leave it to Dad not to miss a major golf tournament!"

To millions of viewers, the bird was nothing more than a nuisance. But the bird held tremendous meaning for us. We interpreted it as a sign from God. Elizabeth's dad wanted us to know that he was in the kingdom and that he had a "bird's eye view" of the tournament's final round of a game he treasured.

Strange? Not at all. Not to us. Believe it or not, it happened.

+++

One night soon after Ken's dad died, his mom awakened for no reason. She opened her eyes and saw a vision of him standing in the doorway of their bedroom. Not taking her eyes off of him, she sat up, called his name, but he vanished. After he left, a sense of calmness washed over her and filled her heart with joy. That night was the first time after his death that she slept peacefully, knowing he is in the kingdom.

Strange? Not at all. Not to us. Believe it or not, it happened.

+++

Ken and his brother-in-law Pete had a very close relationship. When Pete died, Ken's prior commitment to deliver a keynote address at a convention prevented us from attending Pete's funeral. Even though Ken's sister understood, we were devastated.

That summer, Ken and I visited his sister. One Sunday after church, we went with his sister, along with her two girls and their families, to visit Pete's grave. As we paid our respects, we sat in silence. Suddenly, a beautiful butterfly circled overhead and landed on a nearby lamppost. We all noticed it at the same time. One of Ken's nieces approached the butterfly, but it quickly flew away, only to return to the same post. This time, however, the butterfly didn't move; it joined us, and we looked at each other, knowing that the butterfly was a sign from God.

We believed that Pete wanted us to know that he was in the kingdom. Before we left, we said a prayer of thanksgiving to God for such a meaningful moment.

Strange? Not at all. Not to us. Believe it or not…it happened.

+++

As a priest, I have witnessed countless signs at the gravesite that bring the family of the departed peace and comfort, including a butterfly circling the headstone, a bird chirping on a nearby tree limb, the sun breaking through an overcast sky, and a brilliant rainbow appearing as the rain subsides.

Signs like these are often comforting to the grieving family and friends, but in a less meaningful situation, the signs may be interpreted differently. When we see signs on a deeper level, we understand that our eternal souls have no restrictions. We find great comfort knowing that the departed are celebrating with the Communion of the saints. It's a matter of faith or the lack thereof.

We must have faith and accept the unity of this world and the next: *"Faith shows the reality of what we hope for; it is the evidence of things we cannot see"* (Hebrews 11:1). And even though we cannot physically see our departed loved ones, we must trust and have faith they share in God's mercy, forgiveness, and love.

All Saints Day is more than the celebration of eternal life for those who are in the kingdom. It is also an acute awareness of the intermingling between the mortal and the divine. This intermingling that is inconceivable and irrational to us in the mortal world is credible and realistic to those in the spiritual world.

+++

Elizabeth and I were recently in a checkout line at a grocery store. When the cashier finished ringing up our groceries, she asked, "Do you have our store's discount card?" But, of course, we didn't.

The elderly lady behind us tapped me on the shoulder and said, "Here, you can use mine."

We politely thanked her, and the cashier discounted our bill. But the new total put us a nickel short of having to break another dollar, and neither one of us had any coins. The elderly lady reached over and put a nickel on the counter. I turned to her and said, "Well, God put us in front of an angel this morning."

She responded, "As long as you recognize us when you see one!"

That elderly woman's kindness was truly a saintly act. Her kindness gives witness to her vision of the heavenly kingdom. Her kindness connects her to the community of the saints. Living *this* kind of life on earth will enable her and us to live *that* kind of life in the kingdom.

+++

Do you know us?
Do you believe in us?
Do you recognize us?
You ask, "Who are you and from where do you come? Identify yourselves and speak to me!"
They answer, "We are the Communion of the saints. And we hope that now you will know us, believe us, and recognize us! Today is All Saints' Day! Today is our day!"

+++

This week...
Think of a loved one who has died. Go to a quiet space, close your eyes, and visualize that person in the kingdom. Sit quietly and feel your loved one's presence in your heart. Have faith that your loved one is with you.
Strange? Not at all.
If you believe, it will happen.

The Season of Thanksgiving

As we celebrate Thanksgiving Day with family, friends, and neighbors, let us be mindful that God has given us the greatest gift known to humanity: *"For God so loved the world, that he gave his only begotten Son, that whosoever believeth in him should not perish, but have everlasting life" (John 3:16).*

We pray that our reflections not only enhance your spiritual life but also infuse your heart with God's loving presence as you face personal struggles in our ever-changing world. May God's blessings be yours, today and forevermore.

The Greatest Gift

> *When you have eaten your fill, you must bless the Lord, your God, for the good country he has given you. Be careful not to forget the Lord, your God, by neglecting his commandments and decrees and statutes which I enjoin on you today; lest, when you have eaten your fill, and have built fine houses and lived in them, and have increased your herds and flocks, your silver and gold, and all your property, you then become haughty of heart and unmindful of the Lord, your God, who brought you out of the land of Egypt, that place of slavery. Otherwise, you might say to yourself, "It is my own power and the strength of my own hand that has obtained for me this wealth." Remember then, it is the Lord, your God, who gives you the power to acquire wealth, by fulfilling, as He*

> has now done, the covenant which He swore to your fathers. (Deuteronomy 8:10–14, 17, 18)

+++

In their book *Chicken Soup for the Soul,* authors Jack Canfield and Mark Hansen relate a story about Linda Percy, a first-grade teacher in one of the poorest sections of East St. Louis. As Thanksgiving approached, Ms. Linda knew that her students had little to be thankful for compared to other children who enjoyed a more abundant lifestyle. Nevertheless, she wanted them to draw a picture of something for which they were thankful.

Most students drew pictures of turkeys with yellow, orange, and brown feathers, while other students drew turkeys wearing Pilgrim hats, but only a few students drew family members standing in front of a table filled with food. As she walked around the room, looking at and commenting on each student's drawing, she noticed that Douglas, one of her quietest students, had drawn nothing but a simple hand.

After the students finished the assignment, Ms. Linda asked each one to stand and explain his or her drawing. When Douglas proudly displayed his *masterpiece*, his classmates wondered whose hand it could be. Ms. Linda asked him, "Who's hand is that, Douglas?"

"It's your hand, Ms. Linda," explained Douglas. "'Cause every time I have to go somewhere here at school, you take my hand and lead me."

At that moment, Ms. Linda realized that she was even more thankful for giving her hand to him than he was for taking it. True thanksgiving, she concluded, comes not from what we receive but from what we give.

+++

Ms. Linda's hand in Douglas' life is the personification of God's hand in the formation of our faith. In the spring of 1300 BC, God's protective hand led the Israelites out of their oppression in Egypt to their freedom in the promised land of Canaan, an arduous desert journey that lasted forty years. God's omniscient hand created the history of our salvation when He formed the Israelite nation, called the age of the prophets, and sent His Son at the Incarnation. When God takes our hands, He leads us to Him, giving us the freedom of the kingdom. Just as Ms. Linda's hand was a source of trust and comfort in Douglas' life, God's hand is a source of trust and comfort in ours.

Ms. Linda's hand in Douglas' life is also the personification of God's hand in the formation of our country. In the autumn of 1620, God's protective hand led the Pilgrims out of their oppression in England to their freedom in the promised land of America, an arduous ocean journey that lasted sixty-six days. God's omniscient hand created the history of our country when He protected the *Mayflower* on its perilous journey, when He provided a vision for the spirit of America, and when He called our Founding Fathers to fight for freedom and independence.

As American Christians, we recognize God's hand in these momentous journeys. As American Christians, we share not only the Israelites' first Passover and their desert journey, but we also share the Pilgrims' ocean voyage and their first Thanksgiving. As American Christians, we share not only the same church community as the Founders of our Faith: Abraham, Isaac, and Jacob, but we also share the same patriotic vision of the Founders of our country: Washington, Adams, and Jefferson.

As American Christians, we share not only the hope of the Israelites' journey to the promised land of Canaan, but we also share the hope of the Pilgrims' journey to the promised land of America. Even more importantly, as American Christians, we share the vision of the Pilgrim Church on our journey to the kingdom. But if we don't take God's hand and allow Him to lead us, we will either be lost in the desert, drowned in the sea, or abandoned in our eternal life.

+++

In the passage from *the book of Deuteronomy*, Moses initiates a precursor to the first Thanksgiving. In the year 1300 BC, Moses reminds his people to remain humble with their earthly gains: *"Remember then, it is the Lord, your God, who gives you the power to acquire wealth" (Deuteronomy 8:18)*. Moses tells his people that it is only by the hand of God and His blessings that they will be successful; therefore, they must offer Him prayers of thanksgiving. If they do not, they will think that they are solely responsible for their wealth and will offend God.

Seven hundred years after Moses' death, King David, Israel's greatest king, also reminds the Israelites of God's graciousness:

> *May our barns be filled with produce of every kind; may our sheep increase by thousands, by tens of thousands in our fields, and may our cattle be heavy with young. May there be no breach in the walls, no exile, and no cry of distress in our streets. Happy are the people to whom such blessings fall; happy are the people whose God is the Lord. (Psalm 144:13–15)*

Much like Moses, King David tells his people that their successes and happiness come from God's many blessings.

President Lincoln's "Thanksgiving Proclamation" of 1863 echoes Moses' and King David's messages of giving thanks to God for His gracious gifts:

> *No human counsel hath devised nor hath any mortal hand worked out these great things for our nation. They are the gracious gifts of the Most High, who, while dealing with us in anger for our sins, hath nevertheless remembered mercy. It has seemed to me fit and proper that they should solemnly, reverently, and gratefully acknowledge as with one heart and one voice the whole American people. I do therefore invite my fellow citizens in every part of the United States, and also those who are at sea and those who are sojourning in foreign lands, to set*

apart and observe the last Thursday in November next, as a day of Thanksgiving and Praise to our beneficent Father who dwells in the Heavens.

Moses, King David, and Lincoln, an unlikely trinity, understood that their nations' successes were the result of God's graciousness. All three led their people to this truth. All three saw their nations' prosperities in God's benevolence. All three offered prayers of thanksgiving to God for their many blessings.

The momentous events of the Israelites' journey across the desert, the Pilgrim's journey across the ocean, and Lincoln's journey to unite a divided country cannot even compare to the most profound journey known to humankind: a journey of only a half of a mile, made by a single man as He stumbled, crawled, and struggled his way from Pilate's headquarters to Calvary, a small hill outside of Jerusalem.

This was a journey of *Jesus' hands—the hands of God*—as they worked to carry the cross of our redemption. His calloused hands, full of splinters, were nailed to the cross of love so the Pilgrim Church could navigate her way to the eternal promised land of the kingdom.

Of all our blessings, God's Son is a gift for which we should be most grateful. Unfortunately, however, we have strayed from offering God prayers of thanksgiving for His Son, the greatest and most important gift we will ever receive!

+++

During the weeks leading up to Thanksgiving Day, television commercials often portray the quintessential American family gathered around the dinner table, sharing an array of traditional Thanksgiving food, and offering sentiments of gratitude for their family members, their friends, and their accomplishments, but these commercials never mention God. Even though they don't, we should!

However, we should also remember that there is no such thing as a self-made man or woman. God has put you in the right place, at the right time, opened the right doors, and provided the right opportunities for your success. Have you worked hard? Of course. But do you realize that the Lord God has prepared your way? Failure to recognize God's presence in your successes contributes to your false pride and self-promotion. Claiming the glory that rightly belongs to God is un-Christian and un-American.

Sadly, many Americans have removed God from the center of their lives. However, we must realize that when we cut God out of the fabric of our nation, we weaken the thread that binds us. If we do not allow God to stitch us together, we will be a frayed nation, a tattered flag.

With His blessings, God created the vision of America and entrusted us to fulfill it. Imagine if we dedicated ourselves to His purpose. Imagine if our president reminded us that our prosperity comes from our Lord. Imagine if Wall Street opened the New York Stock Exchange every day with a prayer. Imagine if our political leaders did not use economic wealth, improving housing markets, and low unemployment rates as political platforms.

Also imagine if our political leaders emphasized that God is at the center of our successes, and without Him, our lives will be filled with one self-serving step after the next. Imagine if our nation focused on its blessings, rather than its successes: *"Happy are the people to whom such blessings fall; happy are the people whose God is the Lord"* (*Psalm 144:15*). Imagine what a country we would have!

Our lives should be lived as recurring thank you notes to God, who provides us with every opportunity for our success. Losing sight of God's presence in our successes will lead us to arrogance and false pride. How quickly we forget Him when things are going well. How quickly we call out His name when things are not.

The American Dream must not be defined solely as an economic opportunity. It must include a spiritual relationship with God, who provides this opportunity. We must ensure that immigrants coming to our country in search of a better life find one in God. When we remove God from the foundation of our country, we abandon America's soul and the heart of our nation.

+++

As a priest, I have seen glimpses in my ministry of God's vision for America. Some years ago, I gave the invocation and blessing at the opening of a large retail store. On the morning of the grand opening, the manager, the assistant manager, and all of the other employees gathered inside at the front of the store. As I prayed over them, I asked the Holy Spirit to guide my words. My prayer left no doubt in their minds that God created the company's mission statement, guided the store's construction, and called each of the employees. I also reminded them that only by God's gracious hand will their future prosperity be realized.

After my prayer, I walked around the store's interior perimeter, praying and sprinkling holy water at the opening of each aisle. When I returned to the front of the store, I blessed each employee. By some of their inquisitive facial expressions, my blessings were more than they "bargained" for, but no one complained, and no one refused.

God was present that morning, and He entrusted me to lead those employees to Him. Something holy took place in that store: God's abundant love and blessings entered the hearts of each of those employees. What we must remember is that God gives us His blessings and love every day, just as He did with those employees that morning. For this and so much more, we must offer Him prayers of thanksgiving for blessing us with His love and generous gifts, especially the gift of His Son.

+++

A few years before Ken and I met, I had the opportunity to teach at the International School of the Sacred Heart, an all-girls school in Tokyo, Japan, "that for over a century has embraced and provided an education that prepares young women from many countries and faiths for global citizenship" (*International School of the Sacred Heart* website).

During this time, I taught students and worked with colleagues who represented over thirty countries. I not only immersed myself in Japanese culture, but I also learned about my students' and my colleagues' cultures, traditions, holidays, languages, and religions, which provided me with a unique professional and personal experience. My two years in Japan were an exhilarating cornucopia of one learning adventure after another.

However, as exciting as my life was, I missed my family and my American culture and traditions, especially during the holidays. My first Thanksgiving in Tokyo was "different," to say the least. First of all, the fourth Thursday of November was a regular school day, filled with classes, athletic competitions, musical performances, and other after-school activities that took place as usual.

There was no announcement thanking God for blessing America with His abundant gifts, no mention of Lincoln's "Thanksgiving Proclamation," no Thanksgiving assembly or performance, no "feast" at lunch, and not even a passing comment about the Macy's Thanksgiving Day parade or the Dallas Cowboys and the Detroit Lions football game except, of course, among my American colleagues.

Even though I understood why our international school community didn't celebrate or even mention Thanksgiving, as an American Christian, I struggled with my thoughts and my emotions on that first Thanksgiving Day so far away from home. However, God provided me with some comfort when my American friends and I gathered for a meal that evening to celebrate our nation and to give thanks to Him for His many blessings. Although we yearned for our country, our churches, our families and our friends, we relished being together as American Christians.

On my "first" Thanksgiving thousands of miles away from home, I realized that God binds all of us together: guiding, protecting, and blessing us, no matter whom we are with or where we are.

Today and every day, I thank God for blessing us with His love, His peace, and His generous gifts, especially the gift of His Son, our Lord and Savior.

+++

On this Thanksgiving Day and every day, Ken and I wish you, your family, and your friends God's blessings, love, and peace:

The Lord bless you and keep you,
The Lord make His face to shine upon you,
To shine upon you and be gracious, and be gracious unto you.
The Lord lift up the light
Of His countenance upon you,
And give you peace,
And give you peace,
And give you peace.
Amen! Amen! Amen!
Amen! Amen! Amen!"
("The Lord Bless You and Keep You" by John Rutter)

+++

This week…
As you share your Thanksgiving Day with family and friends and
as you break bread together, give thanks to God for your many
blessings, including His Son, the greatest Gift we will ever receive.
If you have never heard "The Lord Bless You and Keep You,"
written and conducted by John Rutter and performed by the
Cathedral of Our Lady of the Angels, February 17, 2008,
take a moment to listen to this moving hymn.
As you listen, keep God in your heart and give Him
thanks for your blessings, today and every day!
May you find His peace in your life!
Happy Thanksgiving!

About the Authors

The Reverend Kenneth Herzog has a Masters in Theology from St. Vincent de Paul Regional Seminary in Boynton Beach, Florida and a Masters in Divinity from The School of Theology at The University of the South in Sewanee, Tennessee where he received The William Porcher DuBose Excellence in Preaching Award, the highest award given to a graduating seminarian.

Ordained an Episcopal priest in 1996, Reverend Herzog has served at three Episcopal churches in Florida, served on the Diocese of Florida Diocesan Council, served as the Spiritual Director for Cursillo, and served as regional canon for the Diocese of Florida. Reverend Herzog has also developed a successful newcomer program for two churches in north Florida, and served as a rector and an assistant rector in the Diocese of Florida. Prior to his ordained ministry, he taught theology at two private secondary schools and was Chair of the Religion Department at Cardinal Newman High School in West Palm Beach, Florida.

Elizabeth Herzog has a Bachelor of Arts degree in Communications and English from Florida Atlantic University in Boca Raton, Florida and has completed advanced class work at The University of the South in Sewanee, Tennessee and at The University of Central Florida in association with the College Board's Advanced Placement curriculum.

Mrs. Herzog taught secondary English, public speaking, journalism, and theater for over forty years in both public and private schools in Florida and at the International School of the Sacred Heart in Tokyo, Japan. Mrs. Herzog served as English Department Chair at St. Johns Country Day School in Orange Park, Florida, where she taught Advanced Placement English Language and Composition, Advanced English Literature and Composition, senior Honors English, public speaking, and journalism.

Printed in the USA
CPSIA information can be obtained
at www.ICGtesting.com
LVHW040510060324
773595LV00001B/178